CO-AVE-885

Alexandria Haddad

SAMS
Teach Yourself
Microsoft® PowerPoint® 2000
in 24 Hours

SAMS

A Division of Macmillan Computer Publishing
201 West 103rd St., Indianapolis, Indiana 46290 USA

Sams Teach Yourself Microsoft® PowerPoint® 2000 in 24 Hours

Copyright © 1999 by Sams Publishing

International Standard Book Number: 0-672-31432-0

Library of Congress Catalog Card Number: 98-86840

First Printing: 1999

00   99   4   3   2   1

Interpretation of the printing code: The rightmost double-digit number is the year of the book's printing; the rightmost single digit, the number of the book's printing. For example, a printing code of 99-1 shows that the first printing of the book occurred in 1999.

Printed in the United States of America

Trademarks

EXECUTIVE EDITOR
Jim Minatel

ACQUISITIONS EDITOR
Jill Byus

DEVELOPMENT EDITOR
Susan Hobbs

TECHNICAL EDITORS
Susan Daffron
Mitch Milam

MANAGING EDITOR
Thomas F. Hayes

PROJECT EDITOR
Leah Kirkpatrick

COPY EDITOR
Nancy Albright

INDEXER
Rebecca Hornyak

PRODUCTION
Steve Balle-Gifford
Louis Porter, Jr.

PROOFREADER
Maribeth Echard

COVER DESIGNER
Aren Howell

BOOK DESIGNER
Gary Adair

Overview

Table of Contents

Acknowledgments

Writing, editing, and producing a technical book takes the dedicated effort of many people. I have been fortunate to be blessed with this opportunity and a group of people who have been not only extremely professional and efficient, but understanding and patient as well. Thanks to Jill Byus for offering me this opportunity and helping to keep me on track when the track disappeared. Suz Hobbs has been a great development editor and her humor has kept me smiling through each step. Both of my technical editors, Mitch Milam and Susan Daffron, were great. The production team who made sure that my spelling and grammar were readable—Nancy Albright, Susan Daffron, Margaret Berson, and Mandie Rowell—all did a great job. There are also countless others at Macmillan whom I haven't met and would like to thank. I would also like to thank my husband for his encouragement and help whenever I needed it. In closing, I would finally like to acknowledge and thank my Lord, for the many blessings He has given me and without Whom none of this would ever have been possible.

About the Author

Alexandria Haddad (alex@cobia.net) has been using computer software applications to improve business communications and operations for almost 15 years. She currently comanages Cobia Communications, a full-service computer consulting firm that operates in a virtual office environment. Her role also includes creating Web sites and writing technical books and manuals for various software products. In addition, Alexandria is a part-time instructor at local colleges. Her specialties include desktop publishing, word processing, spreadsheet design, and (of course) presentation software.

Introduction

Have you ever had to (or do you anticipate having to) stand in front of a group of people and tell them about something? Maybe you need to prepare presentations for someone else to use? Are you thinking of putting together information and making it all available on the World Wide Web? Or, do you have Microsoft PowerPoint 2000 available, because it was included with Microsoft Office 2000, and want to know how, why, and for what you could use it (after all, you did pay for it)? If you answered yes to any of these questions, then you need this book.

For those of you who don't give presentations (and will never give a presentation), you might want to thumb through this book, too. Microsoft has packed a lot of great stuff into PowerPoint 2000. You can create attractive drawings, graphs, and organizational charts. The possibilities are endless once you let your imagination run free.

This book is written for anyone who wants to create dynamic presentations. If you want to put together a few simple pages to hand out for the upcoming PTA budget meeting or maybe create a drawing or company logo, PowerPoint 2000, used with this book as a resource, will have you on the road to infamy before you know it.

I have been a successful software instructor for several years, and have tried to incorporate my teaching style into the pages of this book. I have taught people from all walks of life, from grandmothers to professionals, and believe that whether you're a beginner or an old pro, you will find this book extremely helpful.

This easy-to-follow, step-by-step instruction leaves no questions about what you're supposed to do next. I have thrown in plenty of tips and cautions for good measure and the questions in the Q&A section, at the end of each chapter, come from real people.

The book is divided into six parts that can be reviewed independently or you can read the whole book cover to cover. Each chapter should take about one hour to work through. The basics are covered in Parts I, II, and III. Parts IV, V, and VI cover everything else from creating dynamic drawings to posting your presentation on the World Wide Web. So don't just sit there; the clock is ticking.

To Do: Learn to Use PowerPoint 2000

1. Pay the nice person at the counter.
2. Go home.
3. Turn on your machine.
4. Set your clock and get ready to rock. (Just a small bit of humor ☺)

Tell Us What You Think!

As the reader of this book, *you* are our most important critic and commentator. We value your opinion and want to know what we're doing right, what we could do better, what areas you'd like to see us publish in, and any other words of wisdom you're willing to pass our way.

As the Executive Editor for the General Desktop Applications team at Macmillan Computer Publishing, I welcome your comments. You can fax, email, or write me directly to let me know what you did or didn't like about this book—as well as what we can do to make our books stronger.

> If you have a technical question about this book, call the technical support line at (317) 581-3833 or send email to support@mcp.com.

Please note that I cannot help you with technical problems related to the topic of this book, and that due to the high volume of mail I receive, I might not be able to reply to every message.

When you write, please be sure to include this book's title and author as well as your name and phone or fax number. I will carefully review your comments and share them with the author and editors who worked on the book.

Fax: 317-581-4770

Email: office_sams@mcp.com

Mail: Executive Editor
           General Desktop Applications
           Macmillan Computer Publishing
           201 West 103rd Street
           Indianapolis, IN 46290 USA

PART I
Getting Started

Hour

HOUR 1

PowerPoint 2000 Basics

Welcome to the wonderful world of presentations. A presentation is a structured delivery of information. Teachers, professors, politicians, and sales representatives make a living delivering informative presentations. If you want to create powerful multimedia presentations quickly, you've picked up the right book. Knowing the ins and outs of PowerPoint 2000 will ensure that your message is properly presented, well received, and remembered long after you've left the room.

PowerPoint 2000 helps you structure the ideas and information that you want conveyed to your audience. With it, you can add visual images, animation, supporting documents, and audio recordings to enhance your presentation. For example, you can easily do the following:

- Turbocharge that tired old training speech with animation and sound clips
- Visually demonstrate the importance of the yearly budget numbers by incorporating charts, tables, and high-impact graphics
- Impose structure on a presentation so the audience grasps the message
- Post the presentation on the World Wide Web so others can review it

- Generate an outline for your presentation
- Create audience handouts and speaker's notes

 Multimedia: A format that involves more than one media type, such as a document that contains sound, images, and text.

You have picked an excellent product to help you prepare your presentation. PowerPoint 2000 includes several templates that supply a presentation framework for many common topics. The task of building multimedia slides isn't a chore with PowerPoint 2000 because it has many of the formatting and content-creation tools built into other Office products. It also includes a rich library of clip art and sound files to jazz up the text. PowerPoint 2000 has drawing capabilities that enable you to create a dynamic presentation by including animation and action buttons in the presentation. In addition to slide-creation tools and navigation features, different slide perspectives are available to help you structure your ideas into a coherent presentation.

After you have reviewed your presentation and are ready to publish the content, PowerPoint 2000 supports a variety of display media. You can deliver your presentation with overhead projectors and transparencies (black-and-white or color), with 35mm slides, on the Internet, or simply onscreen. By combining PowerPoint 2000 with your presentation subject and this book, you will enjoy learning to use PowerPoint 2000 to create fantastic presentations.

Before you get started, you should take a few moments and cover the basics. This hour gives you a solid foundation to make sure you get the most out of PowerPoint. Before you create a presentation, you should check to make sure the application has been properly installed. You also should become familiar with what PowerPoint 2000 has to offer in terms of documentation and help desk tools. This first hour covers the following:

- What's new and improved in PowerPoint 2000 (for those who have used previous versions of PowerPoint)
- How to open and exit PowerPoint 2000
- The all-important technical support contact numbers

What's New and Improved

If you've used previous versions of PowerPoint, you're in for some wonderful surprises. Many features have been enhanced to make PowerPoint 2000 an even better application.

To make the upgrade to PowerPoint 2000 even more exciting, Microsoft has added new features, too. These are listed in Table 1.1.

TABLE 1.1. NEW AND IMPROVED FEATURES IN POWERPOINT.

Feature	Description
Font drop-down list	Shows a sample of the font type. (Formatting toolbar)
Clipboard	Holds multiple items. You can activate a toolbar that lists the contents of items you've copied to the Clipboard.
Detect and repair	Help menu command that allows the user to find and fix errors in PowerPoint. (You need to have the installation disk available when you use this option.)
Introductory screen	Displays a list of the most recently used files under the Open Existing Presentation Option. This feature permits quick access to existing files.
New Normal view	The Normal (default) view is a combination of Outline, Slide, and Notes Pages view all on one screen. When you become accustomed to this view, you will wonder how you ever lived without it.
Toolbar enhancements	Toolbars are now easier to customize, and tear-off palettes have been added.
AutoShapes	More of them! The new option is called More AutoShapes. They are simple line drawings of common business-related objects and banners.
Online collaboration	A new option under the Tools menu that starts NetMeeting. NetMeeting is a program that enables you to host a presentation online with people participating from different physical locations.
Online broadcasting	A new feature that allows you to broadcast your presentation to other users on your network. Online broadcasting is capable of sending both audio and video to accompany your broadcast.
Projector Wizard	An option that helps set up a slide show projector.
Enhanced bullets and new numbering formatting	Bullets are now easier to format. You can choose from pictures (good for Web pages) or symbols. The symbols are almost the same as in earlier editions, only you have three categories of Wingdings and a new category called Webdings. PowerPoint 2000 now allows numbered lists as well as bulleted lists.

continues

TABLE 1.1.   CONTINUED.

Feature	Description
Enhanced tables	You can use PowerPoint 2000 to create tables for your presentation, rather than using embedded Word tables—thank goodness! PowerPoint 2000 tables work similarly to tables in Word. Although some of the more advanced Word table features are not available with the PowerPoint 2000 tables, you can still embed Word tables in PowerPoint, if you desire.

You can create dynamic presentations easily by experimenting with the many tools available in PowerPoint. Many of the new features help you create presentations more efficiently. Microsoft has also expanded the scope of the application to step into the 21st century with ease, with the new online collaboration and broadcasting features. To get the most out of PowerPoint, consider installing all the available options.

Starting PowerPoint 2000

Although several methods are available to start any application in the Windows 98 environment, the easiest, by far, is to find and use the Start button in the lower-left corner of your screen.

To start PowerPoint 2000 from the Start button, do the following:

To Do: Starting PowerPoint from the Start Button

1. Click the Start button.
2. Highlight the Programs menu item.
3. Click Microsoft PowerPoint, as shown in Figure 1.1.

Each time you start PowerPoint 2000, a dialog box will display asking what type of presentation you want to start with. For now, simply click Blank presentation and then the OK button. When you see the New Slide dialog box, simply click the OK button again. These two dialog boxes are covered in more detail in Hour 2, "Quick Start: Creating Your First Presentation."

FIGURE 1.1.

Starting PowerPoint 2000 from the Start button is the easiest way to begin creating a presentation.

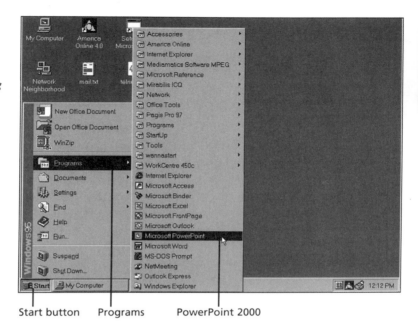

Start button   Programs   PowerPoint 2000

If you have installed the complete Microsoft Office 2000 suite, you can also start the PowerPoint 2000 application by clicking the Microsoft PowerPoint button on the Office shortcut bar, as shown in Figure 1.2.

FIGURE 1.2.

You can also start PowerPoint 2000 from the Microsoft Office shortcut bar.

Getting Help

This section will cover the help features that are available to you from PowerPoint 2000. You probably will not be using these features right away, but you should know what help you have available and how to use it.

When you know what you want to accomplish, but you don't know how to get there, whom are you going to call, especially if you don't have a help desk that's open 24 hours a day, 7 days a week? PowerPoint 2000 has several different options for getting help when you need it, including the Office Assistant, online help files, and access to Office on the Web, to name a few. The help options are very useful in solving a question even when you don't know the correct terminology for what you want to do. Do what the professionals do—use the Help option, and use it frequently. When you have mastered using the Help option, you will have found the framework that can assist you in becoming a PowerPoint expert.

The Office Assistant

The Office Assistant is presented as an animated cartoon. You can have Rocky the puppy, F1 the robot, or one of several other cute, helpful characters who are ready and eager to help you. Unlike real-life office assistants, you can fully customize the Office Assistant. For example, you can change its persona or character; imagine trying that one out on Bob next door. You can customize other Office Assistant attributes, such as whether the character responds when you press the F1 (help) key, includes various noises, displays keyboard shortcuts, as well as other options that you will learn.

Using the Office Assistant

Any time you need help with a feature, the Office Assistant is there to help calmly and politely. You can type your questions in plain English, and the Office Assistant finds the appropriate help file and gives you an answer. To start the Office Assistant, press the F1 function key, or click on the question mark icon on the Standard toolbar (you'll know you've got the correct icon when you place your mouse pointer on it and a ScreenTip displays Microsoft PowerPoint Help). Or you can choose Show the Office Assistant from the Help menu. To use the Office Assistant, use the following steps:

To Do: Using the Office Assistant

1. Open the Office Assistant using any method you choose.

2. Type your question in the Type your question here text box (the text that's already in the box will disappear as you type).

3. Click Search.

4. Select an option item from the help list. If you don't see the item you need in the help list, click See More, if available, to view additional relevant topics, or enter a new question and click Search.

The help file for your question should now be displayed. Figure 1.3 shows an Office Assistant answering a simple question. By clicking on the various options, more information is displayed to the user.

FIGURE 1.3.

Click on the topic closest to your question and get more detailed answers.

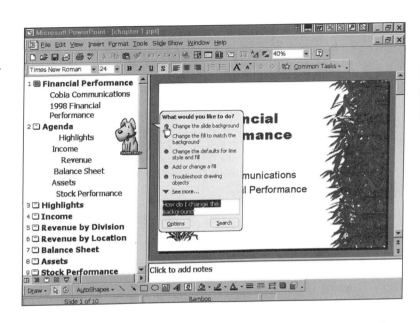

Several customization options are available for defining the Office Assistant's personality. Do you want sound? How about keyboard shortcuts? Do you want the Office Assistant to move out of the way? You can customize all these items, and more, to your liking by following these steps:

To Do: Changing Office Assistant Options

1. Click the Office Assistant to open the dialog box.
2. Click the Options button.
3. Click the Options tab (if it is not showing).
4. Select the options you want, as shown in Figure 1.4.

FIGURE 1.4.

You can view the Office Assistant options in the Office Assistant dialog box.

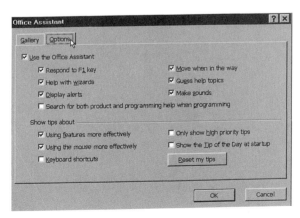

5. Click the Gallery tab to choose a different personality.

▲ 6. Click the OK button when you are done.

> If you would rather not be bothered by the Office Assistant, you can turn off this feature. To turn off the Office Assistant, double-click the Office Assistant to open it, and then click the Options button. On the Options tab, uncheck the Use Office Assistant check box (all the options will be displayed dim) and then click OK. To turn the Office Assistant back on, select Help, Show the Office Assistant from the menu.

Using the Online Help

PowerPoint 2000 includes excellent online help files. With a little patience, you should be able to find answers to your questions quickly. To activate the Microsoft PowerPoint Help window, choose Help, Microsoft PowerPoint Help from the menu. Figure 1.5 shows the Microsoft PowerPoint Help window. The key to successfully using the online help is to understand when to choose the Contents, Answer Wizard, or Index options.

FIGURE 1.5.

The Microsoft PowerPoint Help window aids in finding answers to many questions.

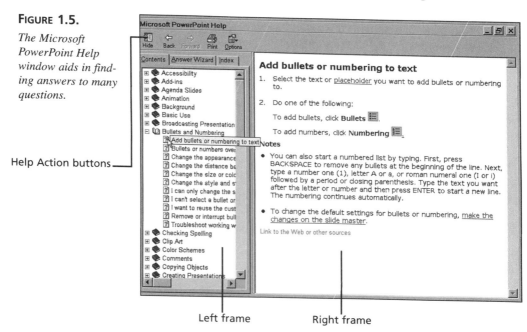

Help Action buttons

Left frame   Right frame

You may want to maximize or resize the PowerPoint Help window while you are researching topics. You can use the scrollbars to view more of a frame or resize the frames.

You should refer to the Contents section of the Help file when you want to find information about a general topic. If you aren't familiar with presentation terms or are new to Office applications, the Contents section is a good place to start. To use the Contents Help option, follow these steps:

To Do: Help Contents

1. With the Help window open, click the Contents tab (see Figure 1.5).
2. Click the plus sign (+) next to any book icon, and the book will open to show available topics.
3. Click the topic title you are interested in to read the documentation in the right frame of the Help window.

You can click any blue underlined text and read more about the particular subject.

The Help index is useful when you need to find help on a very specific topic and don't want to review every option available in the Contents listing. The Index option can quickly advise you on how to perform a specific task because it does a limited context-sensitive search. To use the Help index, follow these steps:

To Do: Help Index

1. With the Help window open, click the Index tab to display the Help index as shown in Figure 1.6.
2. Enter a keyword for which you want to search.
3. Click the Search button.
4. Click the desired keyword or topic to display the information in the text display frame.

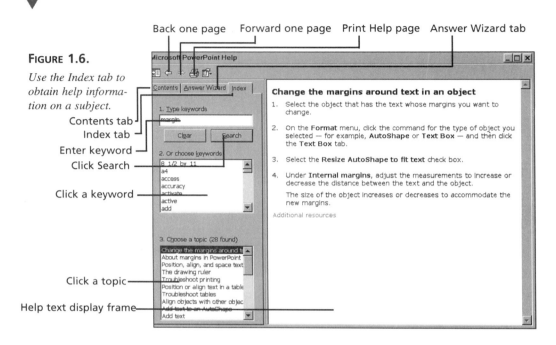

FIGURE 1.6.

Use the Index tab to obtain help information on a subject.

The Answer Wizard

The Answer Wizard works in much the same manner as the Office Assistant. Open the Answer Wizard by clicking on the Answer Wizard tab in the Help window. Then, simply enter your question in the What Would You Like to Do? box, and click the Search button. Help will try its best to give you an appropriate response in the Topic display list box. Read all about a specific topic by double-clicking on it.

When you have finished reading about a topic and using Microsoft PowerPoint Help, you can choose to do any of the following:

- Get help on another subject
- Click the Print button to print the Help file currently displayed
- Click the Back button to return to a previously displayed help topic
- Click the Close button to exit the Help system

Using ScreenTips

You can use the ScreenTips option to display information about any toolbar button on the screen. To activate the ScreenTip, hold the mouse pointer over the button in question to display a pop-up information box. Figure 1.7 demonstrates a ScreenTip for the Print button.

FIGURE 1.7.

ScreenTips provide information about buttons and icons and what they do.

Using Office on the Web

Another new feature included in PowerPoint 2000 is the Microsoft on the Web option, available from the Help menu. If you have Internet access, this is a great option for finding free stuff, getting up-to-date product news, reading frequently asked questions, getting online support, and more. To use Microsoft on the Web, choose Help, Office on the Web from the menu bar.

You must be logged on to the Internet before accessing this option.

This option is great when the Microsoft site is current. But there will be times when Microsoft might not have had time to keep everything up-to-date. Try it out if you feel so inclined, but if it does not work today, it will probably work tomorrow (or next week).

Exiting PowerPoint 2000

When you have finished using PowerPoint 2000 for the day, you will want to exit PowerPoint 2000. There are two quick and simple ways to exit from PowerPoint when the time comes to go home. To exit PowerPoint, you can use one of these two options:

- Choose File, Exit from the menu, or
- Click the application Close button

Technical Support

When it comes to technical support, Microsoft has given you many options. Before you call, make sure you have your product ID number ready, which you can find by choosing Help, About Microsoft PowerPoint from the menu bar. Table 1.3 lists important technical support numbers.

TABLE 1.2. MICROSOFT TECHNICAL SUPPORT.

Option Name	Number	Times Available (All Times Are Pacific Time)	Notes
Standard Support	(206) 635-7145	Weekdays, 6:00 a.m.-6:00 p.m., excluding holidays	If you bought the Microsoft Office Standard Edition, you have unlimited, no-charge, support on this line. You are also entitled to two free calls for assistance with Custom Solutions. If you bought the Microsoft Office Professional Edition, you have four free calls with Custom Solutions.
Priority Support	(900) 555-2000	24 hours a day, 7 days a week, excluding holidays	Calls are $35 each and charges appear on your telephone bill.
Text Telephone	(206) 635-4948	Weekdays, 6:00 a.m.-6:00 p.m., excluding holidays	TT/TDD services are available for the deaf or hearing impaired.

In addition to the technical support options listed in Table 1.2, more options are available to you. To see even more technical support options, follow these steps:

To Do: Getting More Technical Support

1. Choose Help, About Microsoft PowerPoint from the main menu.

2. Click the Tech Support button.

3. From the Contents listing, select the support option you want.

1

Summary

Opening and closing PowerPoint 2000 is no problem for you now! And Microsoft has built many help options into PowerPoint 2000 to assist you with any questions you might have. The Office Assistant establishes a helpful dialog box and asks questions before any confusion arises. ScreenTips display informative phrases, and Microsoft on the Web gives you round-the-clock access to the latest information. In the next hour, you're introduced to the AutoContent Wizard, a helpful tool for automatically creating and structuring your presentation.

Q&A

Q I can't connect to the Office on the Web; what's wrong?

A You need to be logged on to the Internet to activate this feature. Check to make sure that you are logged on and that the phone line is connected to your modem. If you are still experiencing difficulties, see whether you can connect to another, unrelated, site, such as www.yahoo.com. If you cannot connect to anyone, call your Internet service provider (ISP) to obtain assistance. If you can connect to other sites, Microsoft is probably very busy, or is experiencing difficulties. Simply try again another time.

If you do not have an Internet service provider, you will need to first obtain this service. You will need a modem connected to your computer as well. Microsoft offers a service, MSN; and many others are available. Ask your friends whom they use and why. Call and compare pricing. After you choose an ISP, they will help you with the details to get you connected to the Internet.

HOUR 2

Quick Start: Creating Your First Presentation

Congratulations! You made it through the first hour on background information and installing PowerPoint 2000. The rest of this book gives you the information you need to actually start using PowerPoint 2000. Hour 2 is designed to help you quickly create presentations by using the powerful but simple tools built into PowerPoint 2000. In tandem with Hour 3, "Basic PowerPoint File Management: Saving, Opening, and Creating Presentations," you learn the basics of producing great-looking, coherent presentations. If you cover only the next two hours, you could put this book on the shelf and still be able to create basic presentations. However, if you want to learn about all the cool features of PowerPoint 2000 that will impress your audience, you'll read the entire book. In this hour, you will learn the following:

- How to use the AutoContent Wizard
- The correct names for all the PowerPoint screen elements and what they do for you

- How to view your presentation in different ways
- How to use spell check and print your presentation

Starting the AutoContent Wizard

Every time you start PowerPoint 2000, the PowerPoint dialog box is displayed, as shown in Figure 2.1. You can use it to choose the method for starting your PowerPoint 2000 session. The main choices are creating a new presentation or opening an existing presentation. More information about the dialog box options is given in Hour 3.

FIGURE 2.1.

The PowerPoint dialog box enables you to choose different layouts for your slides.

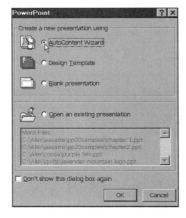

The PowerPoint dialog box shows up only when you first start a PowerPoint 2000 session. After its first appearance, it disappears. You don't see it again until you exit PowerPoint 2000 and start a new session.

The first option in the PowerPoint dialog box list is the AutoContent Wizard, the best method for starting a presentation if you're new to PowerPoint. It's also a great tool to use if you need to create a presentation quickly. The AutoContent Wizard is a guide composed of several screens that help you create professional presentations. It leads you through a series of questions so you can choose the best layout for your presentation. You can select from several predefined content templates. The AutoContent Wizard supplies not only the design for your presentation, but also ideas, starter text, formatting, and organization. It's an excellent tool to use if you don't know where to start.

When the AutoContent Wizard starts, the first screen displayed is the start screen, shown in Figure 2.2. It provides explanatory text that introduces you to the AutoContent Wizard. Look over the text, and then click the Next button. That advances you to the next screen in the AutoContent Wizard.

FIGURE 2.2.

The start screen of the AutoContent Wizard enables you to begin using the wizard.

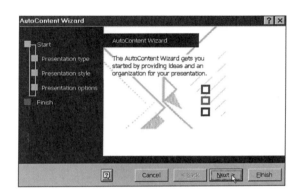

The second screen in the wizard defines the presentation type. You use this screen to select the type of presentation you're going to create. You can scroll through the list of all the available types or click a category button to narrow the list of choices. If you don't see a presentation type that fits your needs, just click the General button and select the Generic presentation type. For example, if you were going to create a presentation on basket weaving, an unsupported topic, click the General button and select the Generic presentation type, as shown in Figure 2.3. After you have selected a presentation type, click the Next button.

FIGURE 2.3.

The AutoContent Wizard's presentation type screen is shown with the Generic presentation type selected.

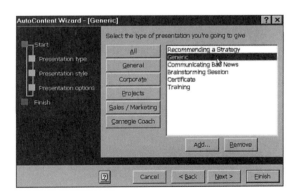

You can add your own presentation types to the AutoContent Wizard by selecting a category and then clicking the Add button. This feature is especially helpful if you have downloaded new presentation designs from the Microsoft site or other sources, and want those designs available when you use the AutoContent Wizard.

The AutoContent Wizard's third screen contains the Presentation style options, as shown in Figure 2.4, where you select the target output format for your presentation. You have five choices:

- Onscreen presentation. Use this option when you give your presentation using an onscreen projector hooked to a computer (usually a laptop). You will then show your presentation using PowerPoint 2000 on the computer.
- Web presentation. Use this option for Internet or kiosk presentations.
- Black and white overheads. This option is used when you will print without color onto slide transparencies.
- Color overheads. Color overheads are similar to black-and-white overheads, only with color.
- 35mm slides. Use slides when you will give your presentation with the use of a slide projector (just like Dad's vacation presentation).

After you have set the Presentation style for your presentation, click the Next button.

FIGURE 2.4.

The Presentation style screen of the AutoContent Wizard gives you many different display options.

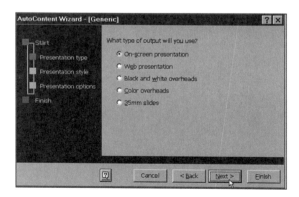

The next screen is the Presentation options screen, as shown in Figure 2.5. Here you get to give your presentation a title, and include a footer if you want. Simply click in the appropriate text box and enter your information. When you have completed this screen, click the Next button.

You can add or delete the footer (text that appears at the bottom of every page) later, if you change your mind. Hour 8, "Working with the Masters," covers this topic in more detail.

FIGURE 2.5.

In the Presentation options screen, you can choose to let PowerPoint 2000 enter the title, footer, date, and slide number automatically.

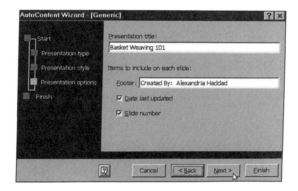

2

The title of your presentation will be placed on the title slide of your presentation. The title slide is the first slide in your presentation.

The last AutoContent Wizard screen is the finish screen, shown in Figure 2.6. The AutoContent Wizard has finished its question-and-answer session, so it's time to generate the presentation file. If you need to change any previously set options, now would be a good time. You can use the Back button to go backward through the wizard screen by screen and change any option you want. You can also just cancel the whole darn thing and go to lunch. If you've decided to take the plunge, all you need to do is click the Finish button to view your generated presentation.

FIGURE 2.6.

Click the Finish button to accept your newly created presentation.

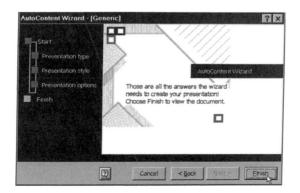

What You See Onscreen

Now that you have finished with the AutoContent Wizard, you will see your presentation in Normal view, as displayed in Figure 2.7. The PowerPoint 2000 screen also displays several toolbars, a color view of your presentation, and the helpful Office Assistant.

For those who have used previous versions of PowerPoint, the new Normal view might take some getting used to. It is a combination of three views: Slide, Outline, and Notes Page. Later in this hour, you will learn more about the different views in PowerPoint 2000.

FIGURE 2.7.

The presentation is shown as it appears in the Normal view.

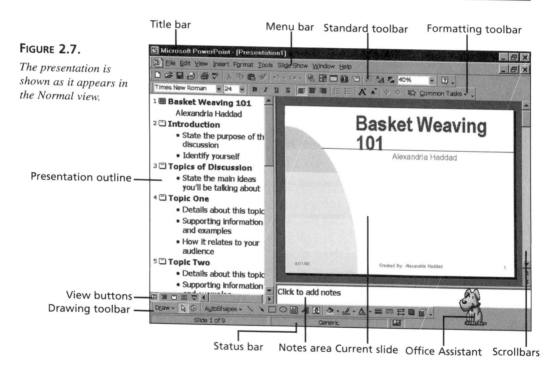

The presentation outline is made up of sample slides that have been generated by the AutoContent Wizard. The slides have suggestions that indicate the type of information to be entered on each slide. Before you begin to customize the presentation with specific information, you should become familiar with the PowerPoint screen elements and what they can do for you.

The Bars

There are several bars on your screen, and they all have a different job to do (but they don't serve any stiff drinks). The following sections give you a brief description of each bar type, starting from the top of the screen and working down.

Title Bar

The title bar sits at the top of your screen. Its job is to display the title of the application you're using and your presentation's name. Because you haven't yet saved your presentation and given it a name (that step comes in Hour 3), the title is a generic name. Presentation1 is the default name for the first unnamed presentation created in this PowerPoint session. The next unnamed presentation would be Presentation2, and so on. The title bar also holds the Minimize, Restore/Maximize, and Close buttons on the far right for the application (PowerPoint 2000).

Menu Bar

The menu bar is where you can choose PowerPoint 2000 commands. The menu bar also contains the Minimize, Restore/Maximize, and Close buttons on the far right. These buttons will affect the presentation window, but not the PowerPoint software as the buttons on the Title bar control the software. Most of PowerPoint 2000's commands can be found in the drop-down menus under one of the main menu titles: File, Edit, View, Insert, Format, Tools, Slide Show, Window, and Help. After you click on any main menu title, you can view other drop-down menus by simply sliding the mouse pointer over a title, and the corresponding menu will open. Take a few minutes to familiarize yourself with the menu by clicking on File and reading the commands (don't click on anything in the drop-down menu, just read); then continue across the menu bar until you have completed reading the Help menu. To close the menu, either click the menu title again, click outside the drop-down menu, or press the Esc key once. If you have a menu plus a submenu open, such as File, Send To and the subsequent submenu that appears, you will need to hit Esc once for each menu displayed to close them.

 A command is a task that you want to do in PowerPoint. There are commands to save, print, change the font, and perform many other operations.

If you have used previous versions of PowerPoint, you may think that PowerPoint 2000 is missing some menu commands. Not so—Microsoft has created new personalized menus that are simplified and with only the most popular choices initially displayed. If you rest your mouse on the menu title for a moment, or click the two down-pointing arrows as shown in Figure 2.8, the full menu will expand, giving you all the available choices. After you have used a command, the menu adapts and the command is added to the menu permanently. You can turn the personalized menu feature off and display all the menus by performing the following steps:

To Do: Turn Off the Personalized Menu Feature

1. Select Tools, Customize from the menu bar to open the Customize dialog box.
2. Click the Options tab, and uncheck the Menus Show Recently Used Commands First check box.
3. Click the Close button.

> The rest of this book will be written with the personalized menu feature turned off. You can turn this feature back on later by checking the Menus Show Recently Used Commands First check box and clicking the Reset My Usage Data button.

FIGURE 2.8.

Use the Customize dialog box to turn off (or on) personalized menus.

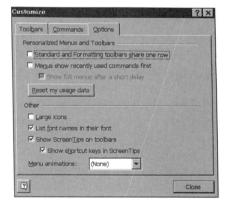

> Changing this setting will affect the way all of the Office 2000 menus operate.

Toolbars

Toolbars are the catchy bars that contain little buttons with graphical images on them; you click the buttons to perform certain tasks. PowerPoint 2000 comes with several predesigned toolbars. You can customize any toolbar or even create your own; PowerPoint gives you total flexibility. You learn more about customization in Hour 24, "PowerPoint Power Hour." The three main toolbars are the Standard, Formatting, and Drawing toolbars. You can display or hide any toolbar by using the following steps:

To Do: Display or Hide a Toolbar

1. Choose View, Toolbars from the menu. A submenu appears listing all the available toolbars.

2. Click the toolbar name you want to display or hide. A check mark indicates that a toolbar is currently displayed.

There's another method for changing the display attributes for the toolbars. You can position the mouse pointer on any toolbar and right-click. This opens up the list of toolbars available to you. Select the toolbar you want to display or hide.

The Standard toolbar has buttons for the most common tasks you perform in PowerPoint 2000, such as saving, printing, or spell checking a presentation.

The Formatting toolbar has buttons that make formatting a snap. You use most of the buttons to format text, such as changing the font type or size, making your text bold or italic, turning bullets off, and so on. Hour 5, "Working with PowerPoint Text Objects," covers in more detail text formatting options.

The Drawing toolbar sits at the bottom of your screen. It contains buttons that are used— you guessed it—when you are working with drawing objects. Many of the commands are not available except from the Drawing toolbar. Hour 11, "Drawing Text-Type Objects," and Hour 12, "Drawing Shapes in PowerPoint," cover using the drawing toolbar in more detail.

Scrollbars

Scrollbars are used to scroll through the current presentation. When you drag the scroll button on the vertical scrollbar, PowerPoint 2000 displays a ScreenTip that indicates which slide you're going to display.

Status Bar

The PowerPoint 2000 status bar is the bar at the bottom of the PowerPoint window. It displays three pieces of information:

- The slide (page) you're currently working on and how many slides are included in the entire presentation.
- The type of the current presentation design.
- Whether Spell Check as You Type is active. If it is active, you will see a small icon that looks like a book with a red check mark. If it is not, you will see nothing in the third section of the status bar.

> To choose a new design for your presentation, you can double-click the design area of the status bar. You can then apply a different presentation design to the presentation. More about presentation designs in Hour 4, "Working with Slides."

Presentation Perspectives

After you have finished answering the questions posed by the AutoContent Wizard, you see the sample presentation displayed in Normal view. Other views are available when you need them. PowerPoint 2000 has six different ways to view your presentation:

- Normal view
- Slide Sorter view
- Notes Page view
- Slide Show view
- Outline view
- Slide view

Each view has a different function. The different views are described in the following sections. To switch views, you can use either the View menu or the view buttons in the lower-left corner of the PowerPoint window.

Normal View

Normal view is a combination of Outline, Slide, and Notes Page views. This is a new view for PowerPoint 2000, as shown in Figure 2.9. You can resize each frame of the view by dragging the frame border to a new location. Normal view facilitates getting your presentation finished in the shortest possible time. This is the view you see first in PowerPoint 2000. You can switch to Normal view by selecting View, Normal from the menu, or by clicking the Normal view button in the lower left of the screen.

FIGURE 2.9.

Normal view combines Outline, Normal, and Notes Page views to give you an overall look at your slide.

Outline Pane ———

Outline View ———

Normal View ———

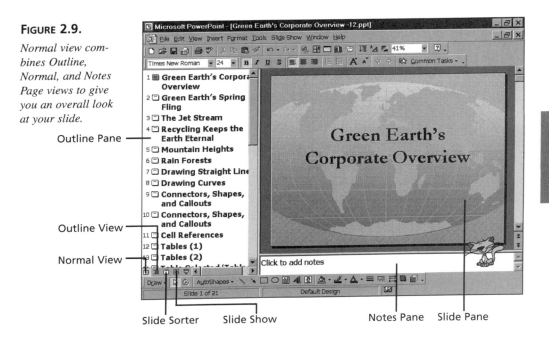

Slide Sorter   Slide Show   Notes Pane   Slide Pane

Normal view is sometimes referred to as Tri-Pane view because it displays a slide in three different views, on one screen, in three panes.

Slide Sorter View

The Slide Sorter view displays a miniature of each slide in your presentation, as shown in Figure 2.10. Use the Slide Sorter view when you want to add some polish to a presentation. You can add transitions to your presentation (see Hour 9, "Basics of Slide Shows," and Hour 10, "Adding Pizzazz to a Slide Show"), or use the Slide Sorter view to easily move, delete, and copy slides. You can switch to Slide Sorter view by selecting View, Slide Sorter from the menu, or clicking the Slide Sorter view button in the lower left of the screen.

FIGURE 2.10.

You can see the different slides that comprise your presentation in Slide Sorter view.

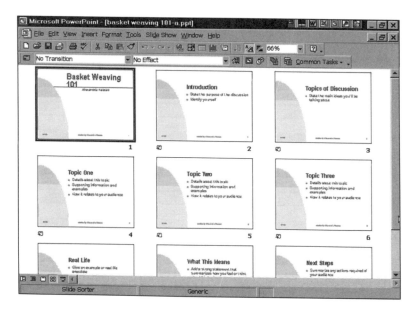

Slide Show View

Slide Show view is the mode in which to operate if you want to display your presentation onscreen or preview it for further editing. To move from slide to slide, simply click the mouse until you reach the end of your presentation. You can start the Slide Show by selecting View, Slide Show from the menu, or clicking the Slide Show button in the lower left of the screen.

> You can always cancel the presentation by pressing the Esc key on your keyboard.

> If you want to see the entire presentation from slide one to the end of the presentation, select View, Slide Show from the menu. If you click the Slide Show button (in the lower-left corner of the screen), your presentation begins from the current slide.

Outline and Slide View

The Outline and Slide views are simply larger views of the Normal view panes. They enable you to work in the selected view, sized for the whole screen. If you need only to edit text, you may find it helpful to use the Outline view. When you are working strictly with graphics, Slide view might prove more beneficial.

Notes Page

This view displays the slide and the notes area as they would print on a page if you chose to print Notes Pages. You can use the Notes Page view to add notes to the slides in your presentation, just as you can add notes in the Normal view. Simply click the notes area and type your notes. You can also add graphics to your notes in the Notes Page view.

Displaying Slides

There are several ways to navigate from slide to slide when you're editing your presentation. The method you choose depends on what view is currently active and whether you prefer using the keyboard or the mouse.

The Notes Page view is sized to show both the slide and the notes area onscreen. You may find it hard to type with the notes area so small. To remedy this, simply click the notes area, and then set the zoom to 75% or 100%.

Using the Keyboard

Table 2.1 lists keyboard navigation you can use to display different slides in your presentation.

TABLE 2.1. COMMON POWERPOINT 2000 NAVIGATION KEYS.

Key Combination	Movement
PgUp	Positions you back one slide at a time.
PgDn	Positions you forward one slide at a time.
Ctrl+Home	Positions you at the beginning of the presentation.
Ctrl+End	Positions you at the end of the presentation.

Using the Mouse

You can also use the mouse to scroll through your presentation. In Normal, Slide, and Notes Page views, the vertical scrollbar also contains Previous Slide and Next Slide buttons. You can click the buttons to move to the previous or next slide.

Zooming

At times, you might find that you need to change the onscreen magnification of a slide. Magnification is commonly referred to as *zoom*. When you start working with the drawing tools or want to create speaker notes, the capability to zoom in and out of a slide is extremely important. To change the zoom options, follow these steps:

To Do: Change the Zoom Options

1. Choose View, Zoom from the menu to open the Zoom dialog box.
2. Select the appropriate zoom percentage, as shown in Figure 2.11.
3. Click OK.

FIGURE 2.11.

Selecting the zoom percentage in the Zoom dialog box.

You also can use the Zoom button on the standard toolbar to quickly zoom in or out of a slide. Click the drop-down arrow next to the Zoom button and select another view percentage. Or click the Zoom button and type in what percentage you want.

When you're in Normal view, you must have the slide frame active to use the Zoom control. To activate the slide frame, simply click anywhere in the frame.

Customizing the Sample Slides

You now should be familiar with all the PowerPoint screen elements and know how to move between your presentation slides. Now you're ready to learn how to customize the generic presentation. The standard sample text previously generated by the AutoContent Wizard needs to be replaced with your specific information. Figure 2.12 illustrates the sample presentation after entering the customized content. You may find that editing the outline is the easiest way to go.

FIGURE 2.12.

The Basket Weaving 101 presentation with more information entered.

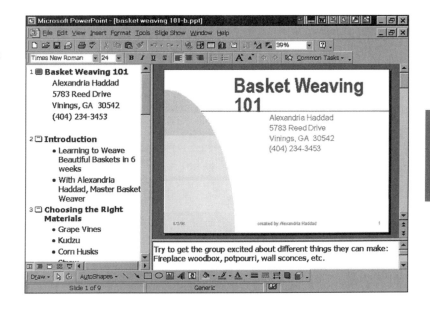

Editing the Outline

The AutoContent Wizard's sample text serves as a guide that gives you an idea of what content should be displayed on each slide. These are only suggestions, however; you can display any message you want in your presentation. PowerPoint's Outline view makes editing slide content very easy. Simply type your own words into the presentation outline and delete the sample text created by the AutoContent Wizard. The modified text automatically appears on the appropriate slide. As you type in the outline, the slides will change to reflect your input.

To get the project done quickly so you can take Friday off, PowerPoint lets you skip a step. You can select the sample text by dragging over it with the mouse, and then simply start typing in your replacement text. This method saves time by not having to delete the generic text first. Hour 5, "Working with PowerPoint Text Objects," covers different ways to select text.

Editing the Slide

You can also edit the text directly on the slides. Editing slides is easy when you understand the basics of working with text objects. To edit a text object, just click the text you want to edit and start typing. PowerPoint displays a cursor, shown in Figure 2.13, showing you where to add and delete text. You might need to move the cursor to the correct position before you edit the text. Use the arrow keys on the keyboard to reposition the cursor.

FIGURE 2.13.

Slide one of the Basket Weaving 101 presentation with the title object selected.

Adding Speaker Notes

PowerPoint 2000 not only helps you create your presentation, but also assists in creating speaker notes, which are paragraphs that serve as your reference material when you give your presentation. You can type speaker notes into your presentation while in Normal view. The notes will print only when you print notes pages. To add speaker notes, follow these steps:

To Do: Add Speaker Notes

1. In Normal view, display the slide to which you want to add notes.
2. Click in the notes frame (lower right, under the slide), as shown in Figure 2.14.
3. Type your notes.
4. Click any area outside the slide (any gray area) when finished.

FIGURE 2.14.

Adding speaker notes is as easy as adding text to your slide.

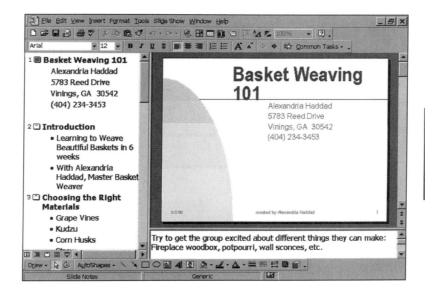

Spell Checking the Presentation

While you have been busy typing all the important information for your presentation, PowerPoint 2000 has been making sure you're spelling the words correctly. You might have noticed the automatic spell check at work when a red wavy underline is displayed beneath a misspelled word. This line appears every time you misspell a word. You can fix your spelling immediately when PowerPoint tells you a mistake has been made, or you can wait until you have finished typing and run a complete spell check. If you've used Microsoft Word before, you will recognize the spell checker in PowerPoint 2000. You can spell check your presentation in one of several ways, including the following:

- Choose Tools, Spelling from the menu.
- Click the Spelling button on the standard toolbar.

With either method, the Spelling dialog box, shown in Figure 2.15, opens and your spell check begins.

FIGURE 2.15.

The PowerPoint 2000 Spelling dialog box highlights each misspelled word, and then gives you the option to correct it.

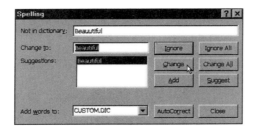

Every misspelled word or word that's not recognized by the spell checker is highlighted in the Not in Dictionary box. PowerPoint usually makes an appropriate suggestion in the Change To box about how the spelling of the word should be changed. PowerPoint sometimes gives you a whole list of suggestions to choose from in the Suggestions list box. To modify the spelling, simply click the correct word, and then click the Change button.

If the word is spelled correctly, but PowerPoint doesn't recognize it as a "real" word, you can tell PowerPoint to ignore the word by clicking the Ignore button. You have a few other options when you run the spell checker. Table 2.2 covers each option and the operation it performs.

TABLE 2.2.   POWERPOINT SPELL CHECK OPTIONS.

Option	What It Does
Ignore	Ignores the word for that one time.
Ignore All	Ignores every occurrence of this word (only in this presentation).
Change	Changes the misspelled word to the word displayed in the Change To box.
Change All	Changes every occurrence of a misspelled word to the word displayed in the Change To box.
Add	Adds the word to the open dictionary file. The default file is CUSTOM.DIC. This is the option you want for words such as your name and your company name.
Suggest	Looks for a similar word in the dictionary.
AutoCorrect	Does the same thing the Change button does with the added bonus of adding the misspelled word and the correctly spelled word to your AutoCorrect dictionary.
Close	Closes the spell checker.

You can correct a misspelled word without running the spell checker on the entire document. You can immediately correct a misspelled word that has a red wavy underline by placing your cursor inside the word, right clicking, and selecting an option from the shortcut menu.

Printing the Presentation

When you have finished editing the presentation contents, you can print your presentation by selecting File, Print from the menu. As you can see in Figure 2.16, you have access to many print options from the Print dialog box. In the PowerPoint Print dialog box, you can select what pages to print, what slide content to print, and how many copies to print. You can also choose to print all the presentation's slides, just the current slide, or a specific combination of slides. You have even more options for determining the contents to be printed. For example, you can print the slides, speaker notes, handouts, or the presentation's outline. Table 2.3 lists the options most often chosen.

TABLE 2.3. POPULAR PRINTING OPTIONS.

Option	Result
Name box	Select the printer that you want PowerPoint 2000 to print to.
Print Range	Select specific slides to print; that is, all slides, the current slide you are viewing, or a range of slides.
Print What	Specify what you want to print by clicking the drop-down arrow and selecting Slides, Handouts, Notes Pages, or Outline. If you select Handouts, you must also specify the options to print from the Handouts area.
Grayscale	Choose this option if you are printing color slides in black and white.
Pure Black and White	Will print the presentation in black or white (no gray).

FIGURE 2.16.

The PowerPoint Print dialog box gives you many different printing options.

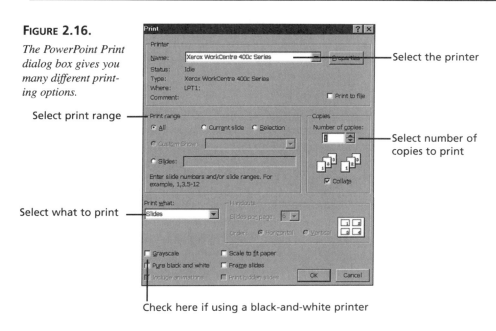

Select print range

Select what to print

Select the printer

Select number of copies to print

Check here if using a black-and-white printer

Although PowerPoint can print more than one copy of your presentation, it's more efficient and cost-effective to photocopy it because printers are slower, and the ink is more costly.

As mentioned earlier, PowerPoint 2000 enables you to print not only the presentation, but audience handouts, speaker notes, and an outline as well. You can print in color or in black and white.

To print your presentation, you can either click the Print button on the Standard toolbar, or follow these steps:

To Do: Print a Presentation

1. Choose File, Print from the menu to open the Print dialog box.
2. Change any settings you want.
3. Click the OK button.

Although clicking the Print button is an option, resist the urge to use it in PowerPoint 2000. All the Microsoft Office applications use the Print button as a shortcut to print the current document using the default settings. When using PowerPoint 2000, you may find that you want to select specific print options before you print. All the Print buttons in Microsoft Office products operate in this manner. The button is usually a great shortcut, but with PowerPoint, you often don't want to print the entire presentation in full color.

Summary

This hour has been jam-packed with information. You have learned how to create a presentation by using the powerful AutoContent Wizard. You've also learned about the screen elements, how to use them, and how they can help you get your work done a little more quickly. PowerPoint has many different views for you to display your slides, and each view helps you perform different tasks.

You can quickly move to another slide in your presentation by using the mouse or the keyboard, and zooming allows you to view a slide either close up or from a distance, depending on your needs. After you have created an initial presentation using the AutoContent Wizard, you can edit the content of the sample slide using either the Outline or Slide in Normal views.

PowerPoint also makes it easy to enter speaker notes. If you're not a great speller, no need to fear; with PowerPoint's handy spell checker, you'll look like the spelling bee champion. If you need to print your presentation on a black-and-white printer, PowerPoint lets you view the presentation with the Black and White view. And printing has never been easier—you can simply click a button to print the entire presentation quickly, or use the menu command to select which slides and what view to print.

Hold on to your hats! Next up is Hour 3, "Basic PowerPoint File Management: Saving, Opening, and Creating Presentations."

Q&A

The following are more questions and helpful answers. They just might answer the question poised on the tip of your tongue.

Q What do all these buttons on all these toolbars do?

A They all do different things, but if you position your mouse pointer on any button without clicking, you get a little ScreenTip that pops up and tells you what task a particular button performs.

Q Why don't I see any ScreenTips?

A For some reason, this option has been turned off. To turn it back on, choose View, Toolbars, Customize from the menu, then click the Options tab. Click Show ScreenTips On Toolbars and click Close. Refer to Hour 24 for more information about customizing the toolbars.

Q I like to check my spelling after I have finished typing the text for my entire presentation. I find the automatic spell checking to be very distracting. Can I turn it off?

A Yes. To turn the automatic spell check off, choose Tools, Options from the menu to open the Options dialog box. Click the Spelling and Style tab; then uncheck the Check Spelling as You Type check box. Click OK.

Q I want to print only slides 4, 5, 6, and 10, but every time I click the Print button, the printer prints all 30 slides of my presentation. How can I print only the slides I need?

A First, don't click the Print button. This is a habit learned from using the other Office applications, but it's usually not a very useful option when you're working in PowerPoint. Instead, use the File, Print menu option, and select the Slides option under Print range. The range you would enter for the sample question would be 4-6, 10.

Hour 3

Basic PowerPoint File Management: Saving, Opening, and Creating Presentations

Welcome to Hour 3. Now that you have created your first presentation, you need to save it and learn the steps for reopening it later. After you save your presentation document, you can give it to colleagues so they can add some final comments or modifications. Here are a few questions that can come up when you're working with files:

- Where is my presentation file located on my computer?
- How do I open the file?
- What concepts and tasks make up file management?

These questions and other intriguing issues are answered in this hour. You might also be at the point where you're thinking, "The AutoContent Wizard is great, but I have my own ideas for my presentation." This hour also covers how to create a new presentation in your own unique format. In this hour, you learn how to do the following:

- How to save and open an existing presentation, or start a new presentation
- How to select a different disk drive or folder in which to store or retrieve a presentation file
- How to search for and locate a specific file
- How to work on more than one file at a time (multitask)

A Few Words on How a PC Stores Presentations

A computer's scariest attribute is the intangible aspect of its contents. As humans, we're used to touching objects before we believe they're real. Computers store presentation files on a storage medium called a disk drive.

The best way to visualize the physical and logical storage of files is to correlate computer concepts with real-world objects, which makes Windows file management much easier to understand. The Windows interface uses disk drives, folders, subfolders, and documents for file management.

A disk drive is analogous to an office filing cabinet. Like a filing cabinet, a disk drive is used to store documents that can contain presentations, spreadsheets, or databases. Each disk drive has a unique name. Typically, you access drives by referring to a corresponding letter, such as A, B, C, D, and so on. Each letter represents a distinct container—a separate filing cabinet—that's used to store information in your computer. Usually, the A: or B: drive is reserved for removable media, such as floppy disks. The C: drive letter designates your computer's hard drive. Other letters commonly represent additional drives—the D: drive can be assigned to the CD-ROM drive, and any additional letter in the alphabet is probably a remote networked drive.

You can understand the folder and subfolder components by expanding the filing cabinet analogy. A filing cabinet has drawers with green hanging file folders in them; these folders might contain smaller manila folders used to store paper documents in an organized fashion. The folder and subfolder concepts correspond to the green hanging folders and manila folders, respectively. As in the real world, you can store document files in either folders or subfolders. In Figure 3.1, the document path C:\My Documents\PowerPoint\ Basket 101.ppt has been broken down to correlate it with real-world objects.

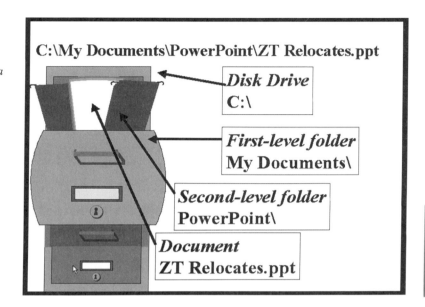

FIGURE 3.1.

A computer document can be compared to objects in a filing

Saving a Presentation

Saving your work is one of the most important tasks you do when you work with PowerPoint. Until you save your work, it doesn't exist in a permanent form. Saving is extremely easy, and you should do it often. When you save a presentation, you must provide a filename for the document that should indicate the presentation's contents. By using an easy-to-remember filename, you can readily locate the presentation in future PowerPoint sessions.

PowerPoint 2000 also includes options for saving your presentation in other formats. For example, you can save a presentation to the HTML (HyperText Markup Language) format so the presentation can be viewed through a standard Web browser, such as Internet Explorer or Netscape. You can post the presentation on the Internet so it's accessible for anyone who can reach your Web site. For more information about formatting a presentation for the World Wide Web, see Part VI, "Multimedia, the World Wide Web, and Other Cool Stuff." You also can save a presentation with information about its runtime characteristics. If you want to distribute the electronic presentation document to an audience, save it in Slide Show view (which is explained in more detail in Hour 9, "Basics of Slide Shows").

There are two types of save operations: Save As or Save. For an unnamed presentation that hasn't been previously saved, both options work in exactly the same way. However, after a presentation has been given a document name, the options work a little differently. Save As lets you specify a new document name and location. The Save operation simply updates the presentation with the same name in the current location, with no questions asked.

The Save button on the standard toolbar works much like the Print button. You won't see anything happen, but your file will be saved using the Save command.

You should use the Save As command when you save a file for the first time. Save As is also used when you want to give a presentation a new name or you want to save it in a different location or folder. You can quickly save a presentation to a floppy disk with the Save As operation by specifying the appropriate drive letter. To save your presentation for the first time or to give a presentation a new name, follow these steps:

To Do: Save a Presentation for the First Time

1. Choose File, Save As from the main menu. This opens the Save As dialog box.
2. In the File Name box, enter a name for your presentation.
3. To save the presentation to a floppy disk or a different folder, select the appropriate location from the Save In drop-down list.
4. Click Save.

Your filename can have up to 255 alphanumeric characters and can also contain the space character, as shown in Figure 3.2.

FIGURE 3.2.

Saving your presentations is easy in the PowerPoint Save As dialog box.

Choose drive and/or folder here

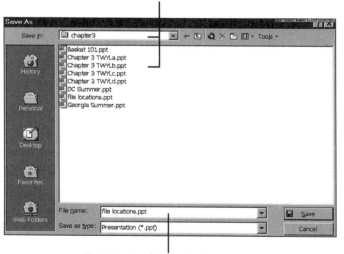

Type name of presentation here

After you save your presentation, the filename appears in the PowerPoint application's title bar instead of the generic PresentationX label. PowerPoint also automatically assigns the .PPT extension to the end of your filename.

The .PPT extension at the end of the filename tells Windows 95/98 that your file is a PowerPoint presentation.

You might not see the .PPT extension, depending on the system options that have been initialized for your operating system (Windows 95/98 or Windows NT).

Changing the Drive or Folders

By default, PowerPoint saves all your presentations on the C:\ disk drive in the My Documents folder. If you want to save a presentation on a different disk drive (such as a floppy disk) or in a different folder, you must indicate the new location by selecting an alternative disk drive and folder from the Save In list box. For example, to save the presentation to the A:\ drive, click the down triangle next to the Save In list box and select the 3 1/2 Floppy (A:) option from the list.

If you want to save a presentation in a different folder on your C:\ drive, you must first select the (C:) option from the Save In list box. You can then open a folder and subsequent subfolders by double-clicking the appropriate folder icon until you reach the location in which you want to save your presentation.

Using the Save Command

To quickly protect your work, use the Save command to periodically update your presentation document. A good rule of thumb is to save every 10 minutes, or after every major modification. Saving takes only a moment, so do it often. If your computer inadvertently crashes between saves, you have a better chance of retrieving all your hard work. You can save and update your presentation in one of two ways:

- Choose File, Save from the menu
- Click the Save button on the toolbar

3

Closing a Presentation

Closing a presentation takes it out of sight and mind. Before you go to lunch or leave for the day, it's best to close your presentation. You can do this in one of two ways:

- Choose File, Close from the main menu
- Click the document Close button on the menu bar

After you have closed a presentation, you have three options available:

- Open an existing presentation
- Start a new presentation
- Exit PowerPoint 2000

Each of these options is covered in the following sections.

Opening an Existing Presentation

You can open any PowerPoint presentation that has been previously created and saved to view or modify it. Opening a presentation is a simple process. In fact, it's almost the same as the steps you use to save a presentation. The only requirement is that you supply the saved presentation's location (drive and folder/subfolders). In PowerPoint, you can see a preview of the presentation file before it's officially opened. Figure 3.3 shows the Open dialog box with the Preview option. Use the following step to open a PowerPoint presentation:

FIGURE 3.3.

You can preview your PowerPoint file in the Open dialog box.

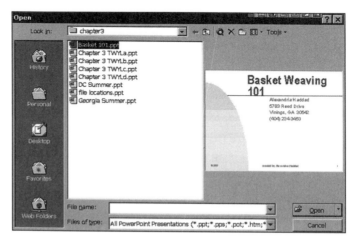

To Do: Open an Existing PowerPoint Presentation

1. Choose File, Open from the menu.

Or, do the following:

1. Click the Open button on the standard toolbar.

2. Select the correct drive or folder.

> To open a presentation document that's in a different location, select the drive or folder from the Look In drop-down list.

3. Select the presentation name from the file list. To see a preview of the presentation (if one is not showing), click the Views button on the Open Dialog Box toolbar (to the right of the Look In textbox) and choose Preview.

4. Click Open.

3

> PowerPoint "remembers" the last four files you have worked on. A quick way to open a presentation you have been working on recently is to select the filename from the bottom of the File menu.

Selecting and Opening Multiple Files

With PowerPoint, you can work on one presentation at a time or open several concurrent sessions. To open several presentations at once, follow these steps:

To Do: Select and Open Multiple Files

1. Choose File, Open from the menu to display the Open dialog box.

2. From the displayed list of files, select the files you want to open.

> To select multiple contiguous files, click the first file, hold down the Shift key, and click the last file. All files will be selected.
>
> To select multiple noncontiguous files, click the first file, and then hold down the Ctrl key while you click each subsequent file. Only the files you clicked will be selected.

3. Click the Open button to open all the selected presentations.

When you have multiple presentations open, you should use the Window menu item to switch between presentation documents. See the "Navigating Open Presentations" section of this hour for more information.

Starting a New Presentation

Starting a new presentation when you first open the PowerPoint application is an easy technique to grasp, as discussed in Hour 2. When you want to create a new presentation in the middle of an active PowerPoint session, the steps are a little different. You still have the same three options for your new presentation, but they are found in different places and are activated with different commands. The following sections explain where to find each of the options that are initially displayed in the PowerPoint dialog box.

AutoContent Wizard

During your PowerPoint session, the friendly AutoContent Wizard has gone into hiding. But don't worry—you can still find it in the New Presentation dialog box. To start a new presentation using the AutoContent Wizard, follow these steps:

To Do: Start a New Presentation Using the AutoContent Wizard

1. Choose File, New from the menu to open the New Presentation dialog box.
2. Click the General tab, if it is not already displayed.
3. Click the AutoContent Wizard, as shown in Figure 3.4.

FIGURE 3.4.

The New Presentation dialog box with the AutoContent Wizard selected.

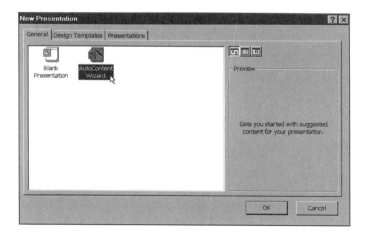

▲ 4. Finally, click OK to start the wizard.

Refer to Hour 2 for information about using the AutoContent Wizard.

Presentation Design (or Template)

When you first create a presentation, choosing the Template option is appropriate if you don't need any help with the logical flow of the ideas in the presentation, especially if you already know the content each slide will contain. Templates allow you to focus on creating the presentation message without worrying too much about the presentation's overall style. The template, which can also be called a presentation design, supplies the artistic theme or style for the slides. The template you choose defines the choice of colors, background graphics, and fonts. This is an excellent choice if you will be giving your presentation on a large screen. Professional commercial artists have created most of these designs. As much fun as PowerPoint 2000 is, you may not have the time to create the entire content for a presentation and worry about the design elements, too. Follow these steps to select an appropriate presentation design for your message:

To Do: Select a Presentation Design

1. Choose File, New from the menu to open the New Presentation dialog box.
2. Click the Design Templates tab (see Figure 3.5).
3. Select an appropriate design.
4. Click OK.

FIGURE 3.5.

The Design Templates tab of the New Presentation dialog box gives you many design options.

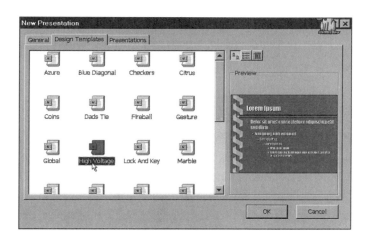

The first few times you select a presentation design, it's a good idea to preview all the designs you have available. You can preview a presentation design template either by clicking once on each design name or by using the arrow keys on your keyboard to highlight each design. You should also realize that the number of designs available on a computer varies. For example, Bob might have downloaded some extra design sets from the Microsoft Web site.

Blank Presentation

The final option available for creating a new presentation is to start a blank presentation. A blank presentation has no color, no design, and not a shred of fancy stuff. PowerPoint leaves all the slide formatting up to you. Unless you need to design a very specialized presentation—for example, when you're using your company's colors, logo, and font choices—you probably would do better choosing from one of the preformatted design Templates. If you need to create a presentation design for your company's use, use the blank presentation option. In general, though, when you start from a blank presentation, you could find yourself putting much more work into a presentation than necessary. Choose the AutoContent Wizard or a premade presentation design, if possible. However, when you need a blank canvas to create an exceptionally unique slide, follow these steps to start a new blank presentation:

To Do: Start a New Blank Presentation

1. Choose File, New from the menu to open the New Presentation dialog box.
2. Click the General tab.
3. Select Blank Presentation.
4. Click OK.

When you want to start a new blank presentation, you can also click the New button. However, if you want to select a presentation design or use the AutoContent Wizard, use the File, New menu command and save yourself some time.

Navigating Open Presentations

You can start a new presentation without closing the currently active presentation. Having several presentations open at once in PowerPoint 2000 is a great way to copy information from one presentation to another and compare different presentations, and has numerous other advantages. If you use this feature, you need to know how to switch between the presentations. At first, having several presentations open at one time may seem a little confusing—it's like having several projects on your desk at one time. You may not be working on them all at once (or you may be), but you need to have them all available to you throughout the day. Just like switching from one project to another on an actual desk, PowerPoint 2000 enables you to do the same thing with presentations.

Any presentation you might have open will be listed in the Window menu. You need only select the actual presentation name from the list. As you can see in Figure 3.6, there are currently three open presentations. The presentation your attention is currently focused on is called the active presentation window, which has a check mark by its name. To switch presentations, simply select the presentation by name and—presto—you're now billing some other client for the work! Here are the steps for switching between open presentations:

To Do: Switch Between Open Presentations

The Window menu has a few other options worth mentioning here. The New Window, Arrange All, and Cascade items all play important roles in the quest for seamless presentation navigation.

1. Click the Window menu title.
2. Click the presentation you want to switch to.

FIGURE 3.6.

The Window menu shows three presentations currently open.

Summary

You now know the fundamentals that allow you to create, print, show, and save a basic presentation. You could put this book down now if that were all you needed to know, but the fun has just begun. You wouldn't really be happy just knowing the basics; the excitement of PowerPoint starts after learning how to change colors, insert clip art, add WordArt, and add animation to a presentation. Also, you haven't yet explored the features that will make Bob actually want to give you that raise in salary, so don't stop now!

Q&A

Q If the power goes out, do I lose all my work?

A Not necessarily. PowerPoint has an AutoRecover feature you can set for just this purpose. Usually, AutoRecover is set to do a backup every 10 minutes. To view your current AutoRecover settings, choose Tools, Options from the menu and click the Save tab. Change the Save AutoRecover info so that it will save in increments of the number of minutes you want (the default is every 10 minutes). Make any other changes you want; then click the OK button.

Q I always save my files to my A: drive. Can I change the default drive and folder in which PowerPoint automatically saves?

A Yes. You can change the default file location to be any drive or folder. If you change the default file location to the A: drive, you need to always have a floppy disk in the disk drive to open a file or save a file, even if you plan on switching to the C: drive. The reason for this is that PowerPoint will attempt to open the default file location first. This is okay if you always work from your A: drive, but if you don't, you might find it annoying to have to constantly stop and put a disk in the computer.

To change the default file location for PowerPoint, choose Tools, Options from the menu to display the Options window and then click the Save tab. In the Default File Location box, type the new file location. For example, type A:\ for the A: drive. When you are finished, click the OK button. Now, every time you want to open or save a presentation, PowerPoint goes to the new location you specified.

PART II

Slides and PowerPoint Objects

Hour

Hour 4

Working with Slides

In the next three hours, you will be creating and formatting a complete presentation from the first slide to the last. During this hour, you learn how to work with the building blocks of a presentation: the slides. At the end of this hour, you will know how to do the following:

- Select the best layout for a slide using the AutoLayout feature
- Create and work with a title slide
- Add, delete, and move slides within a presentation
- Create and work with bulleted slides
- Change the layout of a slide or modify the design of the presentation

Using AutoLayout

When you start a new presentation using either the Design Template or Blank Presentation option, the first screen you see is the New Slide dialog box (see Figure 4.1). You should also see it every time you insert a new slide. The box asks you to select an AutoLayout, which is a preliminary, draft layout for that specific slide. All the AutoLayout formats except Blank have placeholders for different types of PowerPoint objects. PowerPoint has 24 AutoLayout designs from which you can choose, including Title Slide, Bulleted List, Chart, Text & Clip Art, and many others.

FIGURE 4.1.

You can select a slide format from the New Slide dialog box.

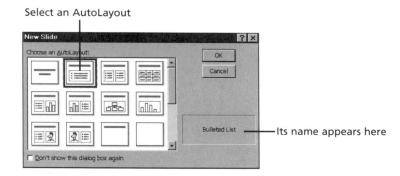

Select an AutoLayout

Its name appears here

 If you're adding text to your slide, you will probably want the information included when you perform a spell check. Rather than start with a blank slide, you need to either start with the AutoLayout option that most closely resembles what the finished slide should look like, or insert the text in the Outline pane of the slide.

Although you can add text to a presentation using the Insert, Text Box command, this text is not included in the outline and therefore is not included in a spell check.

Creating a Title Slide

The Title Slide is the very first presentation slide your audience sees, so it sets the tone for the rest of the presentation. The AutoContent Wizard automatically creates the Title Slide. When you do not use the AutoContent Wizard, you need to create a Title Slide for your presentation by selecting the Title Slide AutoLayout. After creating a title slide, enter your title slide information by simply clicking the title or subtitle placeholder and entering the appropriate text.

 A placeholder is a box with dashed lines on a slide, which contains instructions such as "Click to add title" or subtitle or text, as shown in Figure 4.2. For objects, the placeholder will say, "Double-click to add table" (or chart, org chart, clip art, object, or media clip).

An object is any item that you edit or add to a PowerPoint presentation; text, clip art, chart, and so on. This is unlike a word processor, where you work with mostly text. You work with text in PowerPoint too, but the text is contained in text object placeholders. There are other objects, such as clip art objects and drawing objects.

FIGURE 4.2.

Enter a title and subtitle on the title slide.

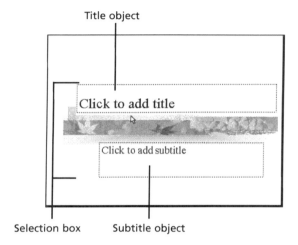

Title object

Click to add title

Click to add subtitle

Selection box   Subtitle object

4

Undoing Your Mistakes

If an action doesn't give you the effect you want, you can reverse it. The Undo feature can be used to undo the last command. To go back one step, you can either choose Edit, Undo from the menu or click the Undo button on the standard toolbar.

PowerPoint is initially set to remember the last 20 actions you have performed, so you could click the Undo button 20 times, if necessary. The Undo button also has a small down-pointing triangle next to it that, when clicked, displays a complete history of your most recent actions. To undo several commands all at once, simply click the last command you want in the list.

Right next to the Undo button is the Redo button. Redo undoes your undo (for all of us who get trigger-happy).

Adding New Slides

Unlike working with a word processing application, you have to explicitly add each new page (slide) in PowerPoint that you want to include in your presentation. Several different methods for adding a new slide are available, one of which is illustrated in Figure 4.3. To create a new slide, simply use one of the following methods. Try each method until you find the one that works best for you.

- Choose Insert, New Slide from the main menu, as shown in Figure 4.3.
- Press the Ctrl+M key combination.
- Click the New Slide button on the Standard toolbar.
- Select Common Tasks, New Slide from the Formatting toolbar.

PowerPoint adds a new slide after the slide that is currently displayed, as opposed to the end of the presentation. If slide two is currently displayed, a new slide added to the presentation is then slide three. If this happens to you, don't worry. You can easily move slides around later. Refer to the section "Moving Slides" later in this chapter for more in-depth information.

Creating and Using Bulleted or Numbered Slides

Most presentations you create contain at least one list of key points. The bulleted list presents this information in a manner your audience can easily understand. The slide in Figure 4.4 shows a simple bulleted slide in my "Letters to Grandma" presentation. In this slide, the bullets are small envelopes rather than the round, black dots you might be used to seeing. You can enter text in a bulleted slide either in the Outline or Slide pane.

An impressive feature of PowerPoint 2000 is its capability to AutoFit text to fit the placeholder. For example, if your bulleted list becomes a bit too long, PowerPoint 2000 will automatically resize the text to fit the placeholder. This also works in reverse; if you delete some items, PowerPoint 2000 will enlarge the text up to the original size.

PowerPoint 2000 now enables you to use numbers in addition to bullets. To use numbers instead of bullets, select the entire text object and click the numbering button on the Formatting toolbar. Refer to Hour 5, "Working with PowerPoint Text Objects," for more information.

Although PowerPoint permits a bulleted slide to have up to five levels, I don't recommend five levels of detail on a single slide. You want to get your point across to your audience, not lose them in too much crowded text. If you have that much to say, use additional slides.

4

FIGURE 4.4.

A bulleted slide is shown with one bulleted level.

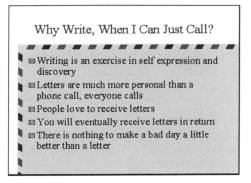

Entering Bulleted Text in the Slide Pane

It's very simple to enter and modify bulleted text in the Slide pane. You can quickly promote (move up in the hierarchy) or demote (move down in the hierarchy) bullet items. To create a multilevel bulleted list as shown in Figure 4.5, use the following steps:

To Do: Create a Multilevel Bulleted List

1. Click on the text object "Click to add text."

2. Type your first item (a first-level bullet) and press Enter.

3. Press the Tab key to demote the next bullet to a second-level bullet.

4. Type the desired text, press Enter, and repeat as needed. Press Enter after the last item. A second-level bullet will be created.

5. To promote the bullet to the first level, press Shift+Tab. Type the desired text and press Enter.

6. Repeat steps 3–5 until your list is complete. Do not press Enter after the very last bullet. If you do, either press Backspace or use the Undo feature.

7. Click anywhere outside the bulleted object to deselect the object.

FIGURE 4.5.

A bulleted slide can support multiple bullet levels.

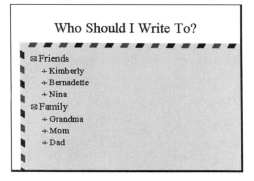

The bullet character for each level is determined by the presentation design that is chosen when you first created the presentation. The bullet style, color, and size can be edited, if desired. Hour 5 explains the steps for customizing bullet characteristics.

Entering Bulleted Text in the Outline Pane

You can also enter bulleted text in the Outline pane almost as easily as you can in Slide view. To enter text in Outline view, use the following steps:

To Do: Enter Bulleted Text in the Outline Pane

1. On a new slide, type the title of the slide and press Enter. PowerPoint then adds a new slide.

2. Press the Tab key to convert the new slide to a first-level bullet.

3. Type the desired text, a first-level bullet, and press Enter.

4. Press the Tab key to demote the next bullet to a second-level bullet (if desired—if not, skip steps 5 and 6).

5. Type the desired text, press Enter, and repeat as needed. Press Enter after the last item. A second-level bullet will be created.

6. To promote the bullet to the first level, press Shift+Tab.

7. Type the desired text and press Enter.

8. Repeat steps 3–7 as necessary.

When you complete the list, you can press Shift+Tab to create a new slide if desired or press Backspace to delete any unwanted bullets.

Moving Slides

When you insert slides, the order of your presentation can become a bit messy. Never fear, though; there's a way to move your slides around quickly and easily. You can use the Outline pane or switch to Slide Sorter view. In the Outline pane, use the following steps:

To Do: Move Slides

1. Place your mouse pointer on the slide icon for the slide you want to move. The mouse pointer looks like a four-headed arrow when it's over the slide icon.

2. Drag the slide icon to the new location.

PowerPoint displays a horizontal line, shown in Figure 4.6, that indicates the final destination for the moved slide.

You can also move slides while you're in Slide Sorter view, which can be a bit easier than the previous method. Simply switch to Slide Sorter view and drag the slide to the new location. It couldn't be easier to rearrange your thoughts or your slides, so let's get moving.

4

FIGURE 4.6.

Moving a slide in the Outline pane is quick and easy.

Horizontal line indicates where slide will be moved

Drag this icon to move a slide

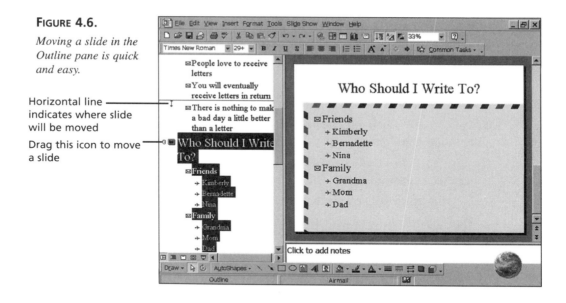

The duplicate slide is inserted after the original. Don't worry—you can always move the slide to a different location if you want.

Deleting Slides

There may come a time when a slide is no longer necessary for your presentation. For example, the slide that covers the reasons you don't write to your mother (she can't cook, she made you wear saddle shoes, she imposed a 9 p.m. curfew on you, and so on). To make the slide disappear, simply delete it by using these two simple steps:

To Do: Delete Slides

1. Display or click the slide you want to delete.
2. Choose Edit, Delete Slide from the menu.

If you aren't paying attention and accidentally delete the wrong slide, just click the Undo button or choose Edit, Undo from the menu.

Determining Page Setup

Use the Page Setup dialog box to set the size, orientation, and type of presentation slides you're creating. By default, your slides are sized for an onscreen show and set to print in Landscape orientation. You can change any page settings, but it's usually best to make changes before you start entering information in your presentation. To change the page setup, follow these steps:

To Do: Change the Page Setup Options

1. Choose File, Page Setup from the menu to open the Page Setup dialog box, as shown in Figure 4.7.

Select type of presentation

FIGURE 4.7.

The Page Setup dialog box enables you to change the size and page orientation of your slides, notes, handouts, and outline.

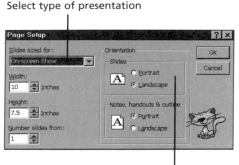

Select orientation

2. From the Slides Sized For drop-down list, select the appropriate slide format.

 Table 4.1 lists the seven different formats from which you can choose. If you select a custom format, you need to specify the presentation's width and height.

3. Select the orientation for the slides.

 Portrait is tall (vertical orientation) and Landscape is wide (horizontal orientation). The picture to the left of the option button demonstrates the difference.

4

▼ 4. Select the orientation for your notes, handouts, and outline.

5. Select the slide number to start with in the Number Slides From box.

▲ 6. Click the OK button.

TABLE 4.1. PAGE SETUP FORMATS.

Slide Type	Description
Onscreen Show	Use this format when you're giving your presentation as an onscreen slide show with a computer, television, projector, or another similar device.
Letter Paper (8.5×11 in.)	Use this setting when the presentation is printed as handouts on standard U.S. letter paper.
A4 Paper (210×297 mm)	Use this setting when the presentation is printed as handouts on International A4 paper.
35mm Slides	Use this setting when the presentation is published on 35mm slides.
Overhead	Use this setting for presentations that use transparencies on an overhead projector.
Banner	Use this setting for designing an 8-inch×1-inch banner.
Custom	This setting is for any other type of presentation that doesn't fit one of the preceding options. You will need to supply the page measurements.

Changing a Slide's Layout

With PowerPoint, you can change a slide's layout template anytime. This feature is especially useful if, for example, you decide you would like to add a chart to a bullet list. To change the layout of a slide, follow these steps:

To Do: Change the Layout of a Slide

1. Click the slide you want to change.

2. Choose Format, Slide Layout from the menu to open the Slide Layout dialog box.

3. Select a new layout.

4. Click the Apply button, shown in Figure 4.8.

FIGURE 4.8.

Different slide types are displayed in the Slide Layout dialog box.

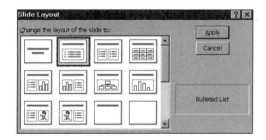

When you change a slide's layout, you're actually applying the layout's specific formatting to the slide. Although you won't lose any presentation information previously typed into a slide (or any objects that have been previously added), you might lose formatting modifications you have made to the text. This process can also be used to reapply the same layout to a slide, just in case you really mess up the formatting.

Changing the Presentation's Design

This hypothetical situation just might happen: You've been working on a presentation for many hours and believe you have the ultimate delivery for it. However, you show it to your colleagues, and they all unanimously agree that they hate the background design. They want a totally different tone for the entire presentation, which is over 30 slides. What to do, what to do... Fortunately, you can simply change the presentation's design by following these steps:

To Do: Change the Presentation Design

1. Choose Format, Apply Design Template from the menu to open the Apply Design dialog box.

2. Select a new design for the presentation, as shown in Figure 4.9.

3. Click the Apply button. The new design is then applied to every slide in your presentation.

FIGURE 4.9.

Choose a new design from the Apply Design dialog box.

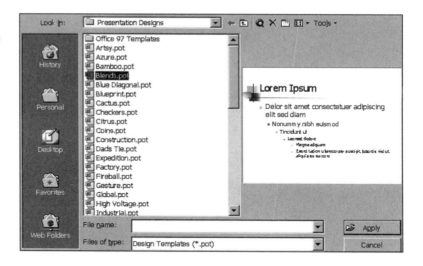

Changing the document's presentation design is similar to changing the layout of an individual slide. When you apply the presentation design's formatting to your presentation, your slides won't lose any text or objects you have entered; however, the formatting may change.

Summary

In this hour, you have covered many important things you need to know when working with slides—from selecting the proper layout for an individual slide to changing the overall design for the whole presentation. You should now be familiar with creating a new presentation and a title slide. You know how to add new slides to your presentation and create, edit, and expand a bulleted slide, so duplicating, moving, and deleting slides should now be easy tasks.

Q&A

Q **I want one slide to be displayed in Portrait orientation and all the other slides to be displayed in Landscape orientation. How can I do this?**

A You can't do this on slides within the same presentation. The Page Setup options apply to all the slides in a single presentation. If you really need to display slides with different orientations or other Page Setup options, you must create separate presentation documents. You can branch to another presentation to make an onscreen show seamless, as discussed in Hour 24, "PowerPoint Power Hour."

Q I've created my presentation and want it to be printed on 35mm slides. How do I print them?

A To print the slides out in 35mm format, you need access to a piece of equipment called a film recorder. Basically, you print the slides to the film recorder instead of a printer. The film recorder photographs your slides and produces undeveloped film, which you can then take to any photo-processing store to have it developed into slides.

If you don't have a film recorder, you can always send your presentation (after formatting it for 35mm slides) to a service bureau that does all the hard work of properly transferring the presentation. Check the Yellow Pages under "Computer Graphics" for local firms. Give them a call beforehand, in case they have specific setup information for you to follow.

Q I have a presentation that was created in Harvard Graphics. Can I use it in PowerPoint?

A Most likely. PowerPoint can import most files that have been created in other presentation software packages, such as Harvard Graphics. To import another file into PowerPoint 2000, you must first start a new blank presentation. Then choose Insert, Slides from Files from the menu to open the Slide Finder dialog box and click the Find Presentation tab. Click the Browse button and select the file you want to import. Click the Display button to view the presentation's slides. Click the Insert All button to insert all the slides from the presentation or you can select individual slides by clicking the Insert button to insert one slide at a time. When you are finished, click the Close button. Before you import a presentation, remember that you must either open an existing presentation or start a new one.

4

HOUR 5

Working with PowerPoint Text Objects

In the next hour, you will learn all the different methods available in PowerPoint 2000 to edit and control text. If you're familiar with operating a word processing program, such as Microsoft Word, you have probably noticed that PowerPoint deals with text in a manner that's slightly different. When you enter text in PowerPoint, you're not only entering the text on a slide, but you're also entering the text into a text object. It's very important to understand that you're not only working with text, but also the underlying object. This next hour covers most of the options available when working with text and text objects. You will learn how to do the following:

- Tell the difference between text objects and text boxes
- Move and copy a text object
- Select text in a text object
- Change font properties, such as font type, size, and color
- Format bulleted or numbered text

- Change text object attributes
- Use the Find and Replace commands

Text Objects Versus Text Boxes

Text is text, isn't it? In PowerPoint, this isn't always entirely accurate, as there are different methods for entering text on a presentation slide. In the Slide pane, simply click the placeholder and type the text. In the Outline pane, position the blinking cursor where you want the text to appear and start typing.

Another method is to insert a text box on the slide and type your text in the box. This is not recommended, however, as the text is not included in the outline, nor in a spell check.

When you enter text in the Outline pane, PowerPoint automatically creates the text object placeholder if there is not one already, and enters the text into the placeholder. Before you enter text in the Slide pane, there must be a placeholder available. If you don't have a text placeholder available, either enter text in the presentation's Outline view or change the slide's layout.

Selecting Text and Text Objects

Before you can move text or change any of the text attributes, you need to know how to select text. Most of the objects and elements that have been selected up to this point have been triggered by simply clicking on the item you want to select. When you're working with text information, the process is slightly different. You will need to either edit only a portion of the text, or apply a formatting option to all of the text. Text is selected when it's highlighted in black.

There are several ways to select text and text objects. In Hour 4, "Working with Slides," you learned about the simplest way to select text: dragging the mouse. Table 5.1 describes a few other quick ways to select text in PowerPoint.

If you want to affect all the text in a text object, you should select the entire object.

TABLE 5.1. SELECTING TEXT IN POWERPOINT.

What to Select	How to Select
Any amount of text	Place the mouse pointer at the beginning of the text; the pointer should be shaped like an I-beam. Hold the mouse button down and drag the pointer over the text you want to select.
Single word	Place the mouse pointer (shaped like an I-beam) anywhere on the word and double-click.
Single sentence	Click once on the sentence; then hold the Ctrl key while clicking anywhere on the sentence.
Single paragraph	Place the mouse pointer (shaped like an I-beam) anywhere on the paragraph and triple-click.
Entire text object	Click once on the text object. You will see the gray placeholder border and a blinking cursor in the text. Position the mouse on the placeholder border and click a second time (you should still see the placeholder border, but not the blinking cursor).

You have probably noticed that the mouse pointer changes shape from time to time. The shape of the mouse pointer tells you what you can do. Appendix B, "Common Mouse Pointer Shapes in PowerPoint 2000," illustrates the most common mouse pointer shapes and describes what the different pointer symbols represent.

Rearranging Text and Text Objects

Now that you know how to select text, you can start moving and copying it. This is very easy to do in PowerPoint. You can rearrange snippets of text, or you can relocate an entire text object. Being able to copy and move text is a feature that makes Microsoft Office applications so much more productive than pen and paper.

Moving or Copying Text and Text Objects

If you have ever moved or copied text in a Windows application, you already know how to move or copy text in PowerPoint. You can move or copy text from either the Slide or Outline pane, depending on your preference. Four basic steps are involved, but one step differs depending on whether you want to move or copy the text. To move or copy text, follow this sequence of steps:

To Do: Move or Copy Text

1. Select the text or text object you want to move or copy.

2. To move text, choose Edit, Cut from the menu, or click the Cut button on the Standard toolbar.

3. To copy text, choose Edit, Copy from the menu, or click the Copy button on the Standard toolbar.

4. For a snippet of text, position the blinking cursor where you want the text to appear. For a text object, display the slide to where you want the object moved or copied.

5. Choose Edit, Paste from the menu, or click the Paste button on the Standard toolbar.

Several methods are available for moving or copying text—keyboard shortcuts and the right mouse button. Common keyboard shortcuts are listed in Appendix A. If you have been using Windows applications for a while, you're probably familiar with the drag-and-drop method. A twist on this method is using the right mouse button. Select the text and then drag with the right mouse button. You can then choose to either move or copy the text from the shortcut menu.

Moving Text Objects on a Slide

When you move and copy text objects to different slides, they usually do not end up in the position that you had envisioned. You may need to move them around. You may also find that at times the AutoLayouts available do not meet the exact layout specifications for your presentation. Figure 5.1, for example, illustrates just such a situation. The slide would look much better if the title were moved up just a bit.

To move text objects on a particular slide, use the Slide pane. You will use the mouse to drag the object to the desired location on the slide. To move a text object, use the following steps:

To Do: Move a Text Object

1. Click once on the text object to select it. You should see a gray outline border around it with eight resizing handles.

The resizing handles are the little boxes at each corner and in the middle of each side of the Text Object border.

FIGURE 5.1.

The title is placed too low on this slide.

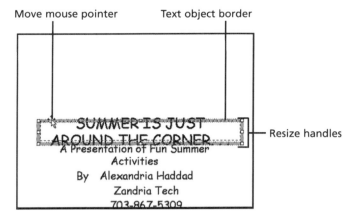

> SUMMER IS JUST
> AROUND THE CORNER. . .
> A Presentation of Fun Summer
> Activities
> By   Alexandria Haddad
> Zandria Tech
> 703-867-5309

2. Place the mouse pointer on any part of the border for the text object, but not on a resizing handle. The pointer should change shape and become a move pointer (the four-headed arrow).

3. Drag the object to the location you want, and release the mouse button (see Figure 5.2).

You must have the mouse pointer on the border of a text object to move it. The pointer looks like a four-headed arrow when PowerPoint is ready to move the text object. If the mouse pointer looks like a double-headed arrow, PowerPoint will resize the text object.

Move mouse pointer   Text object border

5

FIGURE 5.2.

It's easy to move a text object.

> SUMMER IS JUST
> AROUND THE CORNER.   Resize handles
> A Presentation of Fun Summer
> Activities
> By   Alexandria Haddad
> Zandria Tech
> 703-867-5309

Changing Text Properties

Now the real fun starts—changing fonts for intense graphical impact. Fonts are everyone's favorite thing to fool around with. You can change the mood of a whole presentation just by changing the font type. Windows and Office 2000 offer several dozen font types for use in your PowerPoint presentation. Go ahead—be daring and put a little pizzazz in your presentation.

The font drop-down list on the Formatting toolbar displays the name of the font that will actually print—kind of a try-it-before-you-buy-it offer. Font names have descriptors, which can give you some information about the type of font you are selecting. Sample descriptors include script type fonts, such as Brush Script; sans serif fonts (fonts without "tails"), such as Arial; or serif fonts (fonts with "tails"), such as Times Roman. This book was printed in a serif font, with the notes and cautions in a sans serif font. Figure 5.3 shows some examples of these different types of fonts.

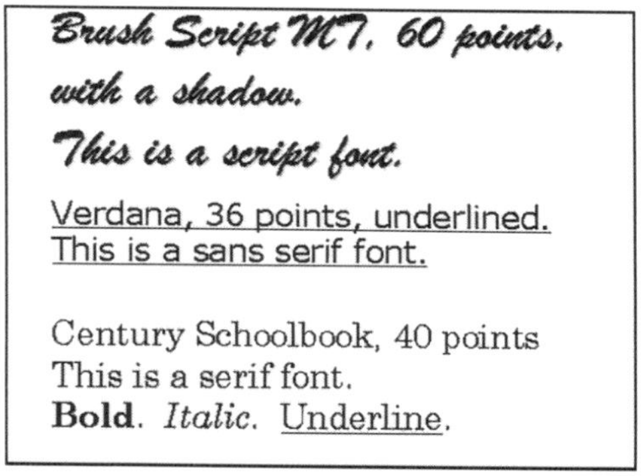

FIGURE 5.3.

Different styles of text fonts can add as much pizzazz to your presentation as graphics.

> *Brush Script MT, 60 points, with a shadow.*
> *This is a script font.*
>
> Verdana, 36 points, underlined.
> This is a sans serif font.
>
> Century Schoolbook, 40 points
> This is a serif font.
> **Bold**. *Italic*. Underline.

Although a lot of really cool fonts are available, keep your audience in mind when choosing a font type. It would not do to use a really "pretty" script font for a board of directors' presentation. Remember, you can change the mood of the whole presentation with fonts, for better or for worse.

Before you change any font attributes, you must first select the text that will be affected by the change. To change the font for a portion of text—for example, just the one word you want in bold—select just that one word. To change the font for an entire text object—if you want the entire title a bit bigger, for instance—select the text object.

Again, you shouldn't select text when you want the font change to affect the entire object. Select the object instead. If you don't, you might notice later that new text added to the slide isn't displayed with the correct font attributes.

If you want to change the font attributes for every slide in your presentation, you could change each slide one by one, or you could change them all at once. The best method for changing slides all at once is to change the font in the Slide or Title Master. Hour 8, "Working with the Masters," covers how to do this. Any changes to the master affect your whole presentation, and you have to make the change only once.

Face, Size, Color, Style, and Effects

You can find most font attributes in the Font dialog box. The attributes available in this dialog include the font, size, color, style, and effects. Remember, if you want to change the font attributes for an entire object, first select the object as described in Table 5.1; if you want to change the attributes for just a portion of text, select only the text that should change.

The Font dialog box, shown in Figure 5.4, has the entire set of font attributes in one location. This makes it easy to change many different attributes and includes a Preview button. This is another kind of try-before-you-buy option, and allows you to view any changes you might have selected before they are applied. To change font attributes from the Font dialog box, use the following steps:

FIGURE 5.4.

Use the Font dialog box to change text attributes.

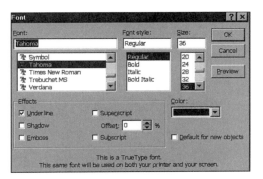

5

To Do: Change Font Attributes from the Font Dialog Box

1. Select the text or text object that will have the new font attributes.
2. Choose Format, Font from the menu to open the Font dialog box.
3. Change any font attributes desired.
4. Click the Preview button to see a preview, if desired.

> When you click the Preview button to see what the change looks like, the change is not permanent until you click the OK button. You might also need to move the dialog box out of the way to see more of the slide. To do that, position the mouse pointer in the title bar of the dialog box and drag the box to the location you want.

5. Click the Default for New Objects check box to change the default font for all new objects, if desired.
6. Click the OK button to accept your changes.

You can also change many font attributes from the Formatting toolbar. Table 5.2 shows the different buttons on the Formatting toolbar and their corresponding attributes.

TABLE 5.2. THE FORMATTING TOOLBAR.

Toolbar Button	Attribute
Comic Sans MS	Font face (the drop-down box also displays how the font will appear)
36	Font size
B	Bold
I	Italic
U	Underline
S	Shadow
A	Font color (on the Drawing toolbar)

Alignment

The alignment of the text on the slide is based on the placeholder bounding box. Figure 5.5 displays three text objects that are affected by different alignment options. Notice that the text isn't aligned with the slide boundaries; it's placed in relation to the placeholder bounding box. If you want an object aligned within the edges of the entire slide, simply resize the bounding box to match the width of the slide. Follow these steps to change the text alignment:

FIGURE 5.5.

Different text alignment options can add different effects to a slide.

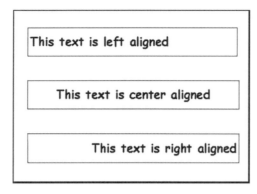

To Do: Change the Text Alignment

1. Select the object you want to change the alignment for.

2. Choose Format, Alignment from the menu to display the submenu.

3. Select the Align Left, Center, Align Right, or Justify menu item.

You can also click the alignment buttons on the Formatting toolbar. Table 5.3 illustrates the buttons and their corresponding alignment attributes.

TABLE 5.3. ALIGNMENT BUTTONS.

Toolbar Button	Alignment
	Align Left
	Center
	Align Right

Working with Bulleted Text

When you have slides with bulleted text, there are a few tricks you can use to achieve a professionally coordinated presentation. In PowerPoint, your slides can have up to five bullet levels. Each level can have a different bullet character, and each descending level is automatically defined with a font size smaller than the preceding bullet level. The two most common operations people want to perform with bulleted text are to modify the bullet symbols (Bob wants check marks instead of smiley faces, for example) and to change the relative font size.

Changing Bullet Symbols

Changing the style of a bullet is fairly simple. The biggest hurdle to overcome is not to get overwhelmed by all the different symbol choices. Keep your audience and presentation subject in mind when choosing bullet symbols. The bullets in Figure 5.6, for example, are congruent with the computer theme for this book. You may also want to use a numbered list instead of bullet symbols. To change the bullet style, use the following steps:

FIGURE 5.6.

Pictures as well as the usual bullet dots can add interest to your slides.

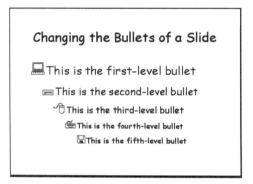

To Do: Change Bullet Styles

1. Click on the line where you want the bullet symbol changed.
2. Choose Format, Bullets and Numbering from the menu.
3. Click the Bulleted tab on the Bullets and Numbering dialog box, if it is not already displayed as shown in Figure 5.7.

FIGURE 5.7.

Use the Bullets and Numbering dialog box to create custom bullets for your slides.

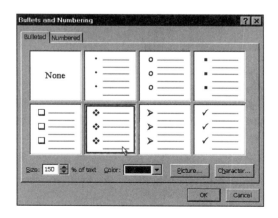

4. Click one of the seven predefined bulleted styles.

5. Change the color or size of the bullet symbol, if you want.

▲   6. Click the OK button.

Repeat these steps for each bullet item you want to change, or you can select all the bullet items to make a global change.

> If you want to change the bullet symbol for every slide in your presentation, you should use the Slide Master, which is covered in Hour 8.

If you do not like any of the pre-existing bullet styles, there are hundreds of other bullet characters or pictures to choose from. To choose a completely different character or picture, use the following steps:

To Do: Change Bullet Characters or Pictures

1. Click on the line where you want the bullet symbol changed.

2. Choose Format, Bullets and Numbering from the menu.

3. Click the Bulleted tab if it is not already displayed.

4. Click the Character button.

5. Select a font from the Bullets From drop-down list.

6. Click a symbol from the symbol grid.

7. Change the color or size of the bullet symbol, if you want.

▲   8. Click the OK button.

5

> Bullet characters are taken from the font sets that are available with a particular system. The first time you see the Bullet dialog box, it's a bit overwhelming. However, here's a little trick you can use: Click on the first symbol in the grid (the symbol "pops up" so you can see it better), and use the arrow keys on the keyboard to review each symbol. If you can't find just the right symbol, try a different font.
>
> PowerPoint 2000 has three new font sets that have been created specifically for use as bullet characters: Wingdings 2, Wingdings 3, and Webdings. These are in addition to the traditional Wingdings and Monotype Sorts that have been available in the past.

Increasing or Decreasing Font Size

As mentioned earlier, each descending bullet level is displayed with a slightly smaller font size than the one before it. If you need to change the font size for a multilevel, bulleted list, you should change the relative size of the text object. This keeps each level's font size bigger or smaller in relation to the rest of the list. To increase or decrease the relative font size, use the following steps:

To Do: Increase or Decrease the Relative Font Size

1. Select the text object.
2. Click the Increase or Decrease Font Size button on the Formatting toolbar.

Line Spacing

When you want to create more distance between lines of text or bullet points, don't press the Enter key an extra time. PowerPoint gives you a much simpler option for changing the line spacing that also gives you much more control than pressing Enter and adding an extra blank line. The Line Spacing option affects any lines of text you have previously selected. You can set the measurement for line spacing in number of lines or by points. Figure 5.8 shows the Line Spacing dialog box.

FIGURE 5.8.

The Line Spacing dialog box enables you to set line spacing.

Point size is the unit of measurement typically used for fonts. One point is 1/72 inch. Therefore, 72 points is 1 inch, 36 points is 1/2 inch, 18 points is 1/4 inch, 9 points is... well, you get the picture. Follow these steps to change the line spacing for selected text:

To Do: Change Line Spacing

1. First, select the lines to modify.
2. Choose Format, Line Spacing from the menu to open the Line Spacing dialog box.
3. Select the amount of space you want between lines of text.
4. Select the unit of measurement for the line spacing.
▲ 5. Click the OK button.

Changing Text Object Attributes

In the first part of this hour, you have learned about different ways to change or enhance the text on your slides. This next section covers how the text object affects the text contained in it and how to control the text object itself. Each of the following sections explains a different option or feature, and the title object is used as the sample object.

Adding a Border or Fill

The first feature is adding a border or fill (shading) to your text object, which is a great way to make text stand out from the crowd. Figure 5.9 shows how a text object can be formatted with borders and shading.

FIGURE 5.9.

A text object shown with a border and a gradient fill.

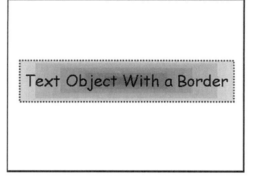

Gradient fill is a very cool special effect that you can use with almost every PowerPoint object. With a gradient fill effect, one color gradually fades into black, white, or another color. PowerPoint 2000 also has several preset color schemes from which you can choose. To add a border or fill to a text object, follow these steps:

To Do: Add a Border or Fill

1. Click anywhere in the text object to which you want to add a border or fill to select it.

2. Choose Format, Placeholder from the menu (the last option in the Format menu), to display the Format AutoShape dialog box.

3. Select the Colors and Lines tab (see Figure 5.10).

FIGURE 5.10.

Use the Colors and Lines tab of the Format AutoShape dialog box to customize the border or fill of a text object.

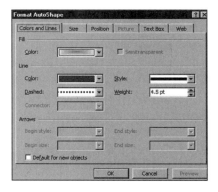

4. If you want to add a fill, select an option from the Color drop-down list in the Fill section.

> Use the Fill Effects option from the Color drop-down list to apply a gradient effect or any other fill effect to your text object. There are several effects to choose from; just remember that your audience must be able to read the message text.

5. If you want a border, select a line color from the Color drop-down list in the Line section of the dialog box.
6. Change the Style, Dashed, and Weight options for the border, if you want.
7. Click the Preview button to preview your changes before accepting them.
8. Click the OK button when you're finished.

Changing the Size of a Text Object Bounding Box

Changing the size of a text object is not the same as modifying the font size of the text. When you change the size of a text object, you're changing the size of the placeholder bounding box that contains the text. Usually, you want the bounding box to be the same size as the text it holds. This rule of thumb is especially true if you're adding a border or fill option to the text object. As you can see in Figure 5.11, when the bounding box is smaller than the text within it and is formatted with a border, things don't look quite right. To set the text bounding box to fit the text it holds, use the following steps:

FIGURE 5.11.

The bounding box is smaller than the text it holds.

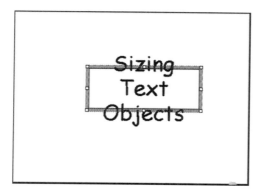

To Do: Set the Text Bounding Box

1. Select the text object.
2. Select Format, Placeholder from the menu.
3. Click the Text Box tab.
4. Click the Resize AutoShape to Fit Text check box to select it with a check mark.
▲ 5. Click the OK button.

Setting the Text Anchor Point

When you're trying to get the best look for your presentation, you can control how the text is anchored within a text object, especially when you have used a border or fill option. The text anchor point is the point where the text sits in the object. Text can be anchored to an object position at the top, middle, bottom, top center, middle center, or bottom center. Figure 5.12 shows two text objects, each with a different anchor point. If you need to change the anchor point, follow these steps:

5

FIGURE 5.12.

Message text is anchored to the middle and bottom of the text box.

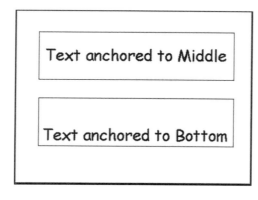

To Do: Change the Anchor Point

1. Select the text object.

2. Choose Format, Placeholder from the menu.

3. Select the Text Box tab, shown in Figure 5.13.

FIGURE 5.13.

The Format AutoShape dialog box displays the Text Box tab.

4. Select a new anchor point from the Text Anchor Point drop-down list.

5. Click the Preview button to see a preview of your change.

 6. Click the OK button.

Using Find and Replace

You can use the PowerPoint Find option to quickly locate a phrase or word in your presentation. PowerPoint searches all the text objects—including all slides and speaker's notes—in your presentation for the text you specify. It is best to use this option in Normal view. To find text, follow these simple steps:

Although you can use the Find or Replace option in Slide Sorter view, it's not as easy to see the recommended changes.

To Do: Find Text

1. Choose Edit, Find from the menu to open the Find dialog box.

2. Type the text you want to find in the Find What box, as shown in Figure 5.14.

FIGURE 5.14.

The Find dialog box makes it a snap to find specific text.

3. Select Match Case to match the case of the text exactly.

▼ 4. Select Find Whole Words Only to find only whole words.

Use the Find Whole Words Only option when you want to find or replace words, such as *form*, that might appear within another word, such as information. In this example, if you wanted to replace form with screen, you wouldn't want to end up with the word *inscreenation*. Using the Find Whole Words Only option can save you a lot of time.

▲ 5. Click the Find Next button to start the search.

The Find dialog box has a Replace button you can use to quickly switch to the Replace dialog box.

If you want to not only find specific text but also replace it with other text, use the Replace option to quickly substitute a phrase or word in your presentation. You can choose to approve (or disapprove) each replacement or have PowerPoint replace all instances of the text you're searching for (sometimes called a global replace). To replace text, follow these steps:

To Do: Replace Text

1. Choose Edit, Replace from the menu to open the Replace dialog box.
2. Type the text you want to find in the Find What box, as shown in Figure 5.15.

FIGURE 5.15.

The Replace dialog box offers different ways of replacing text.

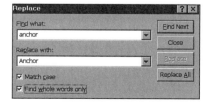

▼   3. Type the text you're substituting in the Replace With box.

4. Select the Match Case check box to match the case of the text exactly.

5. Select the Find Whole Words Only check box to find only whole words.

6. Click the Find Next button to start the find.

7. Click the Replace button to replace the selection with the text in the Replace With box and find the next occurrence of the text.

▲   8. You can also click the Replace All button to replace all occurrences of the text in your document.

Summary

You've had a good hour—you should now be comfortable working with any type of PowerPoint text object and know the difference between a text object and a text box. After you select a text object or just a snippet of text, you can move or copy it to any location. You have seen how to enhance your presentation by changing any text properties you want, but don't get carried away. Although you have a ton of font options available to you, most presentations look best when they're kept simple.

PowerPoint makes it easy to modify bulleted text with a host of tools and options available to you. You can change the bullet symbol used for each level of text, increase or decrease the font size in proportion to the rest of the text, and change the line spacing, if needed.

PowerPoint makes enhancing text objects fun and easy—you can add a border or a fill with a few simple clicks; resizing and repositioning the text object is as easy as clicking the mouse.

Q&A

Q When I try to center a text object in the presentation slide using the exact positioning method, the text is askew. How do I center my text exactly?

A PowerPoint positions the text object by using the upper-left edge of the object. If you want to center a text object, setting the horizontal and vertical positions at 0 inches from the center won't center the text object. To center an object, use the guides by choosing View, Guides from the menu and dragging the object to the center of the window. The object should snap to the guides and automatically center.

Q When I convert a Word outline into a PowerPoint presentation, how do the headings appear on the slides?

A The Word document's Level 1 headings become slides, and lower-level headings are displayed as multilevel bullets.

Hour **6**

Working with Clip Art and Pictures

Enhancing text by making it bold or big is great, but as the old saying goes, "A picture is worth a thousand words." Enter clip art and pictures. In this hour, you will learn all you ever wanted to know about adding clip art and pictures to your presentation. This hour explains how to do the following:

- Insert a clip art image or a picture
- Move, copy, and resize images
- Ungroup clip art to use just a portion of the picture
- Enhance image objects with options such as borders, fill, color, brightness, and shadows
- Animate images
- Add images to the Clip Gallery

Go online! PowerPoint comes with over 1,100 clip art images and pictures. If you still can't find just the right image from the CD-ROM, use the Web. You can use the site http://www.Webplaces.com/search/ to search for all kinds of images, including clip art. Some of the images are for sale, and some are free.

If you're going to publish the clip art in a for-profit project, I'd suggest getting an actual letter of permission and consider having the corporate legal department scrutinize the language for holes.

If you do use an image found on the Web, a word of advice: You should ask permission before using any art you've downloaded. Almost everything published on the Web is copyrighted. Most Webmasters don't mind personal or commercial use of their pictures and will give you permission if you ask. Just dash off an email requesting permission to use the image and wait for a reply.

Inserting Clip Art and Pictures

You can insert a clip art image or picture on any slide even if it does not contain a placeholder. If you do not use a placeholder, the image is placed in the middle of the slide. You will then need to move it to the desired position and resize it, if necessary. When you insert clip art images, PowerPoint displays the Insert ClipArt window, as shown in Figure 6.1. This window allows you to browse through available clip art pictures currently available to you. To insert a clip art image or picture into a slide, use the following steps:

FIGURE 6.1.

You can find lots of graphics ideas in the Insert ClipArt window.

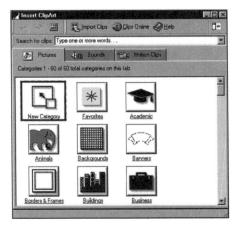

Although PowerPoint 2000 comes with a lot of clip art, click the Clips Online button to quickly connect to the Microsoft Clip Gallery Live site. This site contains hundreds of clip art images, sounds, and movies you can download.

To Do: Insert Clip Art or Pictures

1. Display the slide where you want to add an image.

2. Double-click on the placeholder object where it says `Double click to add clip art`. If there is no placeholder, select Insert, Picture, Clip Art from the menu to open the Insert ClipArt window.

3. Select the Pictures tab to display the categories of available clip art images.

4. Click a category to display the clip art images available.

5. Click an image; then click the Insert Clip button as shown in Figure 6.2, to insert the clip art image on the slide.

6. Click the Insert ClipArt window's Close button to close the window and view your slide.

FIGURE 6.2.

You can use the Insert clip button to place a graphic image into your presentation.

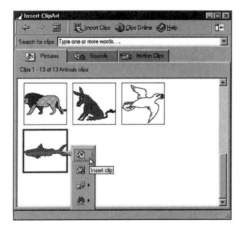

You can also use the Clip Gallery to select sounds and videos for your presentations. Multimedia options are covered in Hour 21, "Multimedia."

6

If you decide that you do not want the image on your slide, click once on it to select it (you will see resizing handles when it is selected), and press the Delete key on your keyboard.

After an image has been inserted on a slide, PowerPoint automatically displays the Picture toolbar (see Figure 6.3). The Picture toolbar is automatically displayed whenever you have an image selected, and closed when you click off an image. Refer to the section "Working with Image Objects" later in this hour to learn how to select an image. This toolbar has several useful buttons with features such as Contrast, Brightness, Cropping, and Reset Picture that are helpful when you're working with images in PowerPoint.

FIGURE 6.3.

Use the many buttons on the Picture toolbar when working with images.

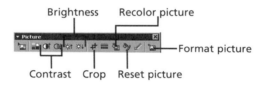

 If you don't see the Picture toolbar, choose View, Toolbars, Picture from the menu to display it.

Adding Images to the Clip Gallery

Adding clip art images and pictures to the Clip Gallery is essential if you have images, like your company's logo, that you use frequently. You can also add sound clips and video clips as well. To add an image to the Clip Gallery, use the following steps:

To Do: Add an Image to the Clip Gallery

1. Open the Clip Gallery by choosing Insert, Picture, Clip Art from the menu.
2. Click the Import Clips button.
3. Select the drive and folder with the clip art or other file you want to add to the Clip Gallery.
4. Select the image file.
5. Select an import option.
6. Click the Import button to open the Clip Properties dialog box, as shown in Figure 6.4.

7. Type a description for the image in the Description of This Clip text box.

8. Click the Categories tab.

9. Select a category where the image is to be displayed.

If there is not an appropriate category for the image, you can create a new category by clicking the New Category button, entering a category name, and clicking the OK button. This will create the category and select it as the holding area for your image.

You must select at least one category, or you will probably not be able to locate your image later. You can select multiple categories.

10. Click the Keywords tab.

11. Click the New Keyword button and enter at least one keyword to help PowerPoint 2000 search for this image later.

FIGURE 6.4.

The Clip Properties dialog box helps you to better organize the many clip art images you may have.

12. Click the OK button.

13. Click the Close button for the Insert ClipArt window.

Working with Image Objects

Before you can move or resize any image, you need to select the image object. It's not nearly as complicated as selecting a text object; with a simple click, the object is selected.

> To select multiple objects, hold the Shift key down while you click on each
> object you want to select.

Now you can move, resize, and format at will. When an object is selected, you can see
selection and resizing handles, as shown in Figure 6.5. Also, the Picture toolbar is automatically displayed.

FIGURE 6.5.

*When you select an
image object, selection
or resizing handles
appear around the
object.*

Resizing handles

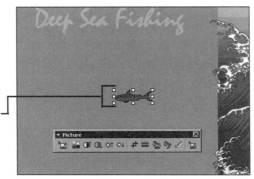

Moving or Copying Image Objects with the Mouse

When you insert a clip art image or picture into a slide that doesn't have a placeholder,
you often need to move or resize the image. The slide you saw in Figure 6.5 contains an
image that needs to be moved and resized. Notice that it's currently in the middle of the
slide and is very small. This image needs to be moved. If you ever need to copy an
image, the process is almost exactly the same; the only difference being you choose copy
instead of move from the menu.

To move or copy images, the simplest method available is to use the mouse. You must be
in Normal or Slide view to move or copy any graphical image. You can also use menu
commands to copy a clip art image or picture, but then you have to move it to the correct
location. You can copy and move an object at the same time. To quickly move or copy a
clip art image or picture:

To Do: Move or Copy an Image

1. Click once on the object to select it; you should see selection and resizing handles
   surrounding it.
2. Place the mouse pointer anywhere on the clip art or picture so that it changes to a
   move pointer, and use the right mouse button to drag the object to the location you
   want and release the mouse button.

3. Select Move Here or Copy Here from the shortcut menu.

 When you want a clip art image on two different slides, you have to use the copy-and-paste method described in Hour 5, "Working with PowerPoint Text Objects." After you paste an object, you usually have to move it to the location you want.

Resizing Image Objects with the Mouse

Unless you need an image to be an exact size, the easiest way to resize it is to use the mouse. To resize an image, simply follow these steps:

To Do: Resize Image Objects with the Mouse

1. Select the image.
2. Place the mouse pointer on any resizing handle, so that it looks like a resize arrow, and drag the object until it's the size you want.

 You can accidentally distort an image when resizing. To avoid this problem, use a corner resize handle and hold the Shift key when resizing. If you do accidentally distort an image, simply click the Undo button and try again. You can also click the Reset Picture button on the Picture toolbar. However, not every image can be reset. For those that can't, you may need to delete the image and reinsert it.

Ungrouping and Grouping Clip Art

PowerPoint gives you the capability to take a piece of clip art and ungroup it. You can then use just a portion of the image. Conversely, you can also group a bunch of images together. The bundled images interact as though they were one large image. In Figure 6.6, one of the clip art images has been ungrouped into separate images; notice that each image is surrounded by selection handles now. To ungroup any image, use the following steps:

To Do: Ungroup Images

1. Select the clip art image.
2. On the Drawing toolbar, choose Draw, Ungroup.
3. If PowerPoint 2000 asks whether you want to convert the object to a Microsoft Drawing, click Yes.

6

FIGURE 6.6.

You can ungroup a clip art image into separate images.

When you ungroup a clip art image, PowerPoint converts the image into a Microsoft Office drawing.

Some clip art images need to be ungrouped several times to get the portion you're looking for. Try ungrouping a simple piece of clip art first, and then work on a more complicated one. You will work more with grouping and ungrouping in Hour 13, "Bringing Drawing Objects Together."

Grouping objects is the opposite of ungrouping them. In Figure 6.7, all the individual images have been grouped so that they will act as one image. This makes copying, moving, and resizing easier. To group several objects together, use the following steps:

FIGURE 6.7.

When images are grouped together, they act as one object, as seen by the selection handles around the images.

To Do: Group Images

1. Select all the objects you want to group together by holding the Shift key and clicking.

2. On the Drawing toolbar, choose Draw, Group.

You can quickly select multiple objects by dragging a lasso around the images. Place the mouse pointer above and to the left of all the images, hold down the mouse button, and drag to the lower right. As you drag the mouse, a lasso surrounding all the images appears. When you let go of the mouse button, all the images within the lasso will be selected.

When you group images, any formatting you apply later, such as borders, are applied to each object in the group. If you want a border around the image, as in the next section, draw an AutoShape and add the formatting to the AutoShape. You may need to rearrange the order of the images. Refer to Hour 12, "Drawing Shapes in PowerPoint," and Hour 13, "Bringing Drawing Objects Together," for more information.

Formatting Image Objects

Now that you know how to resize and move the images, you're ready to learn different ways to control the image object. Some of the formatting options covered in this section include adding a border, controlling brightness and contrast, recoloring, and rotating an image.

Using the Picture toolbar is the fastest and easiest way to perform most of these options.

6

Adding a Border

A border really makes an image stand out; however, when you're "enhancing" slides, always keep in mind that, in the end, "less is more." Don't apply options just because you can. If you don't like the effect, you can always change the image back with the Undo command. Figure 6.8 shows an image object with a border. To add a border to an image object, follow these steps:

To Do: Add a Border

1. Select the object you want to border.
2. Click the Line Style button on the Picture toolbar, and select a border style.

 When you select the More Lines option from the Line Style button, PowerPoint 2000 will open the Format Picture dialog box as shown in Figure 6.9. You can then select Color, Style, Dashed, and Weight options for your line. You must first select a color before any other option is available to you.

FIGURE 6.8.

Many images can be enhanced with a border.

FIGURE 6.9.

The Colors and Lines tab is just one formatting tab in the Format Picture dialog box.

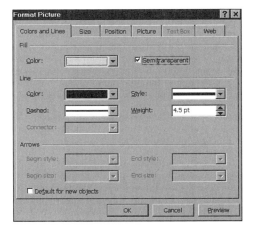

Sizing, Scaling, or Rotating a Picture

With PowerPoint, you have all kinds of control over an image object. You can scale an image or set it to an exact size. You can also rotate image objects in varying degrees, and if you enter a negative number, the object will rotate counterclockwise, from 0 to 359. As with text objects, an image object is rotated in a clockwise direction. To change the size, scale, or rotation of image objects, use the following steps:

You cannot rotate a clip art image. To rotate a clip art image, you must first ungroup it to convert it to a Microsoft Office Drawing. Then group it. Then you can rotate it.

To Do: Change the Size, Scale, or Rotation of an Image Object

1. Click once on the image object to select it.
2. Click the Format Object button on the Picture toolbar to open the Format Object dialog box.
3. Click the Size tab (see Figure 6.10).

FIGURE 6.10.

You can change the size, rotation, or scale of an object by using the Size tab of the Format Object dialog box.

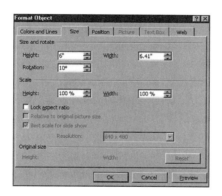

4. Enter an exact height or width for the image.
5. You can also scale the image by entering a percentage for height and width in the Scale section of the dialog box.
6. Enter the amount in degrees by which you want to rotate the image object.
7. Click the Preview button to preview your changes before accepting them.
8. Click the OK button when you're finished.

Setting an exact size is the best method when you know the exact size you need for the image.

6

PowerPoint also allows you to free-rotate or flip any object. These options are covered in Hour 13.

Cropping, Color, Brightness, and Contrast

The Picture tab in the Format Picture dialog box has options for cropping an image and controlling an image's color, brightness, and contrast. Figure 6.11 shows an image that has been cropped. The color has also been set to Watermark, which makes an image dimmer than normal.

Cropping an image is like taking a pair of scissors and cutting out just the portion of the image you need. However, you must crop in a rectangle. When cropping an image, use the cropping tool on the Picture toolbar, as opposed to the measurement boxes in the Format Picture dialog box. It's much easier to crop an image when you can see what you're doing. To use the Picture toolbar to crop an image, follow these steps:

FIGURE 6.11.

An image that has been formatted as a watermark is dimmer than the rest of the text or graphics.

To Do: Crop an Image with the Crop Button

1. Select the image you want to crop.
2. Click the Crop button on the Picture toolbar.
3. Place the mouse pointer on any handle of the image; it should turn into a cropping pointer (which looks like the picture on the Crop button).
4. Drag the handle to crop the image as if you were resizing.
5. Repeat as necessary.

6. Click the Crop button to turn cropping off.

You can choose to change an image into a watermark, to display in the background of your presentation, by setting the color option to Watermark. PowerPoint formats the picture with preset brightness and contrast settings. To set an image as a watermark, follow these steps:

To Do: Set an Image as a Watermark

To Do

1. Select the image you want to set as a watermark.

2. Click the Format Picture (or Object) button on the Picture toolbar to open the Format Picture dialog box.

3. Click the Picture tab.

4. Select Watermark from the Color drop-down list.

5. Click the Preview button to preview your changes before accepting them.

6. Click the OK button when you're finished.

You can also set an image with custom contrast or brightness settings by clicking either the Contrast or Brightness button. The Format Picture dialog box allows you to set an exact contrast or brightness option, as well.

Customizing the Color of Clip Art

PowerPoint 2000 also allows you to customize the colors in a clip art image. This option is great when you have theme colors you want to use for your presentation. It is always best to preview any color changes to save time when editing colors in an image. To customize the colors of a clip art image, use the following steps:

Not all images allow color changes. All the clip art images that come with PowerPoint can be customized, but if you have images from another source, you might not be able to customize the colors.

6

To Do: Customize the Colors of a Clip Art Image

To Do

1. Select the image you want to customize.

2. Click the Recolor Picture button on the Picture toolbar, to display the Recolor Picture dialog box, as shown in Figure 6.12.

FIGURE 6.12.

Use the Recolor Picture dialog box to change a picture's colors.

3. Change the color options by clicking on any drop-down arrow and selecting another color.

4. Click the Preview button to see your changes before accepting them.

▲   5. Click the OK button to accept your changes.

Adding Shadows

Another interesting effect you can apply to an image is a shadow. PowerPoint 2000 enhances the shadow effect by allowing the designer to fully customize the presentation. You can move a shadow up, down, left, or right. To shadow an image, use the following steps:

To Do: Add a Shadow to an Image

1. Select the image you want to place a shadow behind.

2. Click the Shadow button on the Drawing toolbar to display all the shadow options.

3. Click the shadow option you want, as shown in Figure 6.13.

Shadow On/Off button

FIGURE 6.13.

Use the Shadow Settings toolbar to add a shadow to a PowerPoint 2000 object.

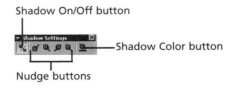

Shadow Color button

Nudge buttons

If you're extremely adventurous, you can add a custom shadow.

To Do: Add a Custom Shadow

1. Select the image you want to place a shadow behind.
2. Click the Shadow button on the Drawing toolbar.
3. Click the Shadow Settings option to display the Shadow Settings toolbar.
4. Click the Shadow On/Off button to turn the shadow on.
5. Click any of the Nudge buttons to move the shadow.
6. Click the Shadow Color button to change the color of the shadow, if you want.
7. Click the Close button to close the Shadow Settings toolbar.

Summary

In this hour, you have learned about all the clip art and other graphical image options available in PowerPoint 2000. You can insert a clip art image or other graphical image into any slide at any time, and you can add your favorite images to the Clip Gallery with a few simple clicks.

Moving or copying an image object is simple, whether you use the mouse or the menu. You can size any image to fit your needs. The Ungroup command lets you separate grouped images so they can be rotated, if needed. Add a border or fill; scale or rotate an object; crop an image; change the color, brightness, and contrast; and even customize the color of clip art images. Don't forget—you can also add any one of numerous shadow options to an image to create the effect of depth.

Congratulations! You're now 1/4 of the way to becoming a PowerPoint 2000 expert. Part III, "Putting Polish on a Presentation," covers how to customize your presentation with even more color options, use and customize the slide masters, and create that extra-special, exciting slide show. You've done a great job so far, and by now you're probably thinking of all kinds of really cool things you can do. What are you waiting for? Show Bob how a real presentation is done.

6

Q&A

Q I have an image that someone gave me on a disk. Can I use it in my presentation?

A Certainly. First, insert the image on your slide by choosing Insert, Picture, From File from the menu. After PowerPoint displays the Insert Picture dialog box, simply specify the drive and/or folder where the file is located, and click the Insert button. Make sure the Files of Type box shows the correct image file type. If you don't know the image type, select the All Files (*.*) option.

Q When I try to rotate a clip art image, the rotate option isn't available. How can I rotate the clip art?

A PowerPoint does not allow the rotation of clip art images. However, you can trick PowerPoint into letting you rotate the clip art image by using the ungroup command. First, select the clip art image; then choose Draw, Ungroup from the Drawing toolbar, and click the Yes button to convert the clip art to a Microsoft drawing object. With all the objects still selected, choose Draw, Group from the Drawing toolbar. You now have one Microsoft drawing object that PowerPoint 2000 will enable you to rotate. Remember that after you ungroup a clip art image, you can't use the Recolor Picture option. You have to color each piece of the object separately. This topic is covered in more depth in Hour 12. If you want to recolor and rotate a clip art image, recolor it first and then ungroup, group, and rotate the object.

Q What happened to the AutoClip Art that was available in PowerPoint 97?

A That feature is no longer available as you are familiar with it. Instead, you can now search for clips in the Insert ClipArt window by using the Search for Clips option. You can search for a clip art from the ClipArt dialog box by clicking in the Search for Clips: box and entering a search word, such as "fish." Insert the clip art as previously discussed in this hour, or search again.

Q I recolored an image and now I don't like the colors that I have chosen. It is too late to use the Undo command, and the Reset button doesn't work. Do I have to reinsert the image and start all over again?

A No. Simply click the Recolor Picture button and unselect all the color boxes that have a check mark in them. This should set the image back to its original colors.

PART III
Putting Polish on a Presentation

Hour

Hour 7

Customizing the Presentation

The next four hours cover all you need to know to customize, polish, and prepare your presentation for audience viewing. You will learn all the tricks for creating fabulous presentations. When you're done, your presentation will look as though a professional marketing firm created it. This hour covers how to apply those all-important custom touches to your presentation. You will learn how to do the following:

- Create a custom color scheme
- Create a custom background
- Create and print speaker's notes
- Create handouts for your audience

Customizing the Color Scheme

When you choose one of PowerPoint's presentation designs or presentation templates, you aren't required to choose coordinating colors for the slide objects. Each design and template has eight coordinating colors for the background, regular text, title text, fills, and accents. The color scheme affects every slide in your presentation. If you want to change the colors for your entire presentation, there's no need to go to each slide and change everything one item at a time. PowerPoint can easily do this for you.

There might also be times when you don't need any color, such as when your presentation will be given on an overhead projector or printed in black and white. You don't want to lose all the panache that the template gives you, but you do need to sell your ideas clearly. PowerPoint 2000 gives you the option of showing the presentation in black and white.

At other times, you may want to use your own custom colors, rather than the standard color scheme those nice folks at Microsoft have created for you. When situations such as these arise, you have two options: You can choose from one of the standard color schemes already created, or you can create your very own custom color scheme.

Keep the format of your presentation in mind when deciding on a color scheme. Will you be presenting using an overhead projector with slide transparencies, a laptop and projector, or 35mm slides? Each of these options—in addition to your target audience—will determine the proper color scheme for your presentation. Use color schemes with light or nonexistent backgrounds for overhead projectors, and darker backgrounds for slide shows (either projectors or 35mm).

Standard Color Schemes

Each presentation design or template has a standard color scheme that is first displayed when you create the presentation. You can also select from at least one other predesigned color scheme, and a black-and-white scheme, as shown in Figure 7.1.

Many of the template designs have more than one color scheme from which to choose. Use the black-and-white scheme for those occasions when you can't use a color printer and need to generate a presentation on transparencies or handouts.

Use these color schemes for transparencies

Use the black-and-white scheme when no color is needed

FIGURE 7.1.

The Color Scheme dialog box gives you several color scheme choices.

Use these color schemes for 35mm or onscreen presentations

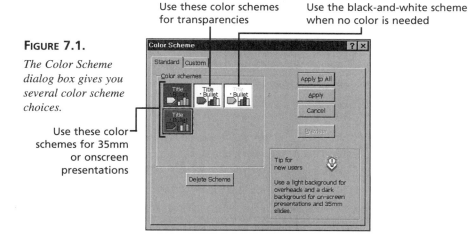

To Do: Select a Predesigned Color Scheme

To select another predesigned color scheme for the entire presentation, follow these steps:

1. Choose Format, Slide Color Scheme to open the Color Scheme dialog box.

2. Click the Standard tab.

3. Click any color scheme; the black-and-white color scheme is usually the top-right color scheme.

4. Click the Preview button to see a preview of the selected scheme.

> You may need to move the dialog box out of the way to see the preview. To move a dialog box, place the mouse pointer in the title bar of the dialog box, click and hold down the mouse button, and drag the box to another location.

▲   5. Click the Apply to All button to accept the change.

7

When you're selecting a color scheme, PowerPoint also enables you to change the color scheme for just one individual slide. This feature lets you add emphasis to a specific slide.

To change the color scheme for just one slide, use the previous steps and click Apply instead of Apply to All.

Custom Color Schemes

If you don't like any of the standard color schemes, you can always create your own custom color scheme. When you create a custom color scheme, you can select a custom color for the following eight options: Background, Text and Lines, Shadows, Title Text, Fills, Accent, Accent and Hyperlink, and Accent and Followed Hyperlink. As you select a new color for each of these eight options, PowerPoint shows you a preview of what your choice will look like. Figure 7.2 shows the Custom tab of the Color Scheme dialog box.

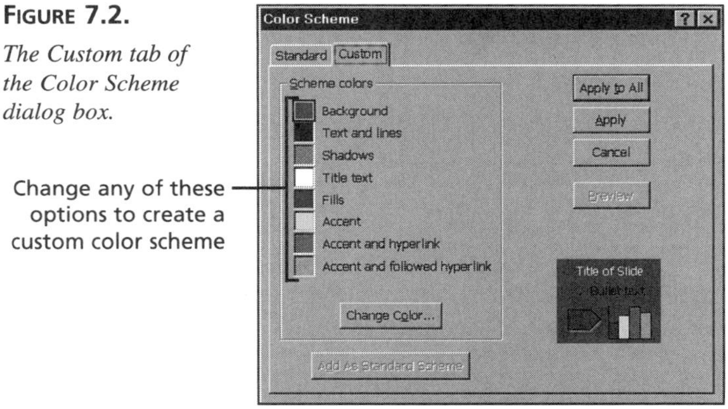

FIGURE 7.2.

The Custom tab of the Color Scheme dialog box.

Change any of these options to create a custom color scheme

To Do: Create a Custom Color Scheme

To create a custom color scheme, follow these steps:

1. Choose Format, Slide Color Scheme from the menu.

2. In the Color Scheme dialog box, click the Custom tab.

3. Click the color box of the feature you want to change in the Scheme Colors section.

4. Click the Change Color button.

The name of the color box you select in step 3 determines the name of the Color dialog box. Figure 7.3 shows that the Background color box was selected before the Change Color button was clicked.

5. Select a standard color, as shown in Figure 7.3, from the Background Color dialog box, or choose a color from the Custom tab.

FIGURE 7.3.

The Background Color dialog box offers you many color choices in the Standard colors tab.

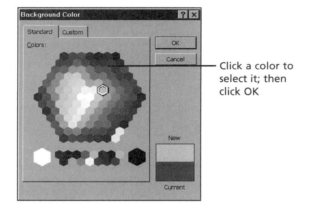

Click a color to select it; then click OK

6. Click the OK button.
7. Repeat the preceding steps for each feature you want to customize.
8. Click the Preview button to see a preview.
9. Click the Apply or Apply to All button to accept the change.

If you want to change the color scheme for only one slide, you must first display the slide.

7

If you want to create a custom color, use the Custom tab in the Background Color dialog box. You can then either drag the crosshair and scroll arrow to select a color, or be more scientific and type in the number (0-255) for the Red/Green/Blue and Hue/Saturation/Luminance color component options.

After you have created a color scheme, you can add that color scheme to the standard list. That can save you time in the future if Bob wants to use the same colors over and over and over.

To Do: Save a Color Scheme

Follow these steps to save a custom color scheme:

1. Choose Format, Slide Color Scheme from the menu.
2. Click the Custom tab.
3. Create a custom color scheme by changing the Scheme Colors.
4. Click the Preview button to see a preview.
5. Click the Add as Standard Scheme button.

PowerPoint permits up to 16 standard color schemes. When you have 16, you will need to delete one before you can create or save more. You can delete a color scheme easily by selecting the scheme from the Standard tab, and clicking the Delete Scheme button.

Customizing the Background

PowerPoint allows you to not only change the color scheme of your slides, but also change the appearance of the presentation or slide background. If you want to change the background, you have many options available: color, shade, pattern, texture, or picture (watermark).

Although you can choose from all these background options, you can use only a single type of background for a specific slide. For example, you can have either a gradient shaded background or a picture as the background, but not both.

Just as you can change the color scheme, you can change the background for only one slide or for the entire presentation.

Changing the Background Color

In addition to changing the background color through the Custom tab of the Color Scheme dialog box, PowerPoint has a quick way to change the background color with the Format, Background command. You can change the background color for just the current slide or for all the slides in your presentation.

To Do: Change the Background Color

To change the background color, follow these steps:

1. Choose Format, Background from the menu. The Background dialog box displays.

2. Click the drop-down list in the Background Fill section of the dialog box, as shown in Figure 7.4.

FIGURE 7.4.

You can select many options for your presentation backgrounds using the Background dialog box.

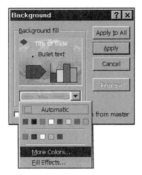

3. Click one of the color boxes.

   or

4. Click More Colors and select another color from the Colors dialog box.

5. Click the OK button (from the Colors dialog box).

6. Click the Preview button to see a preview.

7. Click the Apply or Apply to All button to accept the change.

7

If your slides have graphics, and you want to change only the background color (not add gradient shading or use a pattern), try changing the background color by using the Format, Color Scheme command. When you create the custom color scheme, change only the background color. Although you can change the background color by using the Format, Background command, this option doesn't give you a good display when slides have certain graphical elements.

Changing the Fill Effects

One way to add special effects to a slide is to modify the fill effects for the background. You have four options for the background fill:

- Gradient
- Texture
- Pattern
- Picture

Each option, when used skillfully, can visually enhance a presentation or slide and add emphasis for a particular topic of discussion.

Gradient

Gradient shading is the most frequently used fill effect, not only for the slide background, but for drawing shapes as well. This effect can produce a dazzling visual display. For example, you could gradually transform one solid color into a lighter or darker color, fade two colors from one to the other, or use preset PowerPoint gradient choices with exotic names, such as Early Sunset or Rainbow. Gradient shading also includes six different shading styles, most of which have four different variants to choose from. Table 7.1 illustrates sample variants for the shading options. Explore every avenue—you might be surprised where you end up.

TABLE 7.1. SHADING STYLES AND VARIANT OPTIONS.

Shading Style	Sample Variant
Horizontal	

Shading Style	Sample Variant
Vertical	
Diagonal Up	
Diagonal Down	
From Corner	
From Title	

To Do: Select a Gradient Background Shading Option

To select a gradient shading option for the background, use these steps:

1. Choose Format, Background from the menu to display the Background dialog box.
2. Select Fill Effects from the Background Fill drop-down list.
3. In the Fill Effects dialog box, click the Gradient tab, as shown in Figure 7.5.
4. Select a color option, such as Preset, from the option buttons in the Colors section.
5. Select one of the option buttons, such as Horizontal or Vertical, in the Shading Styles section.
6. Select an option (most shading styles have four) in the Variants section; the one you pick is displayed in the Sample box.
7. Click the OK button.
8. Click the Preview button to see a preview.
9. Click the Apply or Apply to All button to accept the change.

FIGURE 7.5.

The Gradient fill options offer many dynamic possibilities for your presentation.

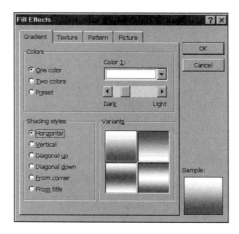

Preparing Speaker's Notes

When you create a presentation, you have done only half the job. Eventually, you have to go before an audience and speak! Showing the slides isn't enough; you need to extrapolate the information on each slide and present it to your audience. What will you say? You've created a stupendous presentation using PowerPoint, but now you need to create some notes pages for the verbal part of the presentation. Unlike other presentation programs, PowerPoint makes it very easy to create speaker's notes. You can do that by using the notes pane in the Normal view.

To Do: Create Speaker's Notes in Normal View

To create speaker's notes in Normal view, use the following steps:

1. Display the slide to which you want to add notes.
2. Click the Notes pane.
3. Type your notes.
4. Click the Slide or Outline pane when finished.

> You can also use the Notes Page view as in previous versions of PowerPoint. Select View, Notes Page from the menu. Click the Notes placeholder and type your notes. Usually the placeholder for your notes is so small that you can't see what you're typing. You might want to zoom in to 75 percent or 100 percent for a more legible display. Change back to Normal view when you are finished.

The Notes pane can be resized if needed. Place the mouse pointer on the Notes pane border until it looks like a double arrow, and drag the border to a different size. Release the mouse button when finished.

Printing Speaker's Notes

Typing your speaker's notes is only half the battle; you will eventually want to print out those notes. You can print notes only when you select the Notes Pages option from the Print dialog box (see Figure 7.6).

FIGURE 7.6.

Use the Print dialog box to print speaker's notes.

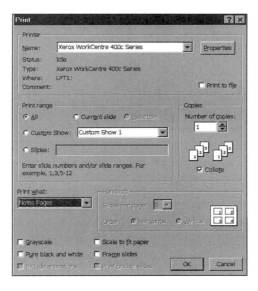

To Do: Print Speaker's Notes

To Do

To print speaker's notes, follow these steps:

1. Choose File, Print from the menu to display the Print dialog box.

 If you want to print speaker's notes, do not click the Print button because that prints your entire presentation, no questions asked. You need to specify that you want to print speaker's notes in the Print dialog box.

7

▼   2. In the Print What drop-down list, select Notes Pages.

       3. Change any other options needed.

▲   4. Click the OK button.

PowerPoint prints a miniature of each slide on the top half of the page, with the corresponding speaker's notes on the bottom half, as shown in Figure 7.7.

FIGURE 7.7.

Speaker's notes show the appropriate slide with the applicable notes.

You can add enhancements to the text in speaker's notes just as you would enhance text in a slide. Hour 5, "Working with PowerPoint Text Objects," covers text enhancements.

Preparing Audience Handouts

Now that you have finished your speaker's notes, wouldn't it be nice to have a printout of your presentation? Audience handouts are useful to keep the audience in step with your presentation. They also can be used to facilitate note-taking. Printing audience handouts couldn't be easier, and you can select the number of slides you want to appear on each printed page. Audience handouts are a nice souvenir to give out. They are great to take notes on and to help your viewers stay on track during your presentation. Keep this fact in mind: People retain 10% of what they hear, 30% of what they hear and see, and 70% of what they hear and see when they have something tangible to remind them, like handouts.

To Do: Print Audience Handouts

To print audience handouts, use the following steps:

       1. Choose File, Print to open the Print dialog box.

▼   2. In the Print What drop-down list, select Handouts.

3. In the Handouts area, select the number of slides per page (2, 3, 4, 6, or 9).

4. Select the order in which to print the slides, either horizontal or vertical.

5. Change any other options you want.

▲   6. Click the OK button.

If you want your audience to have some room on the handouts where they can write their own notes, use the 3 Slides per Page option. This option prints three slides on the left side of the page with lines on the right side for taking notes.

Unless you're printing color audience handouts, make sure the Black and White option in the Print dialog box is checked. Otherwise, you will have some very dark printouts. When you print audience handouts in black and white, PowerPoint prints only the basic information from each slide. All of the text, some of the graphics, and usually none of the background options are printed.

Summary

Even though PowerPoint 2000 creates excellent initial presentation designs, the customization work you add will make the difference between a captivating presentation and just another canned speech. This hour has demonstrated some useful features to help you create a great presentation. Adding a custom color scheme or background can make your presentation stand out, and printing speaker's notes and handouts for your audience is an easy step that shows your preparation for the presentation. In the next hour, you learn how to use master slides to set reusable custom presentation features.

Q&A

Q **I want to change the color scheme for several (but not all) of the slides in my presentation. Is there a quick way to do this without having to change the color scheme one slide at a time?**

A Yes. You need to switch to Slide Sorter View and select all the slides you want to change. Hold the Ctrl key down while you click on each slide. Then simply choose Format, Color Scheme from the menu, make your changes, and click the Apply button to apply the changes to only those slides that have been selected.

7

Q **I love the gradient shading that PowerPoint has, but I want to use a combination of the available options for a background. How can I do this?**

A You can't do this using the Background option. PowerPoint allows you to choose only one shading option per object. You can "trick" PowerPoint, however, and get the effect you want by using drawing objects. If you use this trick, make sure your shapes have no lines. I usually group my shapes and send them to the back, also. Refer to Hour 12, "Drawing Shapes in PowerPoint," and Hour 13, "Bringing Drawing Objects Together," for more information on working with drawing objects.

Q **I have a graphic that would look great as a textured background. Can I use it?**

A Sure. Just click the Other Texture button in the Fill Effects dialog box, and then select the graphics file. Any graphic that displays well as a repeated image can be used as a texture. You can either create your own by using any graphics program or use a graphic created by some other source.

Hour 8

Working with the Masters

PowerPoint 2000 has four hidden slides that control the overall look and feel of your presentation. These slides are called the masters: the Slide Master, Title Master, Handout Master, and Notes Master. You will probably find yourself working with the Slide Master and Title Master most often. These master slides control all the characteristics of your presentation and make it easy for you to place common elements on each slide. For example, if you want your company logo to appear on every slide, there's no need to insert the logo individually on the slides. You can simply place the logo on the Slide (and Title) Master, and it will automatically appear on every slide of your presentation.

If you want a customized, consistent look to your presentation, it's best to make any modifications you want in the Slide or Title Master, rather than slide by slide. Using the masters is a much more efficient way to create that special look. Also, when Bob tells you to make one little change, you have to change only the master, not 57 slides! (Yes, you will get Friday off.)

In this hour, you will learn how to do the following:

- View the four types of masters
- Set the default font for your presentation titles, subtitles, and body text
- Change the default bullet style for the entire presentation
- Add a header, footer, or page numbers to your presentation
- Add your company logo or other graphic to your presentation so that it appears on every slide
- Save a presentation as a template so you can reuse the same formatting options

The Four Types of Masters

A master is a special slide that allows you to define all the formatting attributes and add any common graphical objects that will appear in your presentation. PowerPoint 2000 has four masters, described in Table 8.1.

TABLE 8.1.   THE MASTERS.

Title	Description
Slide Master	Controls most of the slide attributes
Title Master	Controls attributes for title slides
Handout Master	Formats audience handouts
Notes Master	Formats the speaker's notes

If you want to apply a particular slide format, or have the same graphics and/or text appear on every slide, add the attributes to the Slide Master. You can also make the same modifications for the title slide, notes pages, or audience handouts by editing the corresponding master. If you have previously made changes on individual slides, any changes made in the master won't take effect immediately. When customizing a presentation, you should first make changes to the Slide Master. If more specific changes are necessary, change individual slides as needed. If you have made changes to a particular slide and want to switch back to the Slide Master defaults, follow these steps:

To Do: Revert to the Slide Master Defaults

1. Select Format, Slide Layout to open the Slide Layout dialog box.
2. Click the Reapply button.

Reapplying the layout doesn't bring back background graphical items that have been omitted. To redisplay the background graphics, choose Format, Background from the menu, and uncheck the Omit Background Graphics from the Master check box.

8

Think of the Slide Master as Elvis, the King of all the masters. The Slide Master controls every slide of your presentation except for the title slide, which is controlled by—you guessed it—the Title Master. The Slide Master controls how the text is formatted, where it's positioned, what bullet characters are used, the color scheme, and what graphical items appear on every slide in your presentation. Figure 8.1 shows the Slide Master screen. To display the Slide Master, select View, Master, Slide Master from the menu.

FIGURE 8.1.

The Slide Master for a presentation controls the initial format and placement of text and other slide objects.

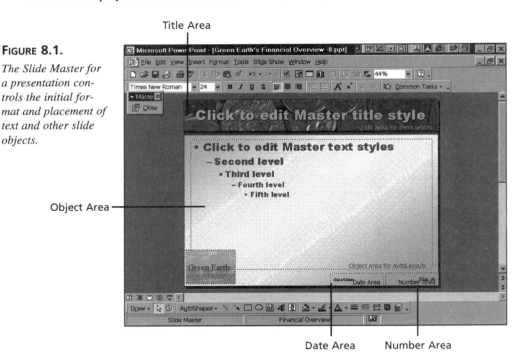

When you make changes to the Slide Master, you shouldn't be concerned with the specific text information. You're more concerned with formatting the text. The Slide Master looks almost identical to a regular bullet slide, but it is different. First, notice that the Slide Master has five placeholders, listed in Table 8.2.

TABLE 8.2.   SLIDE MASTER PLACEHOLDERS.

Placeholder	Description
Title Area	Use to format, position, and size the title text for all slides. You can change the font type, size, color, and any other effects you want.
Object Area	Use to format, position, and size the body text for all slides. You can change the font attributes, just as with the title, and change the bullet style for each bullet level.
Date Area	Use to add, position, resize, and format a date on every slide in the presentation.
Number Area	Use to add, position, resize, and format automatic slide numbering.
Footer Area	Use to add, position, resize, and format footer text for every slide in your presentation.

The Title Master allows you to control the same attributes as the Slide Master by using the Title Slide objects. The Title Master controls how the title and subtitle objects are formatted and positioned. For a graphical object to appear on all slides, those using the title slide layout and all others, you will need to place it on both the Title and Slide Masters. Figure 8.2 shows the Title Master, which you open by choosing View, Master, Title Master from the menu.

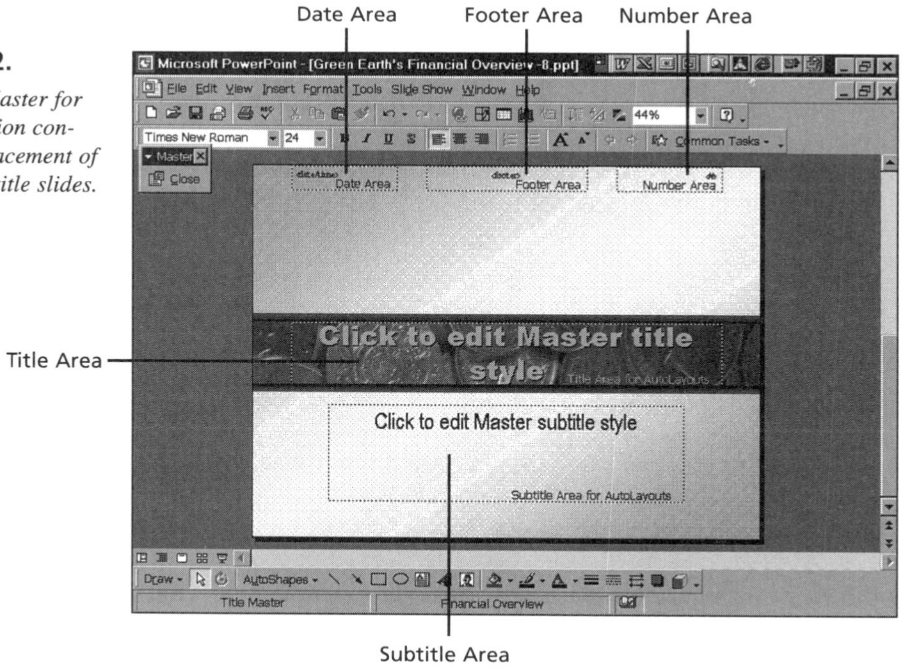

FIGURE 8.2.

The Title Master for a presentation controls the placement of objects on title slides.

If your presentation does not have a slide using the Title Slide layout, you will not be able to select the Title Master option from the menu. If you feel you will not need a title slide, don't worry about it. If you want to format the Title Master, you will need to create a Title Master. To create a Title Master, select Insert, New Title Master from the menu, or click the Insert New Title Master button on the standard toolbar (the Insert New Slide button), while in Slide Master view.

You might want to portray the presentation of the Title Master differently than the Slide Master to add some emphasis to your presentation's title slide. If you create a new presentation with the presentation design template, you will probably notice that the title slide has a slightly different look than the other slides do. However, the presentation is still consistent with the overall theme of the presentation design, as shown in Figure 8.3.

FIGURE 8.3.

The title slide is slightly different from the other slides.

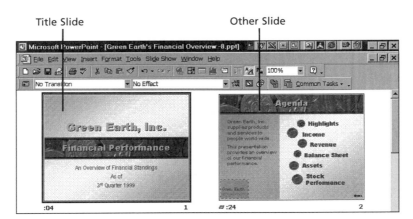

The Title Master, just like the Slide Master, has five placeholders, described in Table 8.3.

TABLE 8.3. TITLE MASTER PLACEHOLDERS.

Placeholder	Description
Title Area	Use to format, position, and size the title text of the title slide. You can change the font type, size, color, and add any other effects you want.
Subtitle Area	Use to format, position, and size the subtitle text of the title slide. You can change the font attributes, just as with the title.
Date Area	Use to add, position, resize, and format a date for the title slide.

continues

TABLE 8.3.   CONTINUED.

Placeholder	Description
Number Area	Use to add, position, resize, and format automatic slide numbering for the title slide.
Footer Area	Use to add, position, resize, and format footer text for the title slide.

The Handout Master is used to format your audience handouts. Like the Slide and Title Masters, you can add graphical and text objects to the Handout Master, shown in Figure 8.4. The Handout Master is associated with a corresponding Handout Master toolbar that enables you to choose from one of the six handout printing options: two, three, four, six, or nine slides per page or an outline of the presentation. To display the Handout Master, select View, Master, Handout Master from the menu.

FIGURE 8.4.

The Handout Master controls the placement of objects on handouts.

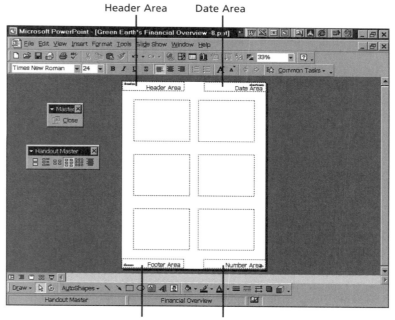

If the Handout Master toolbar isn't automatically displayed, choose View, Toolbars, Handout Master from the menu.

The Handout Master has four small placeholders, two at the top and two at the bottom of the page. Additionally, you can have one, two, three, four, six, or nine placeholders displayed in the middle of the page, depending on the view selected. Table 8.4 covers these placeholders.

TABLE 8.4. HANDOUT MASTER PLACEHOLDERS.

Placeholder	Description
Header Area	Use to add, position, resize, and format text that should appear on the top of every page of the handouts.
Date Area	Use to add, position, resize, and format a date on every page of the handouts.
Footer Area	Use to add, position, resize, and format text that should appear at the bottom of every page of the handouts.
Number Area	Use to add, position, resize, and format automatic page numbering.
Slide or Outline placeholders	Use to show the positioning of the slides or outline in the handouts. These placeholders cannot be moved or resized.

The Notes Master is used to format the presentation of the speaker's note pages. As always, you can add graphical items and text to the Notes Master. The Notes Master also allows you to resize the slide area. To display the Notes Master, select View, Master, Notes Master from the menu. Figure 8.5 displays the Notes Master.

The Notes Master should have six placeholders; they are described in Table 8.5. Two placeholders are located at the top, two at the bottom of the page, and two larger placeholders are in the middle of the page.

TABLE 8.5. NOTES MASTER PLACEHOLDERS.

Placeholder	Description
Header Area	Use to add, position, resize, and format text that should appear on the top of every page in the speaker's notes.
Date Area	Use to add, position, resize, and format a date on every page of speaker's notes.
Footer Area	Use to add, position, resize, and format text that should appear at the bottom of every page in speaker's notes.
Number Area	Use to add, position, resize, and format automatic page numbering for speaker's notes.

continues

TABLE 8.5. CONTINUED.

Placeholder	Description
Slide placeholder	Use to show the positioning of the corresponding slide. This image can be resized or moved.
Notes Body Area	Use to format, position, and resize the body text in the speaker's notes. You can change the font type, size, color, and other attributes.

FIGURE 8.5.

The Notes Master controls object placement on Speaker Notes.

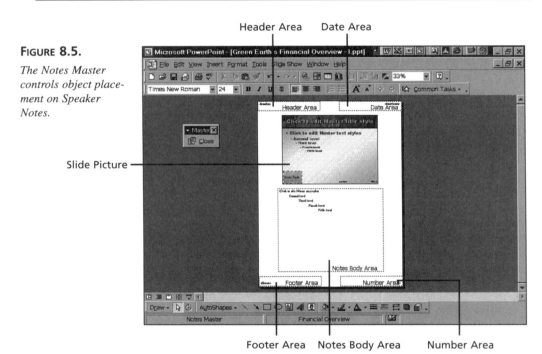

Formatting the Masters

You can change the mood of your entire presentation by simply changing one object or reformatting text. Any changes you make to the Slide Master affect every slide in your presentation, unless you make changes to individual slides. When you make changes to individual slides, those changes override the Slide Master defaults. Therefore, you're not stuck with the default Slide Master items.

Depending on what you want to change, there are two ways to override the Slide Master. For text objects, simply format the object as desired. For graphical objects, select the Omit Background Graphics from the Master check box in the Background dialog box, as discussed previously in Hour 7, "Customizing the Presentation."

Formatting Text

Changing the font face can dramatically affect the tone of your presentation, depending on the font style you select. The font can be changed for the title, subtitle, or body text of your entire presentation by using the Slide and Title Master. Select fonts and font attributes that are appropriate for your presentation, making sure to keep your audience in mind. For example, a financial presentation to a board of directors should use a nice crisp, conservative font such as Times Roman or Arial. If you were creating a presentation for a local garden club, you might want to use a pretty script font in pink or purple. Figures 8.6 and 8.7 show the title slide for a board meeting and garden club.

FIGURE 8.6.

A financial presentation to Green Earth's Board of Directors should be more conservative and may have a money theme.

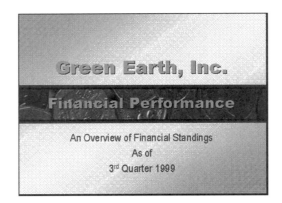

FIGURE 8.7.

The Purple Rose Garden Club's annual meeting presentation can be more informal and may even reflect a softer appearance.

To Do: Set a Default Font for the Title or Subtitle

To set a default font for the title or subtitle, follow these steps:

1. View the Slide Master by choosing View, Master, Slide Master or Title Master from the menu.
2. Click once on the Title or Subtitle area.
3. Choose Format, Font from the menu to open the Font dialog box.
4. Make any font changes desired.
5. Click the OK button.

To Do: Set a Default Font for All Body Text

Follow these steps to set a default font for all the body text:

1. View the Slide Master by choosing View, Master, Slide Master from the menu.
2. Click once on the Object area.
3. Click a second time on the placeholder border to select the entire object.
4. Choose Format, Font to open the Font dialog box.
5. Make any font changes you want, except size (see the following caution).

The font size will usually contain a plus sign. This simply means that the font sizes are different for each bullet level. Do not set the font size to an exact number. Setting an exact number will make every bullet level the same size font. Instead, use the Increase Font Size or Decrease Font Size buttons on the standard toolbar to change the font size.

6. Click the OK button.

You can add some life to your presentation by selecting bullets that fit the theme of the presentation. This feature is one of the easiest ways to customize and coordinate the entire look of the presentation, especially when you're using one of the presentation design templates. Changing the bullet style to reflect the overall theme of the presentation can add that special touch. Your audience will think that you have put hours into designing the presentation. Figure 8.8 shows the fictitious Purple Rose Garden Club presentation with custom bullets.

FIGURE 8.8.

Customize the Purple Rose Garden Club presentation with flower bullets.

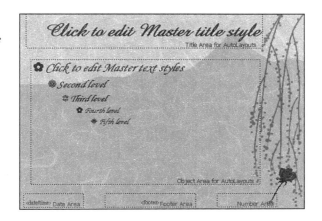

8

To Do: Change the Default Bullet Style for an Entire Presentation

To change the default bullet style for the entire presentation, follow these instructions:

1. View the Slide Master by choosing View, Master, Slide Master from the menu.

2. Click once on the Object area.

3. Click a second time on the bullet level you want to change.

4. Choose Format, Bullets and Numbering from the menu. The Bullets and Numbering dialog box opens.

5. Click the Character button.

6. Select a font from the Bullets From drop-down list.

 7. Click a symbol from the symbol grid.

> The most useful symbols are found in the Monotype Sorts, Wingdings, and Webdings fonts. Click and drag on the symbols in the grid to better view them (the symbol pops up so you can see it better). If you can't find just the right symbol, try a different font.

 8. Click the OK button.

Headers and Footers

If you have ever used a word processing program, you know that the header or footer is any piece of information you want to appear at the top or bottom of every page in your document. Examples of header or footer information are page numbers, dates, or company addresses. In PowerPoint, headers and footers work pretty much the same way. However, PowerPoint has predefined areas for the date and slide number, with a separate area defined for extra header or footer information.

To Do: Add the Date, Slide Number, or Footer to a Slide

To add the date, the slide number, or a footer to the slides in your presentation, follow these steps:

1. Choose View, Header and Footer from the menu to open the Header and Footer dialog box.
2. Select the Slide tab, shown in Figure 8.9.

FIGURE 8.9.

Use the Slide tab of the Header and Footer dialog box to add the date, slide number, and a footer to each slide.

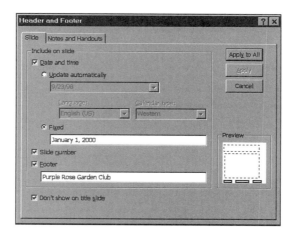

3. Select the items you want displayed on your slides.
4. Type in text for the footer, if you like.
5. Click the OK button.

You can also choose to add the same information in your speaker's notes or audience handouts.

To Do: Add the Date, Slide Number, Header, or Footer to Audience Handouts or Notes Pages

8

To add the date, the slide number, a header, or a footer to your audience handouts or notes pages, follow these steps:

1. Choose View, Header and Footer to display the Header and Footer dialog box.

2. Select the Notes and Handouts tab, shown in Figure 8.10.

FIGURE 8.10.

Use the Notes and Handouts tab of the Header and Footer dialog box to add the date, slide number, header, and footers to handouts and speaker's notes.

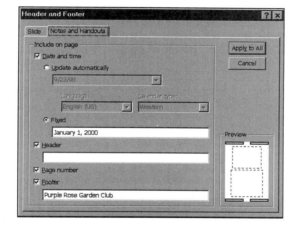

3. Select the items you want displayed on your notes and handouts.

4. Type in text for the header and/or footer, if desired.

5. Click the OK button.

Adding a Company Logo to the Master

You can very easily add your company logo to every slide in the presentation, the handouts, or your speaker's notes. Before you can add your company logo, you need to have the logo already created and saved as a graphic on your system. In Figure 8.11, you can see the company logo added to the master for the fictitious Green Earth, Inc. financial report.

FIGURE 8.11.

The Green Earth, Inc. company logo has been placed in the lower-left corner of the Slide Master.

Green Earth's logo—

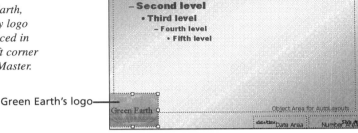

To Do: Add a Logo to the Master

To add your company logo (or any other graphic) to the master, follow these steps:

1. Choose View, Master, Slide Master or Title Master from the menu.

2. Choose Insert, Picture, From File to open the Insert Picture dialog box.

3. Select the drive and folder that contain your company logo.

4. Select the graphics file that contains the company logo.

5. Click the Insert button.

6. Position and resize the graphic as necessary.

7. Switch to Slide view.

You may want to place the logo on both the Title and Slide Master. If so, try placing the logo in a different place on the Title Master to give your presentation a more profressional look. In Figure 8.12, the Green Earth, Inc.'s logo is the background.

FIGURE 8.12.

The Green Earth title slide uses the company logo as the background.

Saving a Presentation As a Template

So far in this hour, you have seen how to fine-tune the format of your presentation using the Slide Master. Choosing the best font and bullet styles, moving the text objects to the perfect position, and adding the company logo all add to the impact of your presentation. Using the Slide Master makes these tasks much easier, but you still may put in a lot of time getting your presentation to look just right. If you need to create presentations frequently for a particular organization, PowerPoint enables you to save your presentations as a template. Why do this? You can create and use your own design templates, just like the design templates that have been created for you by Microsoft. You will never need to duplicate all that formatting again. Not only will you get to take this Friday off, but maybe next Friday as well!

A template is a presentation that has been saved in a special format so that you won't accidentally delete the original file.

A PowerPoint template usually has preformatted text, background graphics, and color schemes. You can also include macros, menu and key assignments, and custom toolbars to a template, if you like. The easiest way to create a template is to use an existing presentation that you have formatted to suit your needs.

To Do: Save a Presentation As a Template Design

Save the presentation as you regularly would, and then use the following steps to save it as a presentation template design:

1. Open the existing presentation, or create a new presentation based on a presentation design.

2. Make any changes you want.

3. Delete any extra text or slides you don't need in every presentation.

Because a template is usually just the overall design of the presentation, not the actual slides themselves, you probably won't need any text or extra slides in your presentation except for the bare minimum (many templates have only one or two slides). To have a complete template, you should make all your changes in the Slide or Title Master.

▼ 4. Choose File, Save As from the menu. The Save As dialog box displays.

5. Type a name for your template in the File Name text box.

6. In the Save as Type drop-down list, select Design Template.

▲ 7. Click the Save button.

> Before you click the Save button, be sure that the Save In box lists either the Templates or Presentation Designs folder as the location for your template. If not, you need to change this option to one of the aforementioned folders.

Summary

If you're modifying a global presentation attribute, use one of the four master slides, which enable you to control all the characteristics of the presentation in addition to offering an easy way to give a consistent look to the presentation slides, notes, and handouts. Modifications to the masters can change the default font, bullet styles, headers, footers, and background graphics for your slides. Changes to the Slide Master, for example, affect every slide in your presentation. After you have taken the time to develop a great presentation, you can even save it as a template and reuse the settings later. In the next hour, you learn how to wrap up the presentation and polish your delivery.

Q&A

Q I have several slides that I made changes to, and now I want them to follow the master slide. Can I reapply the master to all of them at the same time?

A You can reapply the master to all slides that follow the same layout. To reapply the master layout to multiple slides, first switch to Slide Sorter view and select the slides that follow the same layout (hold the Ctrl key and click each slide). A fast way to select all of the slides in your presentation is to select Edit, Select All from the menu or press Ctrl+A. You can also unselect slides by using the Ctrl+clicking method. Once you have the slides selected, choose Format, Slide Layout from the menu and click the Reapply button.

This technique works perfectly if most of the slides follow the same layout (for example, if all the slides in your presentation use the bullet slide layout). If they follow different layouts, you will need to reapply the layouts separately. However, this task is most quickly and efficiently done in Slide Sorter view.

Q **I accidentally deleted the Title placeholder in the Slide Master. How do I get it back?**

A Because you can't reapply the master layout to the master, the Slide Master has a special option for adding missing placeholders to any master. To add a placeholder, select Format, Master Layout from the menu to open the Master Layout dialog box. Click the check box for the placeholder you're missing, and then click the OK button.

Q **How can I get the word Slide to appear in front of the automatic slide numbering in my slides?**

A First, add slide numbering as explained in this hour. Then, while viewing the Slide Master, click once on the Number placeholder and zoom to 75 percent or 100 percent; although this is not necessary, it does make it easier to see what you are typing.

Then click once in front of the (#) symbol. This can be a bit cumbersome—your mouse pointer will look like an I. Type the word Slide (or Page), followed by a space and then zoom back to Fit and switch back to Slide View. You should now have the word Slide in front of the slide number.

8

Hour 9

Basics of Slide Shows

Now that you have created and edited several presentations, you're finally ready to show off all your hard work. This hour and the next cover everything you need to know to get your slide show up and running. In this hour, you will learn how to do the following:

- View the presentation
- Make temporary annotations on the presentation
- Set slide timings, either custom or rehearsed
- Hide a slide
- Create a summary slide

Viewing the Presentation

Viewing your presentation is the easy part, but deciding which option to use can be a bit more difficult. Although there are several ways to view a presentation, you'll learn just two options in this hour:

- Starting the slide show in PowerPoint
- Saving a presentation so that it always starts as a slide show

Hour 10, "Adding Pizzazz to a Slide Show," explains setting up the slide show to run as a self-running presentation at a kiosk.

Starting the Slide Show in PowerPoint

During the initial presentation design, you need to start and view your presentation in PowerPoint. Doing so gives you the opportunity to fine-tune your presentation and add timings, transitions, and any other finishing touches to your show. To start a slide show in PowerPoint, you have four main options:

- Choose View, Slide Show from the menu
- Choose Slide Show, View Show from the menu
- Choose Slide Show, Rehearse Timings from the menu
- Click the Slide Show View button

Each option gives you basically the same result, with a few minor differences. You can view the entire presentation from start to finish, clicking the mouse to advance to the next slide. The Rehearse Timings option gives you the opportunity to rehearse your presentation. While you are rehearsing, PowerPoint 2000 will keep track of the amount of time spent on each slide, and the total amount of time for the entire presentation. Figure 9.1 demonstrates PowerPoint Rehearsal toolbar during such a rehearsal.

The Rehearsal toolbar displays to show you the time spent on each slide. You can click the Next button to advance to the next slide. There is even a Repeat button if you want to start over on a particular slide. The Pause button enables you to pause the presentation, let's say to take an important phone call, and then you can resume the rehearsal without having to start all over again.

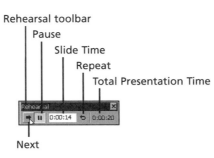

FIGURE 9.1.

Use the Rehearse Timings option to view and rehearse your slide show while recording timings for each slide.

When you click the Slide Show View button, you usually start the slide show from the currently displayed or active slide. If you want to start the presentation from the beginning, go to the first slide before going into Slide Show view.

If you're viewing a presentation and want to stop before you reach the end, press the Esc key on your keyboard. The slide show is then terminated.

To Do: Create a Shortcut on Your Desktop

To create a shortcut on your desktop, follow these steps:

1. Find the file by using My Computer.

2. Right-click the file and drag it to your desktop.

3. Release the mouse button and select Create Shortcut(s) Here.

4. To run the show, simply double-click the icon.

Setting and Using the Slide Show Settings

When you view a slide show, you have several options for its display, most of which are available in the Set Up Show dialog box (see Figure 9.2). From this dialog box, you can choose whether the show is going to be presented by a speaker, browsed by an individual, or run at a kiosk. You can also determine which slides or custom shows to display, how the slides should advance, and the default pen color (explained in the following section, "Using the Pen").

FIGURE 9.2.

The Set Up Show dialog box determines how the slide show will be displayed.

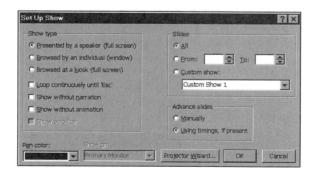

To Do: Change Show Settings

To change any show settings, follow these steps:

1. Choose Slide Show, Set Up Show to display the Set Up Show dialog box.

2. Change any options needed.

 3. Click the OK button.

> If you have a laptop and will be using a projector to display your presentation, PowerPoint 2000 has a Projector Wizard to help with the setup of the projector. Simply click the Projector Wizard button in the Set Up Show dialog box, and follow the instructions. PowerPoint 2000 will attempt to detect your projector and configure everything for you.

Using the Pen

When you're viewing a presentation, you have the capability to temporarily annotate each slide by turning your mouse pointer into a pen. This is a great feature when you have audience participation. To display the pen during a slide show, select one of the following options:

> If you plan on annotating a slide show, it's usually best to manually advance each slide.

> It's a good idea to get some practice using the pen before the actual slide show. Sometimes your annotations can end up as illegible handwriting. Typically, the pen is used to underline or emphasize a specific point during your presentation. A good trick to use to draw straight lines is to hold down the Shift key while you're drawing lines. This keeps your lines straight.

- Press Ctrl+P.

  or

- Right-click and select Pointer Options, Pen from the Menu.

- To use the pen, simply hold down the left mouse button and write or draw annotations by moving the mouse. The annotations you make during the slide show aren't permanent, so they disappear for the next show.

To change the pen back to the pointer arrow, use one of these methods:

- Press Ctrl+A.

  or

- Right-click and select Pointer Options, Arrow from the menu.

Slide Sorter View

When you're adding all the finishing touches to your slide show, you'll find that the Slide Sorter view is the most useful. Slide Sorter view allows you to view several slides simultaneously. You can move slides around, add and view the timings for individual slides, hide slides, add transitions, and include animation (which is covered in Hour 10). Slide Sorter view has its own unique toolbar with buttons that make most tasks just a click away.

 The number of slides displayed at 100% zoom is controlled by the size of your monitor and your screen resolution setting. With screen resolutions set for 640×480, 800×600, or 1024×768, you would see two, six, and nine slides, respectively.

 You can view more slides or fewer slides onscreen by changing the zoom option for the Slide Sorter view.

While in Slide Sorter view, you may see little icons underneath the individual slides. The icons represent transitions, animation, hidden slides, and timings that have been added.

Moving Slides

When you need to rearrange your slides, Slide Sorter view is the place to do it. If possible, set the zoom control so that you can see the slide you want to move and the destination position, as shown in Figure 9.3.

Line indicates new
position of slide

FIGURE 9.3.

You can easily move a slide to any position in the presentation.

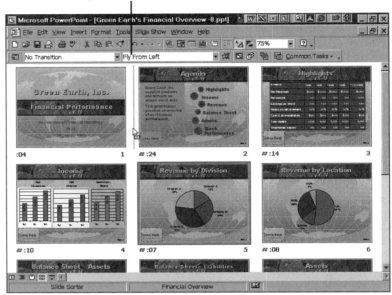

To Do: Move a Slide

To move a slide, follow these steps:

1. Place your mouse pointer on the slide you want to move.

2. Hold down the left mouse button.

3. Drag the mouse pointer to the new position; you should see a vertical line indicating the placement of the slide.

▲   4. Release the mouse button.

Timing

When you want a presentation to run on its own, or a slide show that advances from slide to slide without using the mouse or keyboard, you must set timings for each slide. You can either make an educated guess as to how long the slide should be displayed (custom timings) or rehearse your presentation and have PowerPoint record the duration (rehearsed timings) before you advance to the next slide, as discussed earlier in this hour.

To Do: Set Custom Timings

It's easiest to set custom timings while you're in Slide Sorter view. To set custom timings for your presentation, follow these steps:

1. Select the slide or slides you want to set timings for.

2. Choose Slide Show, Slide Transition from the menu. The Slide Transition dialog box displays.

3. Under Advance, click the Automatically After check box.

4. Type the number of seconds you want the slide to be displayed onscreen.

5. Click the Apply button.

To select a slide, just click on the slide. To select multiple, noncontiguous slides, hold down the Ctrl key and click on each slide you want to select. You can select a contiguous group of slides by clicking on the first slide of the group, holding the Shift key, and clicking on the last slide of the group.

If you want to set the same show timings for all the slides in your presentation, click the Apply to All button in the Slide Transition dialog box.

Rehearse Timings

You can also rehearse your presentation and have PowerPoint automatically add timings for each of your slides. While you're rehearsing your presentation, PowerPoint displays the Rehearsal toolbar as shown previously in this hour.

To Do: Rehearse Timings

To rehearse your presentation and add automatic timings, use the following steps:

1. Choose Slide Show, Rehearse Timings from the menu.

2. Practice your entire presentation as though you were in front of your audience. Click the next button to advance to the next slide and record the time for the current slide.

3. At the end of the show, click the Yes button to record your timings and use them when you view the show.

PowerPoint 2000 will display your slides in Slide Sorter view so that you can either edit them or rehearse your show to get new timing values.

Hiding a Slide

Sometimes when you're creating a presentation, you might not be sure whether a piece of information is relevant. Of course, you always want to be prepared (even if you're not a Boy Scout), no matter what might come up. If you have a slide that doesn't need to be shown, you can always leave it in the presentation file, but hide it from the show by following these steps:

To Do: Hide a Slide

1. Select the slide you want to hide.

2. Choose Slide Show, Hide Slide from the menu.

   or

3. Click the Hide Slide button from the Slide Sorter toolbar.

> If you're hiding slides, you might not want to have them numbered automatically. Although PowerPoint doesn't display a slide that has been hidden, it doesn't renumber the slides automatically.

Creating a Summary Slide

Creating a summary slide quickly is a great feature of PowerPoint 2000. PowerPoint creates the summary (or agenda) slide from the titles of the slides you select.

To Do: Create a Summary Slide

To create a summary slide, follow these steps:

1. Switch to Slide Sorter view.

2. Select the slide(s) that you want included in the summary.

3. Click the Summary Slide button on the Slide Sorter toolbar.

PowerPoint creates the summary slide in front of the first slide selected. Move the summary slide to the end to close your presentation powerfully.

Summary

You have now completed your PowerPoint presentation from design to delivery. Creating a slide show is the finishing touch to your hard work. It's important to apply creativity and thought to the slide show and remember that you're judged on the pacing as well as the overall design of the presentation. It is important to keep in mind that you are what is most important; your presentation is a tool that you are using to help convey your ideas to your audience. The star of the show should not be the presentation itself.

You can now easily view the presentation, make temporary annotations, set slide timings, hide a slide, or create a summary slide. This hour caps the basics. Future hours add more advanced features to your knowledge base.

9

Q&A

Q **When viewing a slide show, can I go back to the previous slide?**

A Yes. You can either display the Slide Show menu or press the P key. (By the way, the N key takes you to the next slide.) If you find you're running a lot of slide shows, it's a good idea to learn the "hot keys" for working with slide shows. Appendix A, "Hotkeys and Menus," has a pretty complete list of the available ones.

Q **How do I redisplay a slide I have hidden?**

A The Hide Slide command works like an on/off button; the option is either on or off. To redisplay a slide that has been hidden, go to Slide Sorter view and select the slide, and then choose Slide Show, Hide Slide from the menu.

Hour **10**

Adding Pizzazz to a Slide Show

Now that you have learned the basics necessary to set up a slide show, it's time to get into the special features that add extra sparkle to your show. In this hour, you will learn about the following:

- Adding special effects, such as slide transitions and animation
- Setting up a show to be browsed by an individual or at a kiosk
- Customizing the same show for two different audiences
- Setting up an Online Broadcast using NetShow

Adding Transitions

When you first view your slide show, advancing (or transitioning) from slide to slide can be a little boring. But never fear—PowerPoint 2000 is here. You can add a special effect called a transition that changes the way individual slides appear onscreen. There are over three dozen types of transitions to choose from. For example, you can indicate that one slide should dissolve into the next or specify a checkerboard transition. Not only do you have a choice of transition effects, but you can also set the speed of each transition. But enough talk; the best way to understand the transition effect is to get in there and try it. To do that, follow these steps:

To Do: Add Transition Effects to a Slide

1. Switch to Slide Sorter view.

2. Select the slide(s) to which you want to add a transition.

3. Choose Slide Show, Slide Transition to open the Slide Transition dialog box, or click the Slide Transition button on the Slide Sorter toolbar.

4. In the Slide Transition dialog box, select a transition from the Effect drop-down list (see Figure 10.1).

FIGURE 10.1.

In the Slide Transition dialog box, the dog changes to a key to display the transition effect you have chosen.

5. Select a speed: Slow, Medium, or Fast.

6. Set an Advance Time and Sound, if desired.

   7. Click the Apply button.

To quickly apply the same transition to every slide in your presentation, click the Apply to All button. You can select the same transition for every slide, or use the Random Transition setting to get a different transition for each slide.

After adding a transition effect to a slide, you will notice that a small slide transition icon appears under the slide's left corner, as shown in Figure 10.2. This icon lets you know that you have been successful in adding the transition effect.

FIGURE 10.2.

Slides with transitions are shown with icons.

Slide transition icon —

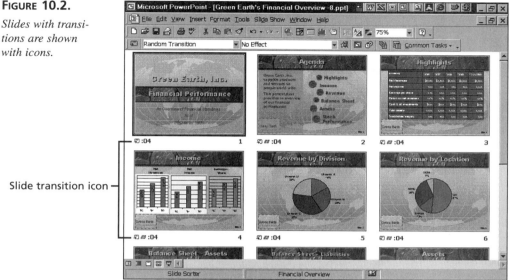

In addition to the initial display that indicates what the transition effect will look like, you can also click the transition icon to see what the effect will look like on the actual slide.

Including Animation

PowerPoint 2000 comes with state-of-the-art animation options for your slide shows. You can animate almost anything. Animation is commonly added to text items, drawing items, charts, and clip art. For more information on charts, refer to Hour 17, "Creating Charts and Graphs with Microsoft Graph," and Hour 19, "Editing Charts and Graphs," later in this book.

Animation effects allow the text and other objects to appear onscreen one item at a time, using the same transition effects available for advancing from slide to slide. Because you can combine these effects, some slides can become quite complex. For example, a slide could have the sound of a drum roll or have the individual letters of a text item fly onto the screen (like a typewriter typing them). When an object is animated, you can see the full effect during the slide show.

You have two options available when setting animation. You can use one of PowerPoint's preset animation settings, or you can create your own custom animation. Preset animation is the way to go when you're in a time crunch, yet want to add a little extra pizzazz to your presentation. Custom animation is an excellent choice when you want full control over the finished show or want to add sound in addition to the visual effects. After you have added animation to the objects on your slide(s), you can preview the animation settings from Slide Sorter view.

Using Preset Animation

PowerPoint 2000 has eight preset animation settings available. Use them to quickly add motion to any PowerPoint object. To set animation using one of the available preset options, follow these steps:

To Do: Format a Slide Object with Preset Animation

1. Switch to Slide Sorter view.
2. Select the slide you want to animate.
3. Choose Slide Show, Preset Animation from the menu.
4. Click the animation setting you want from the submenu.

Many of the preset options include sound effects with the visual animation. Try the laser text option.

Using Custom Animation

The preset animation settings are nice, but when you want to control all facets of the animation effects, you need to roll up those shirtsleeves and get into the custom animation settings. With custom animation, you can choose from over 40 visual effects, multiple sounds, and timings in PowerPoint. You can also set the order in which the objects are animated. Follow these steps to set custom animation:

To Do: Format a Slide Object with Custom Animation

1. Display the slide you want to animate in either Normal or Slide view.
2. Choose Slide Show, Custom Animation from the menu. The Custom Animation dialog box displays.
3. Select the Order & Timing tab (see Figure 10.3).

Select the object(s) you
want to animate here

FIGURE 10.3.

*Use the Order &
Timing tab of the
Custom Animation
dialog box to set the
order and type of
animation for slide
objects.*

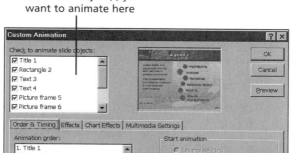

10

4. Check the first object you want to animate. The preview will display the object
   with selection handles. If it is not the right object, select the next one.

5. In the Start Animation section, select either On Mouse Click or Automatically, and
   enter the time for PowerPoint 2000 to wait.

6. Click the Effects tab (see Figure 10.4).

FIGURE 10.4.

*Use the Effects tab
of the Custom
Animation dialog box
to select the anima-
tion and sound effects
you want.*

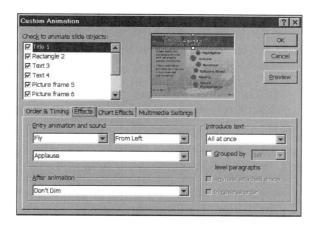

7. In the Entry Animation and Sound section, select the animation and sound settings
   you want.

8. If you're animating a text object, in the Introduce Text section, select how you
   want PowerPoint to introduce the text: All at Once, By Word, or By Letter.

▼   9. Select the paragraph level to introduce the text.

    10. Change any other settings you want.

    11. Repeat steps 3 through 10 for each object to animate.

    12. Click the Preview button to see a preview of the animation settings.

▲   13. Click the OK button when you're done adding animation to the slide.

Previewing Your Animation Effects

You can preview your animation settings at any time by viewing the slide show. PowerPoint 2000 also has an option that lets you preview animation settings for the current slide without starting the entire slide show.

To preview the animation for just one slide, display the slide and choose Slide Show, Animation Preview from the menu. PowerPoint then shows a slide miniature that displays all the currently set animation options for the slide.

> If you already have the slide miniature displayed, you can preview animation settings at any time by simply clicking on the slide miniature.

Running a Slide Show

PowerPoint 2000 gives you three options in the Set Up Show dialog box for running your slide show onscreen: Presented by a Speaker, Browsed by an Individual, or Browsed at a Kiosk. The method selected depends on the type of presentation you have created.

The most common method is Presented by a Speaker (Full Screen). You can run the presentation using a projector of some sort with a speaker controlling the show.

The second option is to create a slide show that people can browse at their convenience. An orientation presentation for new employees is a good example of this kind of presentation method.

The third and final option, a self-running presentation, is useful when the show will be displayed on a kiosk, much like something you might have seen at a trade show.

Presented by a Speaker

Up to this point, you have been viewing the slide shows with the Presented by a Speaker method, because there's usually a speaker who controls the show. If you are broadcasting a presentation, this is also the method to use. To set a slide show to be presented by a speaker in full-screen mode, follow these steps:

To Do

To Do: Format a Slide Show to Be Presented by a Speaker

1. Choose Slide Show, Set Up Show to display the Set Up Show dialog box.
2. Select the Presented by a Speaker (Full Screen) option.
3. Click the OK button.

Deciding Which Slides to Show

As discussed in Hour 9, you can hide slides that shouldn't appear in your slide show. This feature is useful if you want to hide one or two slides. However, if you want to display only a certain range of slides, it's easier to use the Set Up Show dialog box to specify which slides should be included in your show. To specify a range of slides to display in a show, follow these steps:

To Do

To Do: Specify Slides to Be Shown During the Presentation

1. Choose Slide Show, Set Up Show from the menu to display the Set Up Show dialog box as shown in Figure 10.5.

10

FIGURE 10.5.

Use the Set Up Show dialog box to specify which slides to show in your presentation.

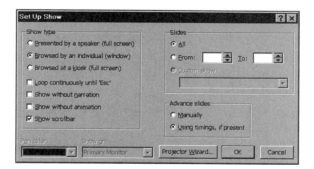

2. In the Slides section, select the From/To option.
3. Type the beginning slide number in the From box and the ending slide number in the To box.

Creating Custom Shows

If you need to create several similar slide shows for different audiences, you will appreciate PowerPoint 2000's new Custom Shows feature. This feature allows you to create a show within a show that specifies which slides to display for each audience, so you don't need to create several shows that are almost the same. To use this feature, you group together the slides that will be different, and then switch to those slides during your custom show.

For example, if you have a slide show for a new employee orientation, you might want one show for new managers and one show for new staff personnel. Both of these shows would have similar slides for all new employees, but the custom shows would have slides specifically tailored for managers or staff, depending on the custom show selected. After showing the first few general slides, the custom show would then move on to the slides directed to the specific audience.

To create a custom show, first create a slide show that has all the slides that will be used for all the shows. After the slides are created, use the following steps:

To Do: Create a Custom Show

1. Choose Slide Show, Custom Shows to open the Custom Shows dialog box.

2. Click the New button to open the Define Custom Show dialog box.

3. Type a name for your custom show, such as Staff or Manager.

4. In the Slides in Presentation box, select the slides you want displayed in the custom show.

> You can select multiple slides by holding down the Ctrl key while you click on each slide.

5. Click the Add >> button to add slides to the Slides in Custom Show list box, as shown in Figure 10.6.

FIGURE 10.6.

Selecting slides for the Products & Services custom show.

> If the slides aren't listed in the order in which they should appear, use the up-arrow or down-arrow buttons to move individual slides to the correct location.

6. When finished, click the OK button to go back to the Custom Show dialog box.

7. Repeat steps 2 through 6 to create another show.

8. Click the Close button to close the Custom Show dialog box when you're finished.

To Do: Add or Remove Slides from a Custom Show

Follow these steps to add or remove slides from a custom show:

1. Choose Slide Show, Custom Shows to display the Custom Shows dialog box.
2. Select the name of the custom show you want to edit.
3. Click the Edit button.
4. Add or remove slides from the Slides in Custom Show list box.
5. If the slides aren't in the order you want, use the up-arrow or down-arrow buttons to move individual slides to the correct location.
6. Click the OK button when you're done.
7. Click the Close button to close the Custom Show dialog box when you're finished.

> You can add hyperlinks from any PowerPoint object to a custom show. The link quickly takes you to another custom show. See Hour 22, "Creating Web Pages," for more information about hyperlinks.

10

Online Broadcasting

The last option covered during this hour explains the steps for setting up and running an Online Broadcast (or presentation). This feature is available to use if you are connected to a network. Online Broadcasting allows you to give your presentation to coworkers on the network, without anyone having to leave his office. This can be extremely powerful if your organization is located in several different, physical buildings such as at a college or university.

> After you create your presentation, you will need to save it in a shared folder, preferably on a network file server. Contact your network administrator if you need help with or access for this task.

PowerPoint 2000 uses the NetShow program to broadcast your presentation over a network. Not only can you broadcast slides, but you can display audio and visual content as well. Because setting up an online broadcast requires some knowledge of your network, type of servers, and access to shared folders you will probably need to contact your network administrator first to help you with this task. To start the setup, select Slide Show, Online Broadcast, Set Up and Schedule from the menu. To set up an online broadcast, use the following steps:

To Do: Set Up an Online Broadcast

1. Select Slide Show, Online Broadcast, Set Up and Schedule from the menu.
2. The NetShow Wizard will start. Select Set Up and Schedule a New Broadcast, and click the OK button as shown in Figure 10.7. The Schedule a New Broadcast dialog box opens.

FIGURE 10.7

The NetShow Wizard start screen is the starting point for presentation broadcasting.

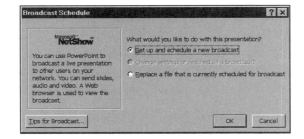

3. On the Description tab, enter a Title, Description, and Speaker.
4. Click the Address Book button to open the address book and select people on your network to invite to the broadcast. If you are asked to select a profile, do so.
5. From the list of name(s) on the left, select the people you want to invite.

> To select one person, click his or her name. To select more than one name, hold the Ctrl key as you click each name. To select the entire list, click the first name, scroll to the bottom of the list, hold the Shift key, and click the last name in the list.

6. Click the To-> button to add the name(s) to the list on the right.
7. Click the OK button when finished.
8. Click the Broadcast Settings tab as shown in Figure 10.8.
9. Select the setting you want to use for the broadcast; if you are unsure of the setting necessary, contact your network administrator.
10. Click the Server Options button to open the Server Options dialog box as shown in Figure 10.9.

FIGURE 10.8.

The Broadcast Settings tab of the Schedule a New Broadcast dialog box.

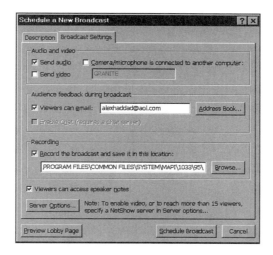

Specify location of presentation

FIGURE 10.9.

Use the Server Options dialog box to specify where the presentation will be located and the server it will be using.

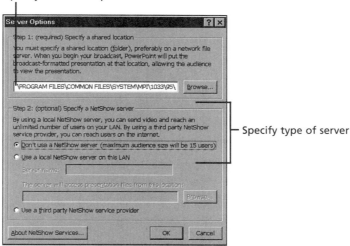

Specify type of server

10

11. Specify the location of the presentation. Again, you may need to check with your network administrator for this step.

12. Click the OK button.

13. Click Schedule Broadcast and your email program should start. You can send a message to inform your audience of the date and time of the broadcast. The location (URL) of the broadcast site should be included in your message.

The presentation broadcasting feature can be either very easy or very complicated. You may want to read the online help files before you start this task. Your Network administrator can be an invaluable resource of information for this procedure. Ask questions first to save time and effort.

Summary

You should now have an excellent understanding of slide show special effects. Experiment with preset and custom slide transitions and animation; the effort will keep your audience from being hypnotized by boring slide flips.

Other features explained during this hour give you the ability to run the show in a stand-alone mode or with a kiosk, or set up an Online Broadcast. The individual and kiosk displays are useful formats when a presenter isn't available to run the show, and NetShow really gives you power when you need to disseminate information to others on your network. For full wizardry, create custom shows so that a single presentation can target multiple audiences. PowerPoint 2000 makes using all these special features an easy task.

Q&A

Q My slide transition is too fast. I can hardly tell that a transition effect was added. How can I fix this?

A Try selecting either Slow or Medium as your transition speed. I always set the speed to Slow because it results in a much nicer show.

Q Can't I just click on the Slide Transition Effects drop-down list on the Slide Sorter toolbar to select a transition?

A You certainly could do that, but then you don't get to see a preview of the effect you have chosen, and you can't change the timing of the transition. To change the timing of the transition, you need to go into the Slide Transition dialog box.

Q Can you animate items that are on the master slide?

A Yes! To quickly set animation for Slide or Title Master items choose View, Master, Slide (or Title) Master from the menu and click the object you want to animate. Then choose Slide Show, Preset Animation from the menu and select the Animation option you prefer. You can also set up a custom animation for any object. Custom animation gives you more animation options.

Q **Can I animate a graph one data series at a time?**

A Once again, yes. Follow the instructions for a custom animation and click the Chart Effects tab. This tab has options similar to the Effects tab (for text), except that they are used for charts and graphs. Refer to Hour 17, "Creating Charts and Graphs with Microsoft Graph," and Hour 19, "Editing Charts and Graphs," for more information about creating and working with charts.

10

PART IV

Drawing with PowerPoint 2000

Hour

Hour 11

Drawing Text-Type Objects

Over the next four hours, you will be learning about the different drawing options available in PowerPoint 2000. Text box and WordArt objects are considered drawing objects, even though they contain text. This hour covers these text drawing objects and using the guides to position objects. You will learn how to work with the following:

- Text boxes
- WordArt
- PowerPoint guides

Text Boxes

You have already been adding text to your slides using the preplaced text object placeholders. These placeholders have been the primary vehicle for your text additions. When you need text added to your slide outside the placeholders, use the Text Box tool on the Drawing toolbar.

Text that's in a text box is included in a spell check of your presentation, but is not included in the Outline of your presentation.

When you add a text box to a slide, it behaves in one of two ways:

- As a label, as shown in Figure 11.1, in which the text within it doesn't word wrap. This option is useful when you need a short caption for a chart or a graphic image.

FIGURE 11.1.
Text labels for charts help describe the information presented.

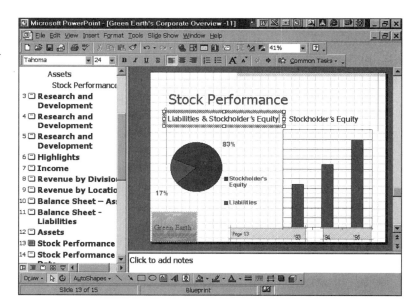

- As a word processing box, as shown in Figure 11.2, in which the text within the text box does word wrap. The text box can expand, if necessary.

FIGURE 11.2.

Use a word processing text box when you want to add a lot of text.

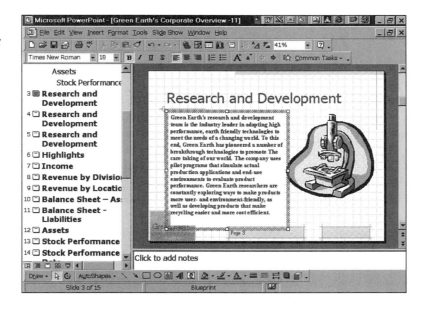

To Do: Create Text Labels

1. Click the Text Box tool on the Drawing toolbar.
2. Click on the slide where you want to position the text label.
3. Start typing.

Be careful when typing text labels. Don't type too much text, or the text box will run off the slide. When there's a chance you might have too much information, create a word processing box instead. If the text does overrun the edge, you can either add hard returns manually or resize the text box object.

Formatting a Text Box

You can add many special effects to a text box for emphasis and impact, such as including a fill or border. PowerPoint also enables you to control the size and position of the text box and change the text anchor point and internal margins of the text. All these options are available in the Format Text Box dialog box.

Adding a Fill or Border

By adding a border or fill to your text box, you can really make the text stand out. Figure 11.3 illustrates how a text box can be formatted by using the fill and border options.

FIGURE 11.3.

Format a text box with a fill and a border to draw attention to the text.

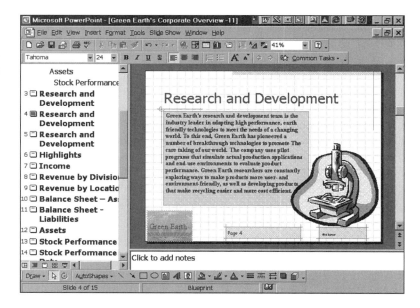

To Do: Add a Fill or Border to a Text Box

1. Select the text box you want to format.
2. Choose Format, Text Box from the menu to display the Format Text Box dialog box.
3. Click the Colors and Lines tab (see Figure 11.4).

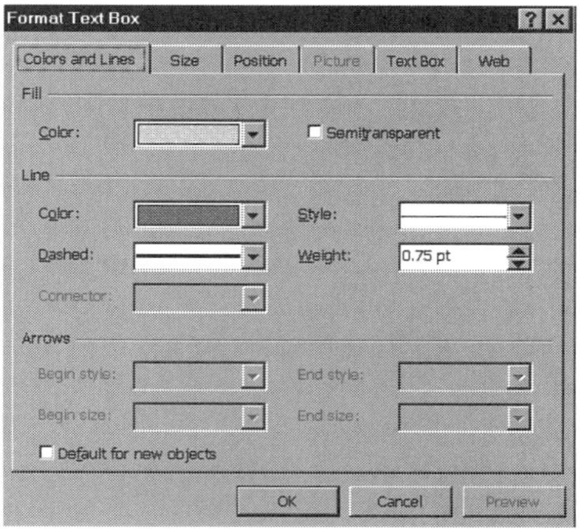

FIGURE 11.4.

The Colors and Lines tab of the Format Text Box dialog box has many options to choose from.

▼ 4. Select a color or fill option from the Color drop-down list in the Fill section.

> Use the Fill Effects option from the Color drop-down list to apply a gradient or other fill effect to your text object. Although it's easy to get carried away with all the special effects, just remember that the text is what you want the audience to focus on, not the fancy formatting.

5. If you want a border, click the Color drop-down list under the Line section.

6. Change the Style, Dashed, and Weight options for the line, if you want.

7. Click the Preview button to preview your changes before accepting them.

▲ 8. Click the OK button when you're finished.

Moving a Text Box

After you create your text box, you might decide later that it needs to be moved to another location on the slide. PowerPoint has two options for moving the text box. You can either drag the text box to a desired position or set an exact position in the Format Text Box dialog box. To drag a text box to a new location, use the following steps:

To Do: Move a Text Box

1. Click once on the text box to select it.

2. Place the mouse pointer on the box's border so you can see the move pointer.

3. Click and hold down the left mouse button.

4. Drag the box to the new location.

5. Release the mouse button.

When you know exactly where you want the text box to be placed on a slide, you can use the Position tab in the Format Text Box dialog box. You must measure the position from either the top left corner or the center of the slide. To position a text box in an exact location, use the following steps:

Changing the Size of a Text Box

Usually, a text box is set to automatically fit the size of the text that it contains. However, on occasion, as in Figure 11.5, you may need the text box to be smaller or larger than the automatic size given by PowerPoint 2000. In this example, because of the border and shading, the overall look would be greatly improved by making the text box a smidgen smaller. To resize the text box manually, you must first turn off the automatic resizing feature.

11

To Do

FIGURE 11.5.

If a text box is too small, simply resize it.

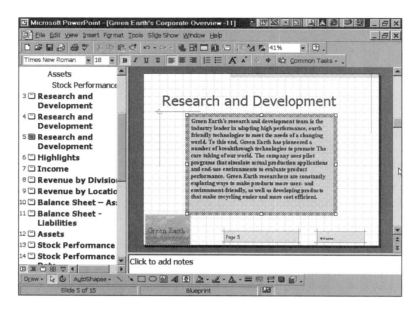

 Remember that when you change the size of a text box, you're not changing the text's font size.

To Do: Resize a Text Box

1. Click once on the text object to select it.
2. Choose Format, Text Box from the menu. The Format Text Box dialog box opens.
3. Click the Text Box tab, shown in Figure 11.6.

FIGURE 11.6.

The Text Box tab of the Format Text Box dialog box give many options to customize how the text will fit in the text box.

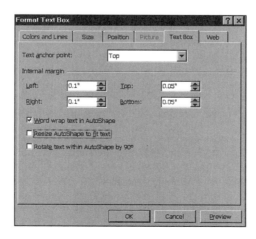

▼ 4. Uncheck the Resize AutoShape to Fit Text option.

5. Click the OK button.

▲ 6. Drag the appropriate resizing handle to resize the text box.

Formatting the Text in a Text Box

You can format the text in a text box by using the Format Font dialog box or by selecting any of the text formatting tools on the Formatting toolbar. Make the text bigger or smaller, select a new font face, or change the color. So many font choices, so little time! To format text in a text box, follow these steps:

> The Drawing toolbar has one button for formatting text: the Text Color button.

To Do: Format Text Box Text

▼ 1. Select the text you want to format. If you want to format all the text in the text box, click once on the text box to select it and a second time on the text box border to select the entire text box.

2. Choose Format, Font from the menu to open the Font dialog box.

3. Change any options you want.

4. Click the Preview button to see a preview of your changes before accepting them.

▲ 5. Click the OK Button.

To Do

11

Using WordArt

The WordArt feature included with PowerPoint 2000 enables you to create dynamic text drawings. Create a new logo or heading by using any of the hundreds of formatting combinations available to you with WordArt. Special effects and other embellishments are only a click away. There are many exciting features, such as 3D effects, shadows, and textured fills. WordArt also gives you several predefined shapes for your text as shown in Figure 11.7.

FIGURE 11.7.

Use WordArt in your presentation slides to create a dramatic effect.

When you create WordArt, the text is changed to a drawing object, so it is not included in a spell check or the Outline view. Keep a dictionary close at hand, just in case you need to check the spelling of a word. A spelling error on a letter will seem like nothing, compared to a spelling error in a presentation that is magnified to two feet or more!

To Do: Create a WordArt Object

1. Select Insert, Picture, WordArt from the menu to open the WordArt Gallery, or click the WordArt button on the Drawing toolbar.

2. Select a style from the WordArt Gallery as shown in Figure 11.8. Don't pay attention to the color of the WordArt, as this can, and probably will, be changed later.

FIGURE 11.8.

The WordArt Gallery has several dozen samples for you to choose from.

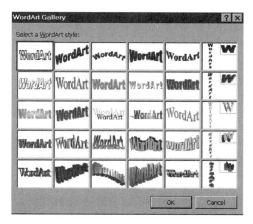

▼   3. Type your text.

4. Change the font style and/or font size, if desired.

5. Add bold or italic, if desired.

▲   6. Click the OK button.

The WordArt object will be added to the middle of your slide, ready to be resized and repositioned as necessary. To resize WordArt, follow the steps:

To Do: Resize a WordArt Object

1. Click once on the WordArt to select it.

2. Position the mouse over any white sizing handle.

3. Hold down the left mouse button and drag the sizing handle to a new location.

> If you use a corner handle and hold the Shift key, the WordArt will resize proportionally.

4. Release the mouse button.

To Do: Move a WordArt Object

1. Position the mouse pointer on the WordArt object (the middle of the object works well).

2. Click and hold down the left mouse button; you should see a move pointer.

3. Drag the WordArt object to a new location on the slide.

4. Release the mouse button.

To Do: Edit the Text in a WordArt Object

1. Double-click the WordArt object.

2. Edit the text.

3. Click the OK button.

Using the WordArt Toolbar

When you click on a WordArt object, the WordArt toolbar usually appears, as shown in Figure 11.9. Use this toolbar to add or change any of the special effects of a WordArt object. Some of the features you can change are the WordArt object's shape and format. You can also rotate the WordArt object and switch the text to a vertical or horizontal orientation.

11

If the WordArt toolbar does not appear, select View, Toolbars, WordArt from the menu.

FIGURE 11.9.

The WordArt toolbar appears when you select a WordArt object.

Changing the WordArt Shape

There are 40 custom shapes you can use for your WordArt object, as shown in Figure 11.10.

FIGURE 11.10.

There are many WordArt shape options available for you to choose from.

To Do: Change the Shape of a WordArt Object

1. Select the WordArt object.
2. On the WordArt toolbar, click the WordArt Shape button.
3. Click a new shape.

Formatting WordArt

You can format WordArt in the same manner as any other object. You can change the color and line options for the WordArt. The Fill option is an excellent method for coloring the WordArt object and making it stand out. To add color and fill to a WordArt object, follow these steps:

To Do: Add Color and Fill to a WordArt Object

1. Select the WordArt object you want to format.
2. Click the Format WordArt button on the WordArt toolbar to display the WordArt Gallery.
3. Click the Colors and Lines tab.
4. Select a fill option from the Color drop-down list.
5. If you want, select Color, Style, Dashed, and Weight options for a border.
6. Click the Preview button to preview your changes before accepting them.
7. Click the OK button when you're done.

Figure 11.11 illustrates vertical WordArt. To make the WordArt text vertical instead of horizontal, use the following steps:

To Do: Format a WordArt Object with Vertical Text

1. Select the WordArt object you want to change.
2. Click the WordArt Vertical Text button on the WordArt toolbar.

> To change the WordArt text back to a horizontal orientation, click the WordArt Vertical Text button again.

You can easily rotate WordArt by using the Free Rotate button on the WordArt toolbar; just follow these steps:

To Do: Rotate a WordArt Object

1. Select the WordArt object you want to rotate.
2. Click the Free Rotate button on the WordArt toolbar. You should see four green rotate handles in each corner of the WordArt object, as shown in Figure 11.12.
3. Place the mouse pointer on any green rotate handle, hold the left mouse button down, and drag to rotate the WordArt object.
4. Release the mouse button when the WordArt object is in the position you want.

11

FIGURE 11.11.

Use the WordArt vertical text option to display the text on the side of a slide.

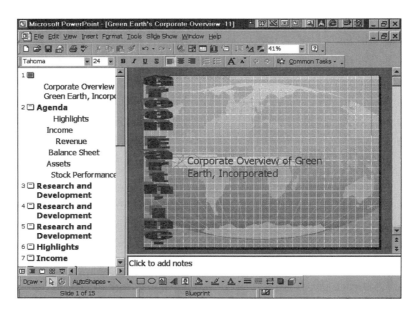

FIGURE 11.12.

Use the Free Rotate button to rotate a WordArt object to any position.

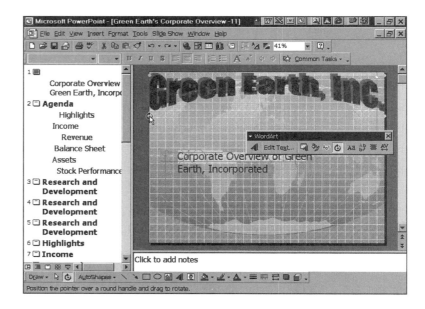

Summary

Drawing objects allow you to add depth to your presentation and more clearly define your message. In this hour, you have learned how to create text objects, use the WordArt program, and follow the steps for using the guides to position objects.

Q&A

Q I created a text box, but now I think I would rather have a shape with the text inside it. Is there an easy way to do this?

A To quickly change a text box to an AutoShape (AutoShapes are covered in the next hour), click once on the text box to select it, and then choose Draw, Change AutoShape from the Drawing toolbar. Select an AutoShape category and click the AutoShape you want.

At first glance, it might not seem that the text box has indeed changed shape. This is usually because text boxes have no lines or fill effects. After you change the shape, you might need to turn on the fill and line options in the Format AutoShapes dialog box. You might also find that the AutoShape needs to be resized. Hour 12, "Drawing Shapes in PowerPoint," covers formatting AutoShapes.

Q What is the little yellow diamond I see when I select a WordArt object?

A This is an adjustment handle. You can use it to change the appearance of the WordArt shape. Simply click and drag the adjustment handle. An adjustment handle's function depends on where it appears on the WordArt; the best thing to do is just experiment with them (they all work a little differently). Don't forget, if you make a change that you really don't like, you can always use the Undo command.

11

HOUR 12

Drawing Shapes in PowerPoint

PowerPoint supplies drawing tools that inspire unlimited creativity. During this hour, you learn the fundamentals of creating eye-catching graphics using PowerPoint 2000. This hour should be very enjoyable because you'll draw interesting objects in PowerPoint. Better than oils and canvas, PowerPoint and a high-resolution monitor enable you to experiment with unique digital effects. If you have the time, creating custom drawing objects in PowerPoint is an energizing, artistic experience. Exciting drawing features are available in PowerPoint 2000. You will be introduced to, and learn the following:

- What an AutoShape is and how to draw it
- How to draw lines and connectors
- How to add text to an AutoShape
- How to apply formatting to AutoShapes and lines

The material in Hours 13, "Bringing Drawing Objects Together," and 14, "Drawing Special Effects," covers even more information needed to bring drawing objects together to use as a standalone graphic image. Although PowerPoint 2000 cannot and should not take the place of a complete graphics package, it gives you many options that are not available in the Paint program. You may even find yourself looking at everyday objects and envisioning ways to reproduce them in PowerPoint 2000. The possibilities are endless!

Drawing AutoShape Objects

When you look at Figure 12.1, you probably see a Manhattan cocktail with a cherry. I see two trapezoids, a rectangle, an oval, a circle, and a curved line. Each of these objects has also been formatted to create a particular effect.

FIGURE 12.1.

You can use PowerPoint 2000's drawing objects to make a simple picture.

Even though you can't tell at a glance, the shapes in this picture have also been grouped to interact as a single vector graphic. The Group and Ungroup features are explained in more detail in Hour 13.

Vector graphics are a type of graphic image composed of grouped shapes. The shapes are stacked in an order that creates a picture in the mind's eye. Think back to when you were in kindergarten. Remember cutting out a bunch of circles, squares, and triangles? After gluing the shapes together, you had formed a picture of a house underneath clouds. Vector graphics work by the same principles.

Are you ready to start drawing? I am. Get ready to learn about the basic PowerPoint object types.

Lines

PowerPoint 2000 has six line styles to choose from: three straight and three curved. Each line style can also be formatted with many options. PowerPoint always has the type of line you need for a project. This hour covers how to work with straight lines, and Hour 14 covers curved lines. The line, arrow, and double-arrow options all draw straight lines. To draw a line, use the following steps:

To Do: Draw a Straight Line

1. Select AutoShapes, Lines from the drawing toolbar to display the Lines submenu.
2. Click a line style: Line, Arrow, or Double Arrow.
3. Move the mouse to the area on the slide where you want the line to start. The mouse pointer should look like Figure 12.2, a thin cross (also called a crosshair).

FIGURE 12.2.

The mouse pointer is ready to draw a line.

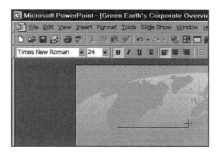

4. Click and hold down the left mouse button.
5. Drag the mouse to the location where the line should end, and then release the mouse button.

12

If you selected Arrow, the arrow appears on the end of the line where you release the mouse button. Therefore, if you're drawing a line from left to right, the arrow appears on the right end of the line. Depending on the settings, the arrow might be so small that you can't see it. The later section, "Using Arrowheads," gives more information on formatting arrowheads.

If you want to draw a straight, or constrained, line, hold down the Shift key while dragging. This method keeps the line constrained to 15-degree angles and makes drawing less tedious.

Holding down the Ctrl key while dragging causes the line to draw in both directions from the starting point.

Use Ctrl+Shift while dragging the mouse to get a straight line drawn in both directions.

Connectors

A *connector* is a valuable, time-saving drawing object used to visually connect two points. Using connector lines instead of normal lines is helpful when you move an object, because the lines stay connected (hence the name *connectors*). To connect any object, use one of PowerPoint 2000's three types of connector lines: straight, angled, or curved. Follow these steps:

To Do: Draw a Connector Line

1. Select AutoShapes, Connectors from the drawing toolbar to display the Connectors submenu.

2. Click the type of connector you want.

3. Position the mouse on the first object to connect.

4. Click a blue connection site.

5. Move the mouse to the second object and click a connection site.

After you have connected two objects, the connection lines show locked connectors as red squares. If a connector isn't locked to an object (unlocked), the connector is shown as a green square. You can also use the yellow adjustment controls to "snake" the connector the way you want.

Basic Shapes, Block Arrows, Flow Chart Symbols, and Stars and Banners

The rest of the AutoShape options behave in basically the same manner. The main difference between the objects is the specific shape. There are many closed shapes that can be easily drawn and grouped to create almost any kind of picture. Remember the sample cocktail shown at the beginning of this chapter? Your drawing can be very simple or extremely complex—enough to create an intricate work of art.

Follow these steps to draw an AutoShape:

To Do: Draw an AutoShape

1. Select AutoShapes from the drawing toolbar to open the AutoShapes submenu.

2. Select Basic Shapes, Block Arrows, Flow Chart Symbols, Stars and Banners, or More AutoShapes to open the corresponding submenu.

3. Select a shape.

4. Click and hold the left mouse button on the upper-left corner of the imaginary box, and then drag to the lower-right corner of the imaginary box.

> When drawing any kind of AutoShape, imagine a box that will contain the AutoShape image. Figure 12.3 demonstrates this using the lightning bolt.

Start here, the upper-left corner

FIGURE 12.3.

Imagine a box that contains the AutoShape.

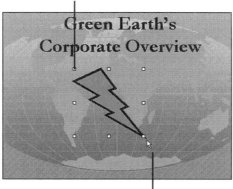

Drag to here, the lower-right corner

12

 5. Release the mouse.

Callouts

A *callout* is a text description for part of a graphical image. Callout objects are useful AutoShapes when you need to use text with a connecting line back to an object. For example, you might need to describe a particular object, as shown in Figure 12.4. To create a callout, use the following steps:

To Do: Draw a Callout

1. Select AutoShapes, Callouts from the drawing toolbar to open the Callouts submenu.

▼ 2. Click the callout you want.

3. Click where you want the callout to be attached and drag to the size you want.

▲ 4. Type the text for the callout.

FIGURE 12.4.

Use callouts to attach text to the object you are referencing (like comics in the newspaper).

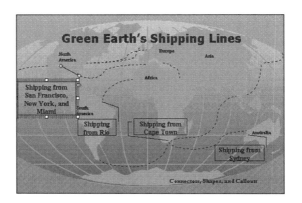

You may need to adjust the callout lines, size, font size, lines, or fill of the callout. Use the yellow triangle adjustment handles to adjust the callout lines. To adjust any other items, refer to the section, "Formatting Drawing Objects," later in this hour.

Action Buttons

Action buttons, the last available option on the AutoShapes menu, enable you to create navigation buttons like the ones you see displayed on World Wide Web pages. You draw these buttons just as you do any other AutoShape. When you release the mouse button, PowerPoint 2000 displays the Actions Settings dialog box, where you can set the specific action you want the button to perform. Action buttons are covered in more detail in Hour 22, "Creating Web Pages."

Adding Text in Drawing Objects

You can add text quickly and easily to almost any AutoShape except lines. Do not draw an AutoShape and then create a text box for text. This creates two separate objects: the AutoShape and the text box, which will cause you unnecessary problems later when you need to move or resize the AutoShape.

To avoid any potential problems, simply select the shape you want to add text to and then start typing. It is almost too easy! The text is automatically centered in the AutoShape and can be formatted in the same manner as other text objects.

Formatting Drawing Objects

Do you want color? Lines? What type of arrows do you want on your lines? Do you need the arrow to be placed at the other end of the line? The drawing objects you have learned to draw in this hour can be formatted in so many different ways. PowerPoint 2000 is like that famous fast-food chain—yes, you can have it your way!

Working with Shapes

The shape of AutoShape objects can easily be formatted with color and lines, which is discussed in this section. The Manhattan cocktail pictured at the beginning of this chapter had different color and line options set for each object. The three shapes that made up the glass were colored white, with no lines. The liquid was colored light brown (a whiskey color) and enhanced with gradient shading and no lines. The cherry, colored red, had gradient shading and no lines, and its stem was a single curved line that was three points thick.

If you have entered text into an AutoShape, you can format its appearance just as you would any other text object. You can use the Format Font dialog box or any of the text formatting tools on the formatting toolbar. You can also move or resize an AutoShape just as you would any other object in PowerPoint 2000.

Using Colors and Lines

You can add or change the color and lines of any AutoShape. How you combine these options depends on the effect you want. At first, it might seem as though it takes a while to figure out how to get a certain special effect, but eventually you will find yourself seeing every object in your home as a combination of PowerPoint AutoShapes with color and lines. To change or add color or lines to any AutoShape, follow these steps:

To Do: Format an AutoShape

1. Select the AutoShape you want to format.
2. Choose Format, AutoShape from the menu to open the Format AutoShape dialog box.
3. Click the Colors and Lines tab.
4. Click the Color drop-down list, as shown in Figure 12.5, and select a fill color or effect.

12

FIGURE 12.5.

Select a fill color or effect from the Color drop-down list.

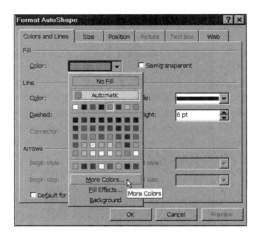

Use the Fill Effects option from the Color drop-down list to apply a gradient or other fill effect to your text object.

5. If you want a border, click the Color drop-down list under the Line section and select a color (or No Line to omit a border).

6. Change the Style, Dashed, and Weight options for the line for different effects.

7. Click the Preview button to preview your changes before accepting them.

8. Click the OK button when finished.

Working with Lines

There are hundreds of ways to format a line. PowerPoint 2000 offers you choices for changing the look for any type of line you might have drawn. The following sections cover the available options for these attributes:

- Line styles
- Color
- Thickness
- Arrowheads
- Connectors

Formatting Line Styles

All the lines you draw can be formatted with many options for just the right look. You can change the line color, select one of PowerPoint's dashed line styles, or choose a custom line pattern. You can also change the line's thickness simply by changing the line weight to a larger point size. On the Green Earth's Shipping Lines slide, the connector lines have been formatted as dashed lines, only .25 point thick. To change the line style, use the following steps:

To Do: Change the Style of a Line

1. Select the line you want to format.
2. Choose Format, AutoShape from the menu to open the Format AutoShape dialog box.
3. Click the Colors and Lines tab.
4. Under the Line section, select a color or pattern option from the Color drop-down list.

> If you use a pattern option for a line, set the line's thickness at 10 or more points so that the pattern is properly displayed.

5. Change the Style, Dashed, and Weight options for the line for different effects as shown in Figure 12.6.

FIGURE 12.6.

Use the Format AutoShape dialog box to change the line style.

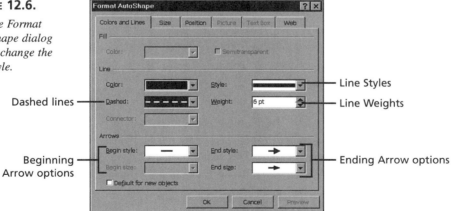

12

> If you use a pattern, you can't select a dashed line, too. You must choose one or the other.

6. Click the Preview button to preview your changes before accepting the modifications.

7. Click the OK button when finished.

Using Arrowheads

You can easily add or edit arrowheads on a line. You might realize that you need arrowheads or that an arrowhead ended up on the wrong side of the line after you drew it. You also have several arrowhead styles to choose from.

The option of adjusting the arrowhead size without changing the line's thickness is a new feature in PowerPoint 2000. Not only can you adjust the size, but for double-arrowhead lines, you can also have a different style and size for each end of the line! Figure 12.7 illustrates a line with different arrowhead styles and varying sizes for each end of the line.

FIGURE **12.7.**

PowerPoint 2000 offers different arrowhead styles.

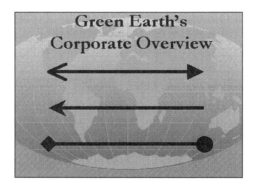

To Do: Add, Move, or Change the Arrowhead Style

1. Select the line you want to format.

2. Choose Format, AutoShape from the menu to open the Format AutoShape dialog box.

3. Click the Colors and Lines tab.

4. Under the Arrows section, select a begin style or end style of arrow for the line.

5. Select a begin size and/or end size for each arrow style.

6. Click the Preview button to preview your changes before accepting them.

7. Click the OK button when finished.

Using Connector Lines

Connector lines can also be formatted with all the options previously discussed. In addition to the standard formatting options, you can change the connector line style, if you want. The connector can have the following styles:

- Straight
- Elbow
- Curved

To Do: Change the Style of a Connector Line

1. Select the line you want to format.

2. Choose Format, AutoShape from the menu to open the Format AutoShape dialog box.

3. Click the Colors and Lines tab.

4. Under the Line section, select the connector style you want from the Connector drop-down list as shown in Figure 12.8.

FIGURE **12.8.**

Choose either a straight, elbow, or curved connector line.

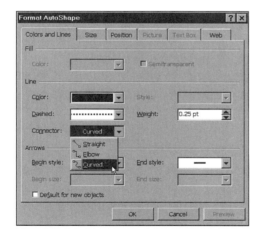

12

5. Click the Preview button to preview your changes before accepting them.

▲ 6. Click the OK button when finished.

Summary

In this hour, you learned about options for drawing and formatting AutoShapes in PowerPoint, and you were introduced to the concept of using the AutoShape features available with PowerPoint 2000 to create a picture. You saw a picture with simple formatting created with AutoShape lines and shapes.

You also learned how to draw straight, curved, and connector lines; explored the quick, easy methods available for drawing any other AutoShape; and learned how to make an AutoShape take on new and exciting dimensions by simply changing the color, fill, line, and other options found in the Format AutoShape dialog box.

Stay tuned, because in the next two hours this book covers more features that will transform you into a novice graphical artist. You'll find that once you start drawing, you won't want to stop.

Q&A

Q **I have seen the AutoShapes menu floating on the left of the screen like a toolbar. How can I do this?**

A Many of the toolbar menus have a thin title bar at the top (like the AutoShape menu). You can "tear away" the menu by dragging the title bar to a new location and creating a floating toolbar. To perform this incredible feat, first select AutoShape from the drawing toolbar. Then move the mouse pointer to the top of the menu into the title bar and click and hold down the left mouse button. Now simply drag the menu to the location you want and release the mouse button.

Q **How do I add text to a line so that the text moves with the line?**

A Unfortunately, there's not really a quick way to add text to a line. You need to create a text box (use the label method discussed in Hour 11, "Drawing Text-Type Objects"). If you want the text to move with the line, you need to select both objects and group them. Grouping is covered in Hour 13.

Q **What's the little yellow diamond that appears on the AutoShapes when selected?**

A This is an adjustment handle. You can use it to change the appearance of the AutoShape object, just as you can with WordArt shapes.

Q **When I type text in my AutoShape, it doesn't word wrap; in fact, it appears outside the shape. Help!**

A Unfortunately, this sometimes happens if you type a lot of text on an AutoShape. I guess those nice folks at Microsoft assumed that you wouldn't be typing anything lengthy on a shape. To fix this particular problem, select the AutoShape and choose Format, AutoShape from the menu. Then click the Text Box tab, select the Word Wrap Text in AutoShape check box, and click the OK button.

You can also use the Resize AutoShape to Fit Text option. Experiment with both options to see which one you prefer.

HOUR 13

Bringing Drawing Objects Together

Now that you know how to draw and format any of PowerPoint 2000's AutoShapes to create a simple picture, you're ready to learn how to create a more complicated picture. This hour covers four important tasks that are often used when creating an image:

- Pulling several objects into a group or ungrouping a single object
- Stacking and using the order of the stack to create the effect you need
- Using different alignment methods
- Rotating objects

Ungrouping and Grouping Objects

As you have seen, there are many wonderful templates that have been designed for you by those nice folks at Microsoft. However, wouldn't it be nice to either customize a template or even create your own? Hour 8, "Working with the Masters," covered the basics on saving a presentation as a template. However, when you really want to customize a presentation for your organization, you might want to edit one of these templates. Many of the predesigned templates use drawing objects to add impact and pizzazz to the look of the presentation. You, too, can create a template using drawing objects, embedded in the Master Slide, using your organization's colors and designs.

The best way to learn how to create your own PowerPoint 2000 drawing objects is by disassembling a few of the templates that Microsoft has created for you. Try it on a simple design first, such as the High Voltage Presentation Design. Simply start a new presentation by using the presentation design you want to explore, view the Slide Master, and start ungrouping as described shortly. Not only will you learn how the experts create really phenomenal drawing objects, but you will find that your creativity, once dormant, will flower.

Clip art is another object that can be taken apart and used as a learning tool. Some of the best lessons are learned simply by inserting a clip art image and ungrouping it to see how the image was created. When you ungroup an image, you can see the components used to create the picture. When you're first learning, start with a simple image and then progress to more complicated clip art.

Object *ungrouping* means taking an image, such as a Master Slide object or clip art, and separating it to see all the smaller pieces that make up the larger image. *Grouping* is the exact opposite: By selecting several objects, you can then bind (or group) them together to make one object. Many of the presentation templates contain objects that are simply a bunch of small shapes that have been grouped to create one image. To ungroup an image, simply select the image and then select Draw, Ungroup from the drawing toolbar.

If PowerPoint 2000 displays the dialog This is an imported picture, not a group. Convert it to a Microsoft Office drawing?, click Yes.

Certain graphic files, such as photographs, bitmaps, jpg, and .gif files, cannot be ungrouped.

Figure 13.1 shows the High Voltage Presentation Design's Master Slide objects after selecting the ungroup command once. Notice that there are selection handles surrounding each separate object in the group.

FIGURE **13.1.**

Selection handles indicate individual objects that make up a drawing image.

Selection handles

Some objects are groups of groups. This makes it easier for the artist to create and manipulate the image. For these types of images, you may need to perform the ungroup command several times to fully ungroup the entire image. The objects in the previous figure are an example of this type of image. In Figure 13.2, the Master Slide objects, of the High Voltage Presentation Design, had to be ungrouped a few times. Notice that there are more selection handles visible as compared with Figure 13.1.

When you have grouped all the objects that make up an image, there are several advantages. First, because the collection of objects becomes a single object, it is much easier to move, resize, or copy that object. To group several objects into a single image, simply select all the objects you want to group, and then choose Draw, Group from the drawing toolbar.

13

You must have at least two objects selected to use the Group command.

FIGURE 13.2.

To see all of the objects that make up the High Voltage Master Slide image, the ungroup command was selected several times.

Selection handles —

You can easily select several objects by using the mouse as a lasso (pretend you are Buffalo Bill), dragging around all the objects you want to select. Figure 13.3 shows a lasso selecting several objects. (Make sure that the mouse pointer looks like an arrow, not a move or resize pointer. Otherwise, some objects might move around. If this happens, simply click the undo button.)

The other option is to hold down the Shift key and click each object you want to select. This also works to deselect objects that may have been accidentally selected by the lasso.

FIGURE 13.3.

Use the mouse and lasso several objects to quickly select them all.

Lasso —

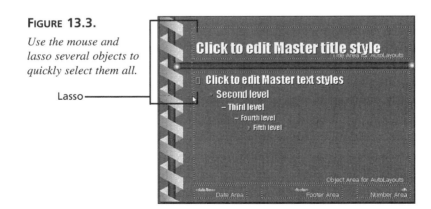

Stacking Objects

When you're drawing AutoShapes or inserting other objects, PowerPoint places (or stacks) each object in the order in which it was drawn. In other words, the object drawn first is on the bottom of the stack, with the object drawn last on top. You can change the way drawing objects are placed together by changing the stacking order of those objects. Objects toward the front of the stack hide and overlap background objects.

When you want to change the stacking order of objects, you can either move an object all the way to the front or back of the stack, or you can send the object forward or backward one layer at a time. The High Voltage Presentation Design displays this feature quite well.

The ribbon is actually two sets of parallelograms, one facing left and one facing right, with a rectangle sandwiched between. The parallelograms were probably all drawn first, and then the rectangle. After the rectangle was drawn, it had to be sent backward once to give the optical illusion of a ribbon wrapped around a bar. To change the stacking order of any object, use the following steps:

To Do: Change the Stacking Order of an Object

1. Select the object.
2. Select Draw, Order from the drawing toolbar to open the Order submenu.
3. Select one of the following order options:

   - Bring to Front sets the object in front of all other objects on the slide.
   - Send to Back sets the object behind all other objects on the slide.
   - Bring Forward brings the object forward one object per click.
   - Send Backward sends the object backward one object per click.

Sometimes you can't select the object you want because other objects are on top of it. If you select any object and then press the Tab key, you can scroll through all the objects available in the picture. PowerPoint selects each object sequentially in the order in which it was drawn.

13

Aligning and Distributing Objects

PowerPoint 2000 has several great features for precisely lining up and distributing objects. When aligning and distributing is combined with the grouping, order, and formatting features, you can create some powerful artwork. Who knows—you might be the next Pablo Picasso.

Aligning Objects

If you have several objects, such as the parallelograms used in the High Voltage Presentation Design, it would be very difficult to line them up manually. Fortunately, PowerPoint 2000 provides the align feature, which arranges all selected objects perfectly, based on the option selected. Use the Left, Center, and Right commands to align vertical objects. Use the Top, Middle, and Bottom commands for horizontal objects. To align vertical objects, as shown in Figure 13.4, use the following steps:

To Do: Align Objects Vertically

1. Select all the objects you want to align.
2. Choose Draw, Align or Distribute from the drawing toolbar to open the Align or Distribute submenu.

FIGURE 13.4.

Choose either Align Left, Center, or Right to align objects vertically.

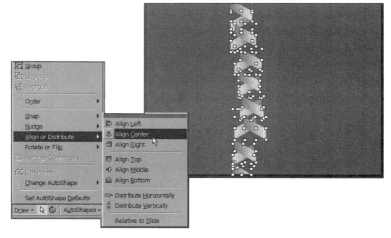

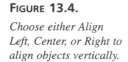   3. Choose either Align Left, Align Center, or Align Right from the submenu.

To align horizontal objects, as shown in Figure 13.5, use the following steps:

> You can also use a combination of the vertical and horizontal alignment options to stack objects precisely.

FIGURE 13.5.

Choose either Align Top, Middle, or Bottom to align objects horizontally.

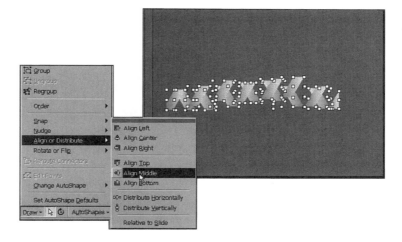

To Do: Align Objects Horizontally

1. Select all the objects you want to align.

2. Choose Draw, Align or Distribute from the drawing toolbar to open the Align or Distribute submenu.

3. Choose either Align Top, Align Middle, or Align Bottom from the submenu.

Distributing Objects

If you have several objects that you would like evenly spaced across a slide, use the Distribute command in the Draw menu. Once again, the parallelograms in the High Voltage Presentation Design demonstrate this command quite well. Distribute takes all the objects selected and spaces them an equal distance apart between the first and last object. You can distribute either horizontally or vertically. To distribute objects, use the following steps:

To Do: Distribute Objects Evenly

1. Select all the objects you want to align.

2. Choose Draw, Align or Distribute from the drawing toolbar to open the Align or Distribute submenu.

3. Choose either Distribute Horizontally or Distribute Vertically from the submenu, as shown in Figure 13.6.

13

FIGURE 13.6.

Distributing parallelograms vertically on a slide is easy when you use the Distribute Vertically option.

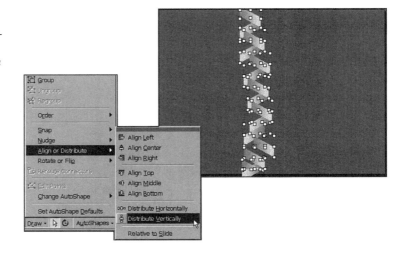

When you are distributing objects, you must have at least three objects selected. However, if the Relative to Slide option is checked (Draw, Align or Distribute, Relative to Slide on the Drawing toolbar), any number of objects, even one, can be distributed.

When you need the same object copied and repeated evenly, use the Edit, Duplicate command, which acts as a combination of the copy and paste commands. When you have the desired number of objects, use the distribute or align options to arrange the objects in the desired pattern.

Summary

This hour covered many different PowerPoint 2000 drawing tools that can be applied to almost any object in your PowerPoint presentations. You learned how to group several drawing objects to create a single object and how to ungroup objects, such as clip art. PowerPoint's alignment and distribution methods can be powerful tools when you need precision object placement. And, last but not least, you learned how to rotate and flip objects to give you more flexibility when you're creating your own drawings.

After the Q&A, you'll want to move right on to Hour 14, "Drawing Special Effects," which will give you even more great tips, tricks, and hints to create phenomenal drawings.

Q&A

Q **I tried to ungroup a graphic that my friend created in Photoshop, but the command was dimmed out. Am I doing something wrong?**

A Probably not. The only types of graphics that can be ungrouped are vector graphics. Graphics that have been created with a drawing program such as Photoshop or Paintbrush can't be ungrouped. This is also true for photographs that you might have scanned.

Q **The Duplicate command you mentioned is great. However, I need to duplicate an object, with the object getting progressively smaller. Will Duplicate do that for me?**

A Duplicate just creates an exact copy of the object at the same size. You have to do a little extra work for this task. First draw the object, and then select it. Then choose Edit, Duplicate from the menu. Next select Format, AutoShape from the menu, click the Size tab and under the Scale section, type the same percentage for height and width, such as 90%, and then click the OK button. Repeat this process until you have the desired number of objects.

You might want to align the objects after you have finished. Use the Draw, Align or Distribute command from the drawing toolbar. You can use this feature to create really cool images.

Q **I want to align several objects by their bottom sides, as well as on the bottom of the slide, to create a border. Can PowerPoint 2000 do that for me?**

A Sure. Simply select Draw, Align or Distribute, Relative to Slide from the drawing toolbar. Then select the objects you want to line up. Then choose Draw, Align or Distribute, Align Bottom from the drawing toolbar. Finally, select Draw, Align or Distribute, Distribute Horizontally from the drawing toolbar.

This procedure aligns the objects not only with one another, but also on the bottom of the slide, and distributes them from edge to edge as well.

13

HOUR 14

Drawing Special Effects

This is the last PowerPoint drawing hour. This hour covers techniques used when drawing fancy lines, such as the Freeform, Curve, and Scribble. In the next hour, you will also learn to add a shadow effect to a drawing object and how to turn on and customize a shape with the 3D feature. Finally, you will learn how to add motion to drawing objects by using animation. In this hour, you will learn about the following:

- Drawing curved lines, freeform objects, and scribbling
- Adding and customizing shadows to your objects
- Adding and customizing 3D effects to your objects
- Animating drawing objects

Drawing Curved Lines

With the Curve tool, you can draw lines with curves easily. Although you can draw curved lines with the Freeform and Scribble tools, the Curve tool gives you more control when you need to draw precise curved lines. PowerPoint 2000 enables you to decide how much of a curve should be applied to the line and where the curve will be placed. You also have full editing power to change or add more curves, if needed. To draw a line with curves, use the following steps:

To Do: Draw a Curved Line

1. Select AutoShapes, Lines, Curve (button) from the drawing toolbar.
2. Move the mouse to the area on the slide where you want the line to start, and then click.
3. Move the mouse to the point where you want the curve to turn, and then click. See Figure 14.1 for an example.

FIGURE 14.1.

Drawing a line with many curves is easy with the Curve tool.

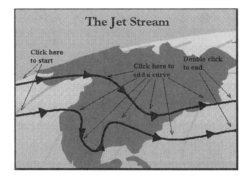

4. Repeat for each curve you need.

5. Double-click to end.

> To create a closed curve, end the line as close to the beginning as possible and then double-click. Figure 14.2 shows a closed curve.

FIGURE 14.2.

Create a closed curve by using the curve tool and ending the line at the beginning.

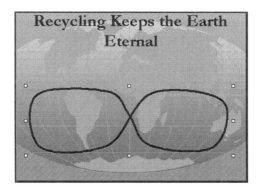

Drawing Freeform Lines

Use the Freeform tool when you need a bit more freedom for your straight lines or when you want to create a shape that's not a stock AutoShape. Drawing freeform is very similar to drawing curves. To draw a freeform object, use this method:

To Do: Draw a Freeform Object

1. Select AutoShapes, Lines, Freeform (button) from the drawing toolbar.

2. Move the mouse to the area on the slide where you want to start the freeform and click.

3. Move the mouse to the first point and click.

4. Repeat for each point you want.

5. Double-click to end the line. (See Figure 14.3.)

FIGURE 14.3.

Use the freeform tool to draw a picture.

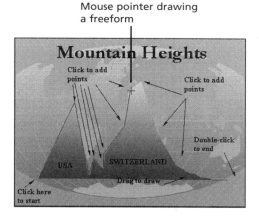

While drawing in Freeform mode, you can add uncontrolled curved lines (scribble) by dragging the mouse.

To close the freeform and create a shape, release the mouse button near the starting point. PowerPoint automatically snaps the endpoints together to signal that the shape is closed.

14

Scribbling

Use the Scribble feature when you want total freedom. Use this feature to create freeform shapes, as shown in Figure 14.4, which are not available otherwise. Scribble allows totally unconstrained drawing at all times in your creative adventures. To scribble (as if you needed instructions), use the following steps:

To Do: Scribble

1. Select AutoShapes, Lines, Scribble (button) from the drawing toolbar. The mouse pointer will turn into a little pencil letting you know that PowerPoint 2000 is ready to scribble.

2. Move the mouse to the area on the slide where you want to start and drag.

FIGURE 14.4.

Use the Scribble feature to create new shapes.

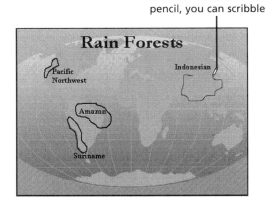

Editing Lines

You can edit the shape of a curved, freeform, or scribble line easily by using the Edit Points option in the Draw menu. When you edit the points of a line object, you're moving a vertex. A *vertex* is the point where two line segments meet or the highest point of a curve. Figure 14.5 shows a closed curve with the Edit Points option turned on and the vertices displayed. To edit a curved, freeform, or scribble line, use the following steps:

To Do: Edit a Curved Line

1. Select a curved, freeform, or scribble line.

2. Choose Draw, Edit Points from the drawing toolbar.

3. Click and drag any vertex point on the object.

Vertex

FIGURE 14.5.

Click and drag a vertex to edit the curve.

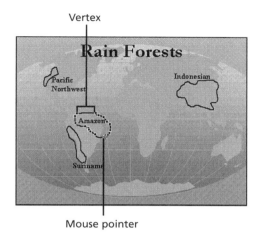

Mouse pointer

▲   4. Click outside of the object to deselect it when you're finished.

Using Shadows and 3D Effects

You can add a shadow or 3D effect to almost any PowerPoint object to add depth. Each effect can be fully customized to create the exact image you want.

Shadows

Shadows add the illusion of depth to PowerPoint objects. You can add a shadow to any PowerPoint object, including text objects, clip art, AutoShapes, lines, freeforms, WordArt, charts, and more. Although PowerPoint has 20 predefined shadow styles to choose from, you can also create your own custom shadow by modifying the shadow position or color. Follow these steps to add a shadow to an object:

To Do: Add a Shadow Effect

1. Select the object to which you want to add a shadow.
2. Click the Shadow button on the drawing toolbar to open the Shadow submenu.
3. Select the shadow style you want as shown in Figure 14.6.

> If you don't like any of the shadow styles available, pick the one closest to the effect you want and then edit the shadow.

14

Figure 14.6.

Adding shadows gives the illusion of depth.

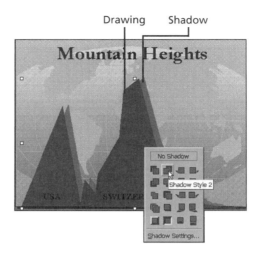

 Not all shadow styles are available for all objects. For example, PowerPoint objects such as clip art, lines, and charts have only eight of the shadow styles available.

To change the shadow's color, use the following steps:

 To Do: Change the Shadow Color

1. Select the object you want to edit.
2. Click the Shadow button on the drawing toolbar to open the Shadow submenu.
3. Click Shadow Settings to display the Shadow Settings toolbar.
4. Click the Shadow Color drop-down arrow as shown in Figure 14.7.

Figure 14.7.

The shadow color can be easily changed for a more dramatic effect.

The Shadow Color drop-down arrow

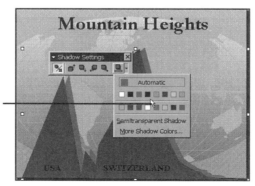

5. Select a color, or click More Shadow Colors, to pick a color from the Color dialog box.

To Do: Move (or Nudge) a Shadow

1. Select the object you want to edit.
2. Click the Shadow button on the drawing toolbar to display the Shadow submenu.
3. Click Shadow Settings to display the Shadow Settings toolbar.
4. Depending on the direction you want to move the shadow, click the Nudge Shadow Up, Down, Left, or Right drop-down arrow.

> Each time you click the Nudge Shadow buttons, the shadow moves one pixel. When you hold down the Shift key and click a Nudge Shadow button, the shadow moves six pixels.

If you decide that the shadow doesn't add the effect you want, you can remove it by using the following steps:

To Do: Remove a Shadow Effect

1. Select the object you want to edit.
2. Click the Shadow button on the drawing toolbar to display the Shadow submenu.
3. Click the No Shadow button.

3D Effects

With PowerPoint 2000's 3D feature, you can add a 3D effect to AutoShapes, lines, and freeform objects, and customize the 3D settings after they have been applied. You can change the rotation (or tilt), depth, direction, lighting, and surface texture. Figure 14.8 shows a PowerPoint drawing object with 3D effects.

To Do: Add a 3D Effect to an Object

1. Select the object you want to add 3D to.
2. Click the 3-D button on the drawing toolbar to open the 3-D submenu.
3. Select the 3D style you want.

> If you don't like any of the 3D styles available, pick the one closest to the effect you want, and then edit the effect.

14

FIGURE 14.8.

Use the 3D effects to create a dramatic illusion of depth.

To Do: Change the Color of the 3D Effect

1. Select the object you want to edit.
2. Click the 3-D button on the drawing toolbar to open the 3-D submenu.
3. Click 3-D Settings to display the 3-D Settings toolbar.
4. Click the 3-D Color drop-down arrow as shown in Figure 14.9 to display color submenu options for the shadow.

FIGURE 14.9.

Change the 3-D color to add more emphasis on the new dimension.

5. Select a color, or click More 3-D Colors to pick a color from the Color dialog box.

The Tilt option rotates the 3D object around a horizontal or vertical axis. The object appears to turn onscreen and present different sides. To tilt a 3D object, follow these steps:

To Do: Tilt a 3D Object

1. Select the object you want to edit.
2. Click the 3-D button on the drawing toolbar to open the 3-D submenu.
3. Click 3-D Settings to display the 3-D Settings toolbar.
4. Depending on the direction you want to tilt the object, click the Tilt Down, Up, Left, or Right button.

> When you click the Tilt buttons, the object moves in six-degree increments. If you hold down the Shift key while you click a Tilt button, however, the object moves in 45-degree increments.

> Use the Direction button before using the Tilt buttons. You might find that a simple change in direction gives you the effect you're looking for without having to use several Tilt commands.

If all these 3D effects were just too much dazzle for the monthly budget, you might want to remove them. Here's how you can do that quickly:

To Do: Remove a 3D Effect

1. Select the object you want to edit.
2. Click the 3-D button on the drawing toolbar to open the 3-D submenu.
3. Click the No 3-D button.

Summary

In this hour, you have covered the PowerPoint 2000 basics for including professional drawing effects in your presentations. Curves, freeform objects, and scribbling give you extra flexibility when you're drawing lines. In addition, you can add depth to almost any two-dimensional object by adding either a shadow or a 3D effect; both can be fully customized. For example, you can change the color or create a custom theme. You have also seen the dazzling animation features available with PowerPoint 2000.

You've spent the last four hours learning how PowerPoint's drawing features can help you create simple graphics. If you really want to do some serious drawing with PowerPoint's tools, the best way is learning from other people. When I first started drawing, I would insert a clip art image and ungroup it to see what shapes were beneath the final creation. I learned how they were colored and discovered how the image was composed. Experimentation and reverse engineering are the best methods of learning about expert tricks that can be used to draw PowerPoint pictures.

14

Q&A

Q I've been drawing with the Scribble tool, trying to write my name, but it still looks awful. How can I fix it?

A You can try editing the points of the scribble line, as previously explained in this hour. If you're still having a tough time getting a legible image, try zooming in to get a better view of what you're working on. Setting the zoom to 150 percent or higher can make a big difference. Also, you might want to go into the Windows Control Panel and set the mouse pointer speed as slow as possible. A slow pointer speed helps when you're creating freeforms and scribbles.

Q Whenever I add a shadow to an object that has a 3D effect, the 3D disappears. What's going on?

A PowerPoint 2000 doesn't allow you to have both a shadow and a 3D effect. You must choose one or the other.

Q I used the Text Shadow tool to add a shadow to my text. How can I change the color and edit the shadow?

A When you use the Text Shadow tool on the formatting toolbar, you can't edit the shadow. The shadow is preset. If you want full shadow-editing capabilities with text, your best bet is to add a shadow to the text object. As long as the object has no fill, the text takes the shadow of the object.

Q How do you add a 3D effect to a clip art image?

A You can't add a 3D effect to a clip art image unless you ungroup the image first. Be careful when choosing clip art for this effect. Usually the simple clip art looks just fine with 3D, but the more complicated clip art doesn't.

PART V

Inserting Tables, Worksheets, Graphs, and Organizational Charts

Hour

HOUR 15

Creating and Using Tables

Tables are a great way to convey information that would best be formatted in rows and columns. Some examples include calendars, forms, itineraries, and meeting agendas. You have seen several examples of tables throughout this book. The next two hours will cover using the new PowerPoint 2000 table feature. This hour will cover the basics, and Hour 16, "Formatting Tables," will cover formatting and creating a custom table. In this hour, you will learn about the following:

- Creating a table using the table AutoLayout
- Inserting a table onto a slide
- Inserting text and graphics into a table
- Formatting text in a table

If you're familiar with Microsoft Word and have used the table feature before, you will find the PowerPoint 2000 table feature, although not quite as powerful, very similar. You may want to quickly glance over the information provided here. You might find tips or tricks that could prove extremely useful both in PowerPoint 2000 and Word 2000.

Creating a Table

There are two basic ways to create a table in PowerPoint 2000. You can either use the AutoLayout feature, which has a predesignated placeholder for a table, or you can insert a table into any slide when and where you need one.

Using the Table AutoLayout

When you want to create a slide that contains only a table for your presentation, use the AutoLayout feature. This is the easiest method available, as shown in Figure 15.1. Using the table AutoLayout feature provides you with a predesignated placeholder for a table object. To create a table slide using the table AutoLayout, use the following steps:

To Do: Create a Slide with a Table

1. Insert a new slide by selecting Insert, New Slide from the menu (or any way you like). Select the Table AutoLayout from the New Slide dialog box as shown in Figure 15.1.

FIGURE 15.1.

Use the Table AutoLayout when you want a table included in a slide.

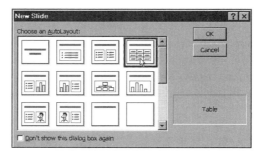

2. Select the Table layout and click the OK button.
3. Click the title placeholder and enter a title for the slide (if desired).
4. Double-click the table placeholder to display the Insert Table dialog box.
▼ 5. Enter the number of columns and rows desired, as shown in Figure 15.2.

▼

FIGURE 15.2.

Select the number of columns and rows for your table.

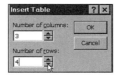

▲   6. Click the OK button.

 After you have created the table, you may notice that your mouse pointer looks like a little pencil. This is the Draw Table feature. Do not worry about this; as soon as you enter text in your table, this feature will turn off.

Inserting a Table in a Slide

When you already have a slide created and want to display a table in addition to other objects, you can use the Insert menu to create the table. To insert a table into any slide, use the following steps:

To Do: Insert a Table into a Slide

1. Display the slide where you want to insert a table.

2. Select Insert, Table from the menu to display the Insert Table dialog box.

3. Enter the number of columns and rows desired.

▲   4. Click the OK button.

 Although you can add rows and columns to the table later, it's best to specify the exact number of columns and rows when you first create the table. When you add rows or columns later, you will need to resize the table and possibly reformat any text.

After you have inserted a table, PowerPoint should be ready for you to insert text and edit the table. This is referred to as *table edit mode*. The mouse pointer will look like a little pencil, and you should see the Tables and Borders toolbar. To exit quickly from table edit mode, click anywhere outside the table.

Parts of a Table

Before you jump right in and start entering data into your table, let's take just a minute to understand the parts of a table. A table is made up of rows and columns. The *rows* are drawn using horizontal lines, and the *columns* are drawn using vertical lines. At every intersection of a row and column is a *cell*.

Although PowerPoint 2000 does not label the rows and columns, it is sometimes helpful to do so. Some people reference cells by indicating the row and column the particular cell is in, such as "The information in row 3, column 3 demonstrates the need for more education in vaccination." Another method used is to designate each row by a number and each column by a letter. This is the method used in the PowerPoint 2000 chart program and in many spreadsheet programs, such as Excel 2000. This naming process makes it easy to reference the individual cells. Although PowerPoint does not reference cells in this manner, Figure 15.3 shows a table with the cell references typed in.

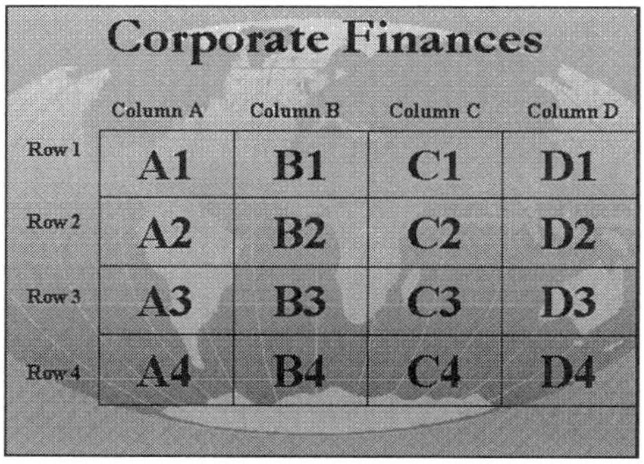

FIGURE 15.3.

The columns, rows, and cells can be easily referenced by letters and numbers.

Navigating a Table

Before you can enter text in a specific cell, you must first position the blinking cursor in that cell. You have several options available to you:

- Click with the mouse in the cell.
- Use the up-, down-, left-, or right-arrow keys on the keyboard.
- Press the Tab key to move the cursor to the next cell.
- Press the Shift+Tab key combination to move the cursor to the previous cell.

Using the Tab key or Shift+Tab key combination is a quick way to move the cursor to another cell in a table. However, PowerPoint 2000 is actually selecting the entire cell when you use this method. This is not really apparent, nor does it matter if there is no text in a cell.

However, if you have information already entered in a cell, this could potentially cause a problem. When a cell is selected and you start typing, you replace the current contents with the new data you are typing. If this happens to you, use the undo button right away. To avoid this problem, use the mouse or the arrow keys to navigate a table.

If you press the Tab key while in the last cell of the table, you will add a row to the end of the table. If you don't want the additional row, just click the undo button on the standard toolbar.

Entering Text

After a table has been inserted into a slide, you can enter the text that you want the table to display. To enter text in a table, simply position the cursor in the appropriate cell and begin typing.

Remember that a presentation slide shouldn't have too much information jammed into the display area. The table text should be short, sweet, and to the point.

Formatting Text in a Table

Formatting text that is in a table is pretty much the same as formatting any other text object. There are one or two tricks, however, that make this task a little easier. There is even an option to center the text vertically in a cell in addition to the standard center option.

Selecting the Table, Columns, Rows, or Cells

The best shortcut to formatting text in a table is to select the entire column or row you want to format (you can even select multiple columns, rows, or cells or the entire table to format). Table 15.1 lists available selection options.

TABLE 15.1. SELECTING PARTS OF A POWERPOINT TABLE.

Table Part	How to Select
Table	Click in the table and then select Table, Select Table from the Tables and Borders toolbar.
Row	Click in the row and then select Table, Select Row from the Tables and Borders toolbar.
Column	Click in the column and then select Table, Select Column from the Tables and Borders toolbar.
Cell	Click in the cell. To select multiple cells, drag through them using the mouse. Use this method to select multiple rows or columns as well.

To Do: Format Text in a Table

1. Select the text, cells, rows, or columns you want to edit.

2. Choose Format, Font from the menu, to display the Font dialog box as shown in Figure 15.4.

FIGURE 15.4.

Use the font dialog box to change any font attributes you want.

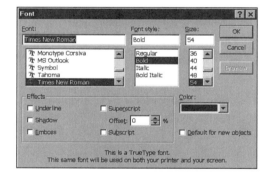

3. Make any changes you want from the Font dialog box.

 4. Click the OK button.

> You also can use the buttons on the formatting toolbar to quickly format text.

You might want to change the alignment of the text in the cells of your table. To change the alignment, use the following steps:

To Do: Change the Alignment of Text

1. Select the cells where you want to change the alignment.

2. Select Format, Alignment to open the Alignment submenu. Choose Align Left, Center, Align Right, or Justify from the menu, as shown in Figure 15.5.

15

You can also click the Align Left, Center, Align Right, or Justify button on the Formatting toolbar.

FIGURE 15.5.

You can change the alignment of text from the menu or by clicking buttons on the Formatting toolbar.

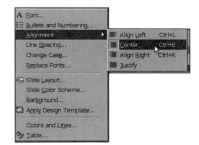

You can also vertically align text in a cell, either at the top, center, or bottom of the cell. The center option frames the text nicely in the cell and gives a much more professional appearance. To vertically align text in a cell, use the following steps:

To Do: Vertically Align Text in a Cell

1. Select the cells where you want to change the alignment.

2. Click either the Align Top, Center Vertically, or Align Bottom button from the Tables and Borders toolbar, as shown in Figure 15.6.

Align Top   Align Bottom

FIGURE 15.6.

Select a vertical alignment option from the Tables and Borders toolbar.

Center Vertically

Summary

In this hour, you learned how to create a table in a PowerPoint 2000 slide. There are two methods available: using the table AutoLayout or inserting a table. Navigating within a table is easy by using the mouse or arrow keys on the keyboard. You can now enter and edit text that has been added to a table. Setting the alignment of text is also easy when you use the buttons available on the Formatting toolbar and the Tables and Borders toolbar.

Q&A

Q I already have a table created in Microsoft Word that I want to use. Can I use it in PowerPoint 2000?

A Yes, you can, but you will need to be careful. You can copy it from Word and paste it in PowerPoint. The table will then be an embedded object, a Word Table (the object) embedded in a PowerPoint slide. You will be working with embedded objects in Hours 17, "Excel Worksheets," 18, "Creating Charts and Graphs with Microsoft Graph," and 20, "Using Microsoft Organization Chart." Embedded objects require that you double-click the object to open it in its "parent application"—in this case, Microsoft Word—before you can edit it.

You need to be particularly careful when you resize embedded objects. Word tables turn into ugly monsters when they are not resized proportionately with the corner handles.

To copy information from one application (such as Word) into another application (such as PowerPoint), it is best to have both programs started. When you have two (or more) programs running, you should see buttons on the Windows taskbar representing each program.

Although there are several ways to copy information from one application into another, the following method has been found to be the most foolproof. To copy a table from a Word document into a PowerPoint slide, first make sure both programs are running and that the Word document and PowerPoint slide are open. Next, switch to Word by clicking the appropriate button on the Windows Taskbar, and select the table by clicking anywhere in the table and selecting Table, Select Table from the Word menu. Then select Edit, Copy from the Word menu. Next, switch to PowerPoint by clicking the PowerPoint button on the Windows taskbar and display the slide you want to place the table on. Finally choose Edit, Paste from the PowerPoint menu.

You can also link the table in your presentation to the original table in the Word document. If the table is linked, later modifications to the Word table are updated and displayed in the PowerPoint presentation. To link a table, copy it from Word as previously discussed. When you switch to PowerPoint, display the slide you want to place the table on and choose Edit, Paste Special from the menu; this will open the Paste Special dialog box. In the Paste Special dialog box, select Paste Link and select Microsoft Word Document Object; then click the OK button.

Now you can make changes to your original Microsoft Word document, and the changes will show up in your presentation.

One final note when linking information—you should save your Microsoft Word document before you perform the steps needed to link the object to PowerPoint. When you create a link, PowerPoint uses the name of the original document to make any necessary updates. If you haven't saved the original document, PowerPoint gets confused and doesn't know where to find the linked information when you view the presentation later. You also do not want to move or rename the document, because this can also break the link.

Q My linked objects aren't updating. What's wrong?

A Usually, the links have somehow been turned to manual update. You can fix this attribute in two ways. You can manually update your links or change them to automatically update. To manually update links, choose Edit, Links from the menu to open the Links dialog box. From the list of links, select the links you want to update. Then simply click the Update Now button and then click the Close button.

To change the links to automatically update while in the Links dialog box, select the Automatic option button from the Update: choices.

Q I want one cell at the top of the table as a title. Excel has a Merge and Center button. Does PowerPoint 2000? How can I get this same look?

A The same effect can be achieved in PowerPoint 2000. Those nice folks at Microsoft have not given us a one-click step, such as the Merge and Center button in Excel. To get the same results in a PowerPoint 2000 table, simply select the cells you want to merge and center, and then click the Merge Cells button on the Tables and Borders toolbar. Next, click the Center button on the Formatting toolbar. As a final option, you can then click the Center Vertically button on the Tables and Borders toolbar.

HOUR 16

Formatting Tables

Creating tables is only half the fun. The more exciting part is when you get to add your personal design signature with custom formatting. After all the information has been inserted into the table, quite possibly you will want to jazz it up with a bit of customization. You may need to resize the table or columns to better fit the text displayed or add an extra row or column (or two). This hour will cover the options available when you customize a PowerPoint 2000 table. You will learn the following:

- How to select parts of the table for formatting
- How to insert or delete additional columns or rows
- How to resize the table, columns, or rows
- How to change the line and shading style

Selecting Cells, Rows, Columns, and the Entire Table

Before you can truly customize the look of the table, you should take a moment to consider how you want the final product to look. Figures 16.1 and 16.2 show the same information in two tables with completely different looks.

FIGURE **16.1.**

A Green Earth table with custom formatting.

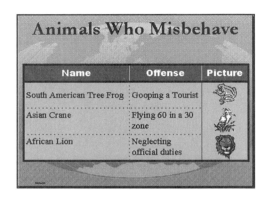

FIGURE **16.2.**

The same Green Earth table with different formatting.

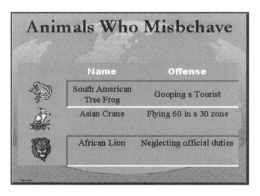

When you create custom tables, you may want to format the entire table or parts of that table. To format a part of a table, you select the part you want to format (more about formatting with custom borders and shading later this hour). Refer to Table 15.1, in Hour 15, "Creating and Using Tables," to review selecting different parts of a table.

When the table is selected, nothing is highlighted. The table placeholder border will change from diagonal dashed lines to a dotted line.

When the table is selected, all formatting changes—that is, border, shading, font, and so on—will affect the entire table.

To select multiple columns, rows, or cells, use the mouse to drag through the items you want to select.

You can also select a column by placing the mouse pointer above the column (so that the pointer becomes a down-pointing black arrow, as shown in Figure 16.3) and clicking.

Column selection

16

FIGURE 16.3.

When the mouse changes to a down arrow, you can select a column.

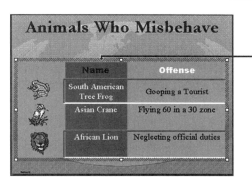

Inserting and Deleting Columns and Rows

You can add extra columns or rows easily to a table at any time. When you add extra columns or rows to a table, the table object will probably become bigger than the slide. You may need to resize the table so that it will fit.

Inserting and Deleting Columns

To insert a column to the left of the current insertion point's position, position the cursor (insertion point) in a cell to the right of where you want the new column. Then simply select Table, Insert Columns to the Left from the Tables and Borders toolbar.

To insert a column to the right of the current insertion point's position, position the cursor (insertion point) in a cell to the left of where you want the new column. Now you should select Table, Insert Columns to the Right from the Tables and Borders toolbar.

To insert more than one column, select the number of columns you want to insert. For example, to insert two columns, you should select two columns and then select Table, Insert Columns to the Left (or Right) from the Tables and Borders toolbar.

Deleting a column is comparably easy. To delete a column, click in any cell in the column you want to delete. Now select Table, Delete Columns from the Tables and Borders toolbar.

 To delete more than one column, select the number of columns you want to delete and then select Table, Delete Columns from the Tables and Borders toolbar.

Inserting and Deleting Rows

Inserting rows is just as simple. To insert a row above the current insertion point's position, position the cursor (insertion point) in a cell below where you want the new row. Now from the Tables and Borders toolbar, select Table, Insert Rows Above.

To insert a row below the current insertion point's position, first position the cursor (insertion point) in a cell above where you want the new row. Now go to the Tables and Borders toolbar and select Table, Insert Rows Below.

 To insert a row quickly at the end of the table, position the cursor in the last cell and press the Tab key on the keyboard.

 To insert more than one row, select the number of rows you want to insert. For example, to insert three rows, you select three rows and then select Table, Insert Rows Above (or Below) from the Tables and Borders toolbar.

Deleting a row is comparably easy. To delete a row, first click in any cell in the row you want to delete. Now, from the Tables and Borders toolbar select Table, Delete Rows.

 To delete more than one row, select the number of rows you want to delete and then select Table, Delete Rows from the Tables and Borders toolbar.

Adjusting the Size and Position of the Table, Column Width, and Row Height

After inserting columns or rows, you might find that the table is too big for the slide. You have several choices: Resize the entire table, adjust column widths, adjust row heights, or use a combination of each of these tasks. To resize the entire table to fit on the slide, use the following steps:

To Do: Resize a Table

1. Click the table and select Table, Select Table from the Tables and Borders toolbar.

2. Place the mouse pointer on any resizing handle (the lower right works great) and drag the handle to fit the table on the slide, as shown in Figure 16.4. The mouse pointer changes to a two-headed arrow when it's over the handle.

▲ 3. Repeat step 2 as necessary.

FIGURE 16.4.

Adjust the table size by dragging the resizing handles.

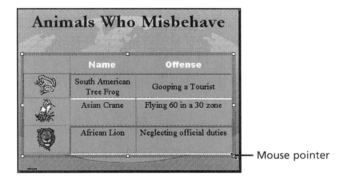

— Mouse pointer

You may need to scroll down and to the right to see the lower-right handle.

To adjust the width of a column, simply place the mouse pointer on a border line of a column, so that the mouse pointer changes to a double-headed arrow pointing left and right. Then click and drag the border to the desired column width, as shown in Figure 16.5.

Mouse pointer

FIGURE 16.5.

Adjust the size of a column by dragging a column border.

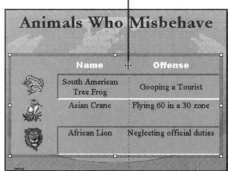

 You can double-click the right border of a column to automatically size the column to the width of the largest entry in that column.

To change the height of a row the procedure is almost the same. First place the mouse pointer on a borderline of a row, so that the mouse pointer changes to a double-headed arrow pointing up and down. Now click and drag the border to the desired row height, as shown in Figure 16.6.

Mouse pointer

FIGURE 16.6.

Adjust the size of a row by dragging a row border.

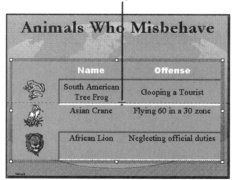

 If the table fits on the slide, but the row seems too large for the text, consider centering the text vertically in the row instead of changing the height.

You cannot resize a row any smaller than the last line of text in any individual cell in the row.

If you have multiple cells selected when you're resizing rows or columns, chances are you might end up resizing only certain cells, instead of the entire row or column. This is great if that effect is your intention, but usually it isn't. If this does happen, just click the Undo button on the Standard toolbar.

16

Moving a Table

After a table has been resized, you may want to reposition it on the slide. To move a table, position the mouse on the left, right, or bottom placeholder border (the mouse pointer changes into a four-headed arrow). Then click and drag the table to the desired location. Figure 16.7 shows a table being moved.

FIGURE 16.7.

Move a table simply by clicking and dragging the mouse to the desired position.

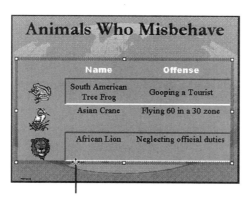

Mouse pointer changes to
a four-headed arrow

Adding Impact with Custom Borders and Shading

When you really want to dazzle your audience and make them sit up and pay attention, customize the table with borders and shading. The table in Figure 16.8 (also shown at the beginning of the hour) shows a table that has been formatted with customized borders and shading.

FIGURE **16.8.**

A table with customized borders and shading draws the attention of an audience.

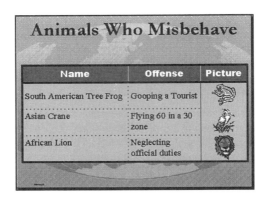

When you create a table in PowerPoint 2000, it is usually formatted with a border around each cell and no fill (or shading). Changes made to the border and fill style affect only those cells that are selected. This enables you to have different borders and fill styles for different table elements, as shown previously. Changing the border or fill style of a table is easy to do. You have two choices: Use the Format Table dialog box or use the Tables and Borders toolbar buttons.

The following steps illustrate making changes using the Format Table dialog box. This dialog box offers a few additional options that are not available from the Tables and Borders toolbar.

If you want to change the border or shading style for the table, use the following steps:

To Do: Change the Border or Shading of a Table

1. Select the cell, row, column or table you want to format.

2. Chose Table, Borders and Fill from the Tables and Borders toolbar to open the Format Table dialog box.

3. Click the Borders tab in the Format Table dialog box if it is not currently displayed (see Figure 16.9).

FIGURE 16.9.

Click the Borders tab to make changes to the border.

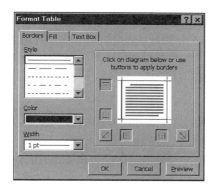

4. Select a border style, color, and width.

5. Click the diagram borders or buttons to change the border style.

> If you click the buttons, you need to click twice. The first click turns the border off, and the second click turns it back on with the new style settings.

6. Click the Preview button to see a preview of your changes.

7. Click the Fill tab.

8. Select a fill color from the fill drop-down list.

9. Click the Preview button to see a preview of your changes.

10. Click the OK button when finished.

> You can also select from any of the many previously discussed fill options, such as gradient shading for the shading of a table, row, column, or cell.

Summary

This hour, you learned how to customize your tables by inserting or deleting columns or rows. You also learned how to adjust the width of columns, the height of rows, and the size of a table. You explored how some simple changes to a table's border and shading options can add impact to your table.

Q&A

Q How can I format a table to have a 3D effect?

A This effect looks very professional and complicated, but it is really a simple feat. The table used in the Green Earth example was formatted as follows: no borders for the table, medium gray shading for the table, and cells B2 and C2 were selected and formatted with a dark gray top and left border and a white bottom border. The same was done for cells B3 and C3.

Q Can I select more than one, noncontiguous row (or column)—such as rows 1, 3, and 5—as I can in Excel?

A No, not in this version. Moreover, the format painter is not a big help, either. You have to format each row one at a time. Maybe if those nice folks at Microsoft get enough input from the users, they will make that an upgrade for the next version of PowerPoint.

HOUR 17

Excel Worksheets

You can easily copy or embed a Microsoft Excel worksheet into your presentation. PowerPoint 2000 enables you to copy an externally created worksheet into a slide show or embed a new worksheet. This hour covers Microsoft Excel worksheets. When you're trying to decide whether to use an Excel worksheet or a table, ask yourself whether you need to work with numbers or text. If the answer is more numbers and calculations than text, use an Excel worksheet. If the answer is more text than numbers, you should look at Hour 15, "Creating and Using Tables," and Hour 16, "Formatting Tables." For example, if you're adding, subtracting, multiplying, or dividing, a worksheet is preferred.

Inserting an Excel worksheet into a slide can be done in two ways. You can either copy a worksheet that has been previously created, or you can create a new worksheet from scratch right in PowerPoint! In this hour, you learn how to do the following:

- Embed or link a preexisting Excel worksheet into a PowerPoint slide
- Insert (or embed) a new Excel worksheet into a PowerPoint slide
- Add information to an embedded Excel worksheet
- Edit and format an embedded Excel worksheet

If you're already familiar with Microsoft Excel, you probably don't need to study this entire hour in depth. However, even proficient Excel experts might want to at least skim through this hour. You could find a useful trick or two.

This hour assumes that you understand the basics of using, and switching between, two applications using Windows. You also should have a basic understanding of Excel 2000. If you do not, consider purchasing *Sams Teach Yourself Office 2000 in 24 Hours*, also produced by Macmillan Computer Publishing.

You can copy a preexisting Excel worksheet, or at least part of it, into your PowerPoint presentation. Try walking through the steps for copying a sample worksheet. Figure 17.1 shows a Microsoft Excel worksheet with information that should be included in the presentation.

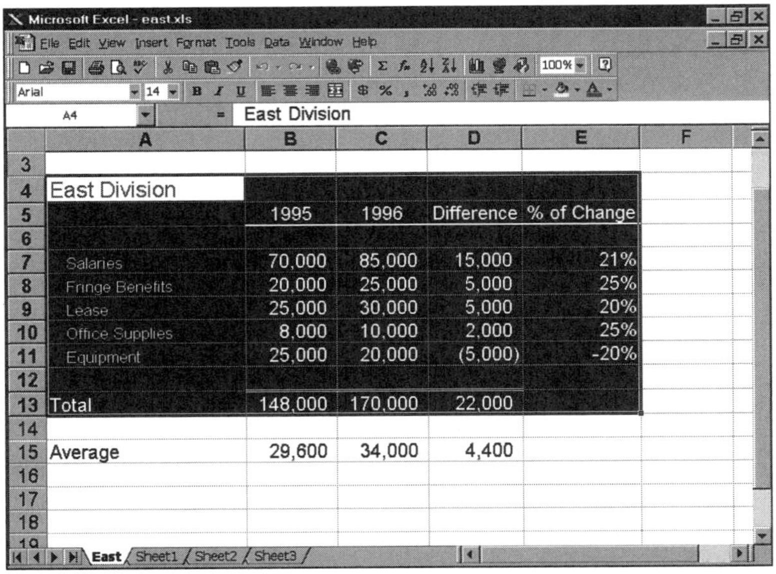

FIGURE 17.1.

A Microsoft Excel worksheet can be copied easily into a PowerPoint presentation.

	A	B	C	D	E	F
3						
4	East Division					
5		1995	1996	Difference	% of Change	
6						
7	Salaries	70,000	85,000	15,000	21%	
8	Fringe Benefits	20,000	25,000	5,000	25%	
9	Lease	25,000	30,000	5,000	20%	
10	Office Supplies	8,000	10,000	2,000	25%	
11	Equipment	25,000	20,000	(5,000)	-20%	
12						
13	Total	148,000	170,000	22,000		
14						
15	Average	29,600	34,000	4,400		
16						
17						
18						

Microsoft Excel - east.xls
File Edit View Insert Format Tools Data Window Help
Arial — 14 — B I U
A4 = East Division
East / Sheet1 / Sheet2 / Sheet3 /

Most worksheets can be quite large, so you should copy only the information that's needed to make your point for a particular presentation. Remember that the fundamental design concept for a presentation is "Less Is More." You can always expand on any information when you're giving the presentation.

When copying information from one application (such as Microsoft Excel) into another (such as Microsoft PowerPoint), you should have both programs running. You should see buttons on the Windows taskbar that represent both applications (Excel and PowerPoint).

There are several ways to copy information from one application into another; you can use Edit, Copy with the Edit, Paste command, toolbar buttons, the drag-and-drop procedure, or hot keys. Although all the methods work, the following steps demonstrate the task by using the menu commands. To copy worksheet information from Excel to PowerPoint, follow these steps:

To Do: Copy an Excel Worksheet onto a PowerPoint Slide

▼ To Do

1. Make sure both programs are running, the worksheet you want to copy from is open and onscreen in Excel, and the presentation and appropriate slide are open and onscreen in PowerPoint.

2. Switch to Excel.

3. Select the cells you want to copy.

17

 The easiest way to select cells is to simply drag through the cells you want to select.

4. Choose Edit, Copy from the menu.

5. Switch to PowerPoint by clicking the PowerPoint button on the Windows taskbar.

6. View the slide where you want to place the information.

▲ 7. Choose Edit, Paste from the menu. The worksheet is now copied onto your slide.

You might want to link the worksheet information in your presentation to the original worksheet in the Excel workbook. If the information is linked, later modifications to the Excel worksheet are displayed in the presentation. Use the following steps to link the worksheet information:

To Do: Copy and Link an Excel Worksheet onto a PowerPoint Slide

▼ To Do

1. Follow the previous steps 1–6.

2. Choose Edit, Paste Special from the menu. The Paste Special dialog box opens.

3. Select Paste Link (see Figure 17.2).

FIGURE 17.2.

Use the Paste Special dialog box when you want to link information.

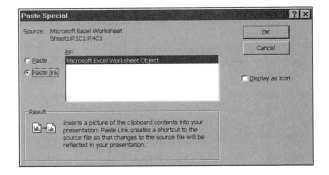

4. Select Microsoft Excel Worksheet Object.

5. Click the OK button.

Over time, you might find that you prefer to use another method, such as toolbar buttons or the drag-and-drop technique. There's usually no problem with doing that. Experiment with different methods and use the method you prefer. The only exception is when you want to link information from the original document to the destination document. In that case, you need to use the menu to paste the information.

Now you know how to make changes to your original Microsoft Excel worksheet and have the changes displayed in your presentation. When you open your presentation file, PowerPoint displays a window asking whether you want to update your links. Simply click the Yes button to update your presentation.

You should save your Microsoft Excel worksheet before you perform the steps for linking the object to PowerPoint. When you create a link, PowerPoint uses the name of the original document to make any necessary updates. If you haven't saved the original document, PowerPoint may become confused and won't know where to find the original information when you view the presentation at a later date. If you rename or move the document, the link will be broken.

After you have inserted a worksheet into a presentation, it becomes an embedded object. The object might need information inserted or require the cells to be reformatted. If you want to directly edit the worksheet, simply double-click the worksheet object and you will find yourself back in the land of Excel.

When you first insert an Excel worksheet into a slide, the worksheet is often too small to see. You can change the zoom control to 100 percent or 150 percent. Before you enter any information, you should resize the worksheet object so that it's big enough to work with and big enough to see later. To resize the worksheet object, follow these steps:

To Do: Resize an Excel Worksheet

1. Click outside the object to exit from Excel editing.
2. Click once on the worksheet to select it (do not double-click).
3. With the worksheet selected, drag a corner-sizing handle to resize the worksheet.

> Don't drag a top, bottom, left, or right sizing handle. This resizes the worksheet, but it doesn't maintain the proportions for the information it will eventually contain.

To insert information in your worksheet, you must be in Excel edit mode. If you do not see the row and column labels on the left and top of the worksheet, double-click the worksheet to go into edit mode. Click the cell where you want to add information and type the information.

You can quickly move from cell to cell while typing information by pressing the Tab key. Pressing the Shift+Tab key combination moves the cursor backward one cell at a time.

After all the information has been inserted into the table, you will probably want to add lines to the worksheet, format the text and numbers, and change the size of the columns or rows. Figure 17.3 shows a finished worksheet that has been formatted with lines and shading, as well as text and number formatting.

FIGURE **17.3.**

A formatted work-sheet can be a pow-erful slide.

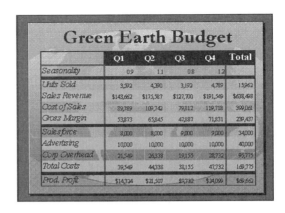

Although Excel automatically adds gridlines to the worksheet, they are a bit dim. You might want to enhance the lines or add shading. To add a border to a worksheet, follow these steps:

To Do: Add a Border to a Worksheet

1. Double-click the worksheet to go into Excel editing.

2. Select the cells, columns, or rows you want to enhance.

3. Click the Borders button drop-down arrow on the formatting toolbar (see Figure 17.4).

FIGURE **17.4.**

Select a border from the formatting tool-bar.

4. Select a border style.

To Do: Add Shading to a Worksheet

1. Double-click the worksheet to go into Excel editing.

2. Select the cells, columns, or rows you want to enhance.

3. Click the Shading button drop-down arrow on the formatting toolbar (see Figure 17.5).

FIGURE **17.5.**

Select shading from the formatting toolbar.

4. Select a shading color.

Choose Format, AutoFormat from the menu to select from many preformatted worksheet styles from the AutoFormat dialog box.

Excel offers easy access to a number of formatting styles. Depending on the type of numbers you're working with, you have several options available, including currency, accounting, dates, and percentages.

To Do: Format Numbers in a Worksheet

1. Select the numbers you want to format.
2. Choose Format, Cells from the menu to open the Format Cells dialog box as shown in Figure 17.6.

17

FIGURE 17.6.

The Format Cells dialog box gives many options for formatting numbers.

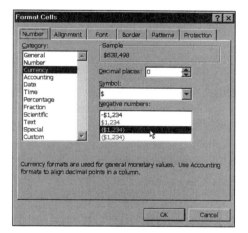

3. Click the Number tab.
4. Select the category that matches the type of numbers you're using.
5. Select the number of decimal places to show.
6. Change any other options available, if you want.
7. Click the OK button.

When working with numbers, one of the most common tasks is to total a column or row of numbers. Excel gives you a quick way to do this.

To Do: Quickly Sum Numbers

1. Click the cell where you want the total to appear.

2. Click the AutoSum button (Figure 17.7) on the Standard toolbar.

AutoSum button

FIGURE 17.7.

Click the AutoSum button to quickly total numbers.

▲   3. Press Enter.

After you have formatted the text or numbers in a worksheet, you might find that the width of the columns should be smaller or larger. You can either manually adjust the size of columns, or you can let Excel quickly change the column width based on the information in the column.

To Do: Manually Adjust Column Width

1. Place the mouse pointer over the border of the column you want to adjust so that it looks like a double-headed arrow, as shown in Figure 17.8.

Double-headed arrow

FIGURE 17.8.

Adjust the size of a column by dragging a column border.

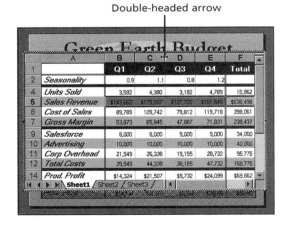

2. Click and hold the mouse button.

3. Drag the border to the new size.

▲   4. Release the mouse button.

You can quickly resize a column to get the best fit. Just double-click a column border.

If you want the columns in your worksheet to be an exact size, use the following steps:

To Do: Format Columns to an Exact Size

1. Select the column you want to resize.
2. Choose Format, Column, Width from the menu. The Column Width dialog box opens.
3. Enter an amount in the Column Width dialog box, as shown in Figure 17.9.

FIGURE 17.9.

Set an exact column width for all columns in a worksheet.

17

 4. Click the OK button.

Summary

This hour covered the different methods for inserting a Microsoft Excel worksheet into a presentation. You can either copy an existing worksheet or embed a new worksheet into your presentation. When you copy an existing worksheet, you can link the PowerPoint copy to the original Microsoft Excel worksheet if modifications or updates are likely.

When editing an embedded worksheet, you have access to all the tools and commands that would normally be available in Microsoft Excel. You can format the worksheet by adding lines or shading or by changing the number format. Microsoft Excel enables you to quickly resize columns and to sum a group of numbers.

Q&A

Q I just tried to copy some information from my Excel worksheet, but the Paste command is dimmed. Why can't I paste?

A Excel has a little quirk. When you select information and then choose Copy, you should see little dashes running around your selection (a marquee). If you press the Esc key (or any other key that makes the marquee disappear), the Paste command won't paste the worksheet cells. All you need to do is make sure you don't press Esc.

Q I would like an average of the numbers in my worksheet. Is there an easy way to do this?

A Yes, Excel has a function that gives you the average of a range of numbers. To perform this task, simply click in the cell where you want the average to display and then click the Paste Function button on the Standard toolbar (the button next to the AutoSum button that has an f and x on it). Then, from the Function Category list, select Statistical, and from the Function Name list, select AVERAGE. Now click the OK button. In the Number 1 box, Excel makes a guess as to the correct range of numbers to average for you. (If this range isn't correct, click the button that looks like a worksheet with a red arrow, select the correct range, and then click the button next to the new, selected range with the little red arrow pointing down.) Finally, click the OK button to accept the range.

You should see an average of the numbers you have selected. The Office Assistant is a great help with this feature, especially from step 5 on. If you don't see him hanging around asking whether you want help, press the F1 key on your keyboard.

Excel has tons of other functions to make your number life easier. If you want more information on using Excel, consider purchasing the *Sams Teach Yourself Excel 2000 in 24 Hours* (Macmillan Computer Publishing) companion book.

Hour 18

Creating Charts and Graphs with Microsoft Graph

In addition to worksheets, you can also embed a chart or graph into your presentation. Charts and graphs are an excellent medium for visually presenting numeric data. PowerPoint 2000 relies on the Microsoft Graph program for creating the charts and graphs that will be embedded in your presentation. Several chart types are available, and each chart type has several subtypes as well, ensuring that there's a chart for any need. Most charts can be displayed in either two or three dimensions, and almost every aspect of a chart can be formatted to suit your requirements. The next two hours should give you a solid foundation for creating and inserting fantastic charts. This hour covers the basic chart tasks:

- Inserting and viewing a chart
- Entering the data that will be displayed on the chart
- Choosing the correct chart type for the job

Inserting and Viewing a Chart

It's easy to create a chart in PowerPoint when you use one of the available AutoLayouts. Figure 18.1 displays the chart layout selections. If you want to insert a chart on any other slide, just use the Insert Chart button on the standard toolbar.

FIGURE 18.1.

Select the chart lay-out that best fits your needs.

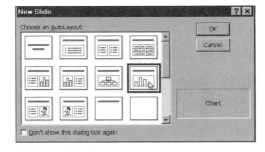

To Do: Create a Chart Using the Chart AutoLayout

1. Insert a new slide based on either the Chart, Text and Chart, or Chart and Text AutoLayout.
2. Double-click the chart placeholder, as shown in Figure 18.2. (Don't forget to add the slide title.)

FIGURE 18.2.

Double-click the chart placeholder to start a new chart.

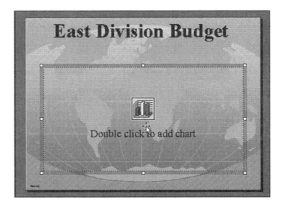

Another method for inserting a chart into any slide is to simply display the slide where you want to insert a chart and then click the Insert Chart button on the standard toolbar.

> If you use the Insert Chart button, the chart is inserted in the middle of the current slide. If you have other objects on the slide, you might need to resize or move the chart. After you have finished creating the chart, and are no longer in chart edit mode, you can use the corner handles to resize the chart. Move the chart in the same manner as you would move a graphic object.

After you have inserted the chart, you will be in what might be referred to as chart edit mode. While in chart edit mode, you're actually working in Microsoft Graph. This graphing software is an extra program that is installed with PowerPoint 2000. Working with Microsoft Graph is very similar to working with Microsoft Excel. Take note that the toolbars and menu commands have changed to reflect that you're now in Microsoft Graph. Any formatting or changes to the chart must be done in Microsoft Graph. You "turn on" Microsoft Graph by double-clicking any chart. You "exit" Microsoft Graph (and return to PowerPoint) by clicking any slide area outside the chart.

Entering Information in the Datasheet

The first item to take note of when you're in chart edit mode is the chart datasheet, which is simply a small worksheet you can use to fill in the appropriate information that serves as the basis for your chart. Microsoft has given you a sample datasheet and corresponding chart (it's hiding behind the datasheet) to get you started. The first row and column are reserved for text (or data labels) that identifies the actual numbers you will eventually enter. Figure 18.3 shows the sample datasheet and underlying chart.

After you have inserted the information for your chart, you can turn the datasheet off, which gives you more room to format the chart. If you need to edit the chart data later, you can turn the datasheet back on with a simple mouse click. To turn the datasheet off or on, use one of the following steps:

- Choose View, Datasheet from the menu.
- Click the View Datasheet button on the Graph Standard toolbar.

> To move the datasheet, place the mouse pointer in the datasheet title bar and drag the datasheet window to a new location.

FIGURE 18.3.

*Moving the datasheet
to work on the chart.*

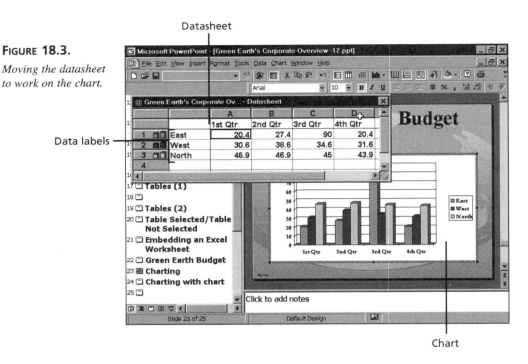

To create a chart, all you need to do is replace the sample information in the datasheet with your real information.

Entering Information

Entering information in a Microsoft Graph datasheet is really no different from entering information in a table or worksheet. Although you can change the column width in a datasheet, you don't really need to worry about this option unless you want to see the information as you work. The information you enter in the datasheet (whether you can see it or not) is displayed on the chart, and the chart is what your audience sees. To enter information in the datasheet, simply click in the cell where you want to enter or change information and start typing.

Here are some helpful datasheet tips:

- Use the first row and column to label the information.
- Use the Tab key to move one cell to the right.
- Use the Shift+Tab key combination to move one cell to the left.
- Use the Enter key to move one cell down.
- Use the arrow keys to move one cell in the arrow direction.

- The cell with the dark border is the current selected cell.
- To edit cell information, select the cell and press F2.

When entering information on a datasheet, keep in mind the type of chart you will eventually be using. For example, if you're using a pie chart like the one shown in Figure 18.4, you should enter only one row of information. On the other hand, if you're using a bar chart, you can enter as many columns and rows of information as needed.

FIGURE 18.4.

A pie chart uses only one row and many columns.

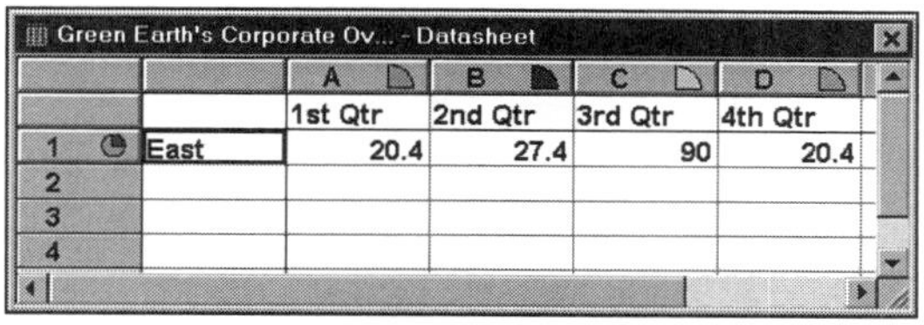

Green Earth's Corporate Ov... - Datasheet				
	A	B	C	D
	1st Qtr	2nd Qtr	3rd Qtr	4th Qtr
1 East	20.4	27.4	90	20.4
2				
3				
4				

If you have a lot of information you need to chart, you might want to create several slides.

As always, remember that you don't want to get too detailed when entering information. Your audience has to be able to read and quickly understand the information onscreen. You can always expound on the information when you give the presentation.

Selecting Cells

When editing chart information, it's important to know how to select multiple cells, columns, rows, or the entire datasheet. You can select multiple cells by simply using the mouse and dragging, as shown in Figure 18.5.

FIGURE 18.5.

You can select several cells by dragging the mouse.

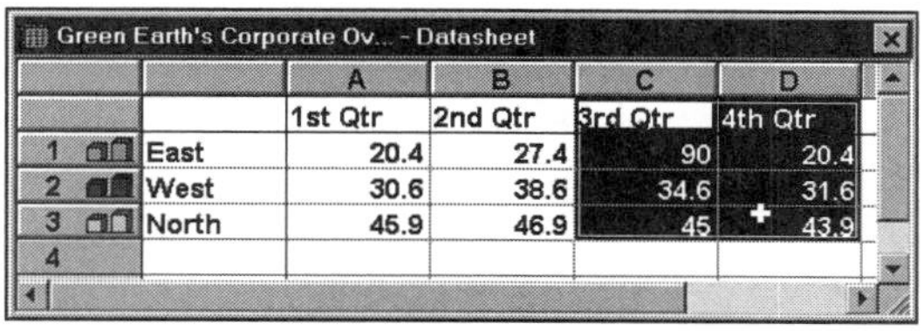

Green Earth's Corporate Ov... - Datasheet				
	A	B	C	D
	1st Qtr	2nd Qtr	3rd Qtr	4th Qtr
1 East	20.4	27.4	90	20.4
2 West	30.6	38.6	34.6	31.6
3 North	45.9	46.9	45	43.9
4				

To select entire columns or rows, click the appropriate headings on the datasheet. The column or row headings are the lettered or numbered gray areas at the top of each column or to the left of each row. Figure 18.6 demonstrates selecting column A, and Figure 18.7 shows row 2 selected.

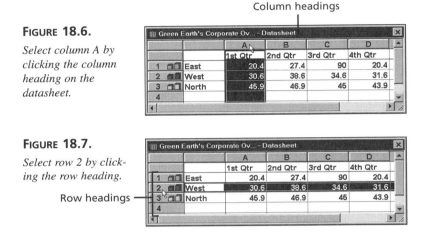

FIGURE 18.6.

Select column A by clicking the column heading on the datasheet.

FIGURE 18.7.

Select row 2 by clicking the row heading.

Selecting the entire datasheet is just as easy. Click the Select All button, as shown in Figure 18.8. (If you press the delete key, you can clear the entire datasheet in one fell swoop.)

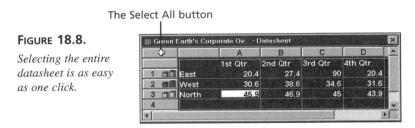

FIGURE 18.8.

Selecting the entire datasheet is as easy as one click.

A Word About Undo

You're probably used to having unlimited access to undoing your mistakes in PowerPoint 2000. Although Microsoft Graph does have an Undo command, you get only one chance as opposed to when you are working solely in PowerPoint 2000. In other words, if you make a mistake, don't do anything else—click the Undo button right away. To undo a mistake, you have these two choices:

- Choose Edit, Undo from the menu.
- Click the Undo button on the standard toolbar.

Choosing a Chart Type

Now that you have fully entered all your charting information into the datasheet, you are ready to select the type of chart you want to use to convey the information. There are 14 chart types available for you to choose. The default chart is the standard 3D Column chart, as shown in Figure 18.9.

FIGURE 18.9.

The default chart type is a 3D column.

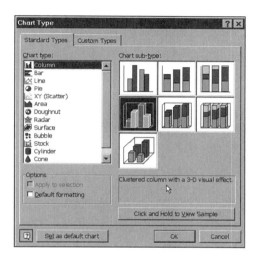

Most of the standard chart types also have several subtypes that you can select. In total, there are over 70 different charts from which to choose. In addition to all the standard charts that come with Microsoft Graph, there are 20 predesigned custom chart types to choose from. For even more flexibility, you can create your own custom chart types to use in the future.

If you find that you're always changing the chart type to your favorite variation, such as a 3D pie chart, you can change the default chart type.

All the instructions that follow assume that you're already in chart edit mode. The instructions don't apply if you're in PowerPoint slide edit mode. To edit a chart and enter chart edit mode, double-click a chart object.

18

Standard Types

You can change the type of chart at any time. When you do, you're usually affecting the entire chart. To change the type of the entire chart, use the following steps:

To Do: Change the Chart Type

1. Choose Chart, Chart Type from the menu to open the Chart Type dialog box.
2. Click the Standard Types tab.
3. Select a chart type from the list.
4. Select a chart subtype from the samples in the right pane of the dialog box.
5. Click the Press and Hold to View Sample button to see a sample of your chart before accepting any changes, as shown in Figure 18.10.

FIGURE 18.10.

Preview a chart type selection before accepting your change.

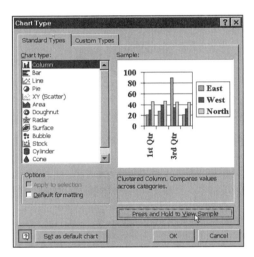

6. Click the OK button to accept the new chart type.

You can also combine some chart types, such as the column and line types, as shown in Figure 18.11. This feature enables you to change the chart type for one data series in your chart. The combination feature is available when using 2D charts, with the exception of the XY (Scatter) and Bubble types.

FIGURE 18.11.

You can combine a number of chart types on one PowerPoint slide.

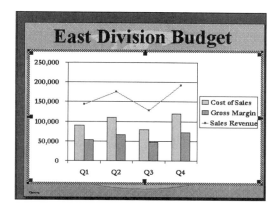

The 3D Column and Bar types also enable you to use a Cylinder, Cone, or Pyramid type. To change the chart type for a single data series, follow these steps:

To Do: Combine Chart Types

1. Select the data series you want to change.

> You can select any item on a chart by single-clicking it. You also can select a chart item by choosing the item from the Chart Objects drop-down box on the standard toolbar, as shown in Figure 18.12.

FIGURE 18.12.

Select a chart item from the Chart Objects drop-down box on the Standard toolbar.

2. Choose Chart, Chart Type from the menu to open the Chart Type dialog box.
3. Click the Standard Types tab.
4. Select a chart type from the list.
5. Select a chart subtype from the samples at the right side of the window.
6. Make sure the Apply to Selection check box is checked.
7. Click the Press and Hold to View Sample button to view a sample of your chart before accepting any changes.
8. Click the OK button to accept the new Chart type.

Custom Types

A custom chart type is similar to a template that stores all the custom formatting information. Usually the coherent, custom formatting of a chart takes considerable time to create. If you think there's even a remote chance you will want to create a similar chart, it's worthwhile to save the chart as a custom chart type.

Take a peek at all the predefined custom chart types available to help give you ideas for your own custom chart types. To save a chart as a custom chart type, use the following steps:

To Do: Save a Chart As a Custom Chart Type

1. Format the chart as desired.
2. Choose Chart, Chart Type from the menu to open the Chart Types dialog box.
3. Click the Custom Types tab (see Figure 18.13).

FIGURE 18.13.

Use the Custom Types tab for adding or selecting a custom chart type.

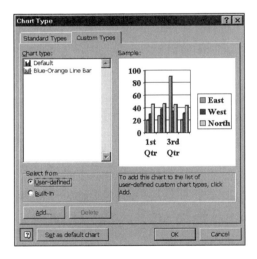

4. Select User-Defined for the chart type.
5. Click the Add button to open the Add Custom Chart Type dialog box.
6. Type a name for your chart type in the Name box.
7. Type a description, if you like, in the Description box (see Figure 18.14).

FIGURE 18.14.

Type a name and description for your custom chart type.

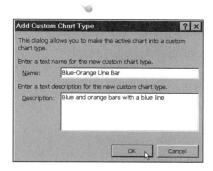

▲   8. Click the OK button.

Later, when you want to use your custom chart type (or one of Microsoft's), all you need to do is follow these steps:

To Do: Use a Custom Chart Type

1. Choose Chart, Chart Type from the menu to open the Chart Type dialog box.
2. Click the Custom Types tab.
3. Select either User-Defined (for your custom charts) or Built-In (for Microsoft's custom charts).
4. Select a chart type from the list on the left.

▲   5. Click the OK button to accept the new chart type.

Changing the Default Chart Type

If you find that you are always selecting your custom chart type whenever you create a chart, you may want to modify the default chart type. You can set the default chart type to any chart that is available in the Chart Type dialog box. Microsoft Graph makes it easy to change the default chart type; follow these steps:

To Do: Change the Default Chart Type

1. Choose Chart, Chart Type from the menu to open the Chart Types dialog box.
2. Click the Standard Types tab or the Custom Types tab.
3. Select a chart type from the list.
4. Select a chart subtype (if applicable) from the samples at the right side of the window.
5. Click the Press and Hold to View Sample button to see a sample of your chart before accepting any changes.
6. Click the Set As Default chart button.
7. Click the Yes button to accept the change to the default chart.

▲   8. Click the OK button to accept the new chart type.

Exiting from Microsoft Graph

As with all embedded objects, you exit from Microsoft Graph by clicking outside the chart area. To edit a chart, simply double-click the chart.

Summary

This hour introduced you to the power available with Microsoft Graph. You can display any type of numeric information imaginable with a visual chart. There are several methods available for inserting a chart into your presentation, but the easiest is to use the Chart AutoLayout.

Every chart is derived from a base dataset. Entering data on the chart datasheet is easy. If you already have the information in an Excel worksheet, you can quickly copy or import the information into your chart datasheet. If you make a mistake, use the Undo feature right away, because Microsoft Graph remembers only the last thing you have done.

Microsoft Graph has dozens of chart types available and also has many built-in custom chart types. If you still can't find just the right chart type, you have the option of creating your own custom chart type.

Stay tuned, because the next hour covers all the different formatting options to really make those charts stand out.

Q&A

Q I have all my chart information in an Excel worksheet as well as an Excel chart. Can't I just use the chart I have already created in Excel?

A By all means, please do. The charting features in Excel are actually better than those available with Microsoft Graph. If you know how to use the chart feature in Excel or have charts already created, the best thing to do is to select the chart in your Excel worksheet and copy it into your PowerPoint presentation slide. No need to do extra work if the job is already done (remember, you want to take Friday off).

Q When I change the chart type, I lose all the formatting that took me hours to do. Help!

A Whenever you change the chart type, Microsoft Graph will, by default, apply the formatting of the chart type to your chart. If you have made formatting changes to your chart, such as changing the font face, font size, color, background, or anything else, you might want to uncheck the Default formatting box under Options in the Chart Type dialog box.

Hour **19**

Editing Charts and Graphs

Now that you can insert and create a graph using the Microsoft Graph program, it's time to talk about editing the graph so that it looks just the way you want. When a graph is successfully customized, there's no need to do all that hard work again next week. You can save extra effort by saving the graph as a custom chart type to use over, and over, and over again. With custom chart types, you not only get to take this Friday off, but next Friday as well!

In this hour, you learn the necessary basics for customizing a graph and creating a quality presentation. The basics to be covered give you the details for doing the following:

- Editing datasheet items
- Selecting chart objects
- Changing the attributes of the axis, legend, or a data series
- Plotting your chart by row (default) or by column

Editing Data Items

Sometimes the best work can be rendered useless. Just as you've finished the presentation for the board of directors, you are told that the sales numbers are all wrong. Just say, "No problem." All you need to do is edit the information that Microsoft Graph 2000 used to create your chart. You can do this task quickly and easily by editing the chart's datasheet, as shown in Figure 19.1.

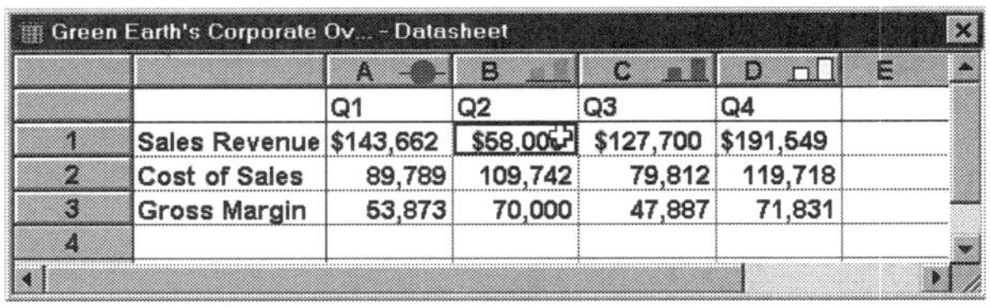

FIGURE 19.1.

Edit the Microsoft Graph datasheet to change information in a chart.

		A	B	C	D	E
		Q1	Q2	Q3	Q4	
1	Sales Revenue	$143,662	$58,000	$127,700	$191,549	
2	Cost of Sales	89,789	109,742	79,812	119,718	
3	Gross Margin	53,873	70,000	47,887	71,831	
4						

Green Earth's Corporate Ov... - Datasheet

Displaying the Datasheet

If you have already exited from chart edit mode (or from PowerPoint for that matter), finding the datasheet is easy. Just double-click on your chart to return to chart edit mode and—bata-boom-bata-bing—the datasheet pops into view. You can also display a datasheet with one of these two methods:

- Choose View, Datasheet from the Microsoft Graph menu.
- Click the View Datasheet button from the Microsoft Graph standard toolbar, as shown in Figure 19.2.

View Datasheet button

FIGURE 19.2.

Use the View Datasheet button to quickly display the Microsoft Graph datasheet.

When the datasheet is displayed, you can easily change any information needed.

Changing Information Using the Datasheet

When you need to change information in a cell of the datasheet, you have two choices. Microsoft Graph gives you the option of either completely replacing the existing information or merely editing the existing information.

To Do: Change Information on the Datasheet

To replace the existing information, use the following steps:

1. Click the cell you need to change.
2. Type in the new information.
3. Press Enter.

To edit existing information (if you misspelled a name, for example), use the following steps:

To Do: Edit Information on the Datasheet

1. Click the cell you need to edit.
2. Press the F2 key.
3. Position the blinking cursor where you need to edit, as shown in Figure 19.3.

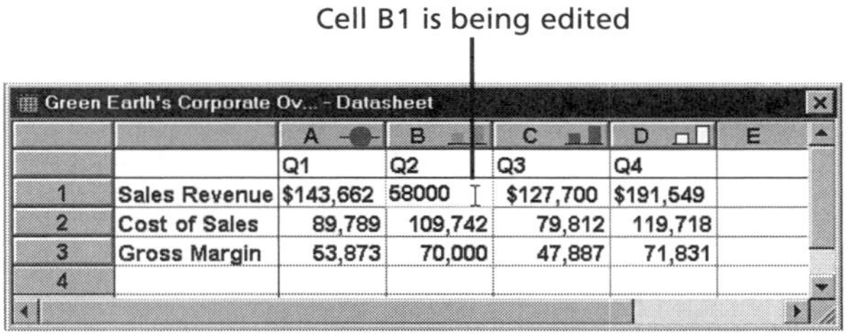

Cell B1 is being edited

FIGURE 19.3.

Press F2 and position the cursor to change information in a cell of the datasheet.

		A	B	C	D	E
		Q1	Q2	Q3	Q4	
1	Sales Revenue	$143,662	58000	$127,700	$191,549	
2	Cost of Sales	89,789	109,742	79,812	119,718	
3	Gross Margin	53,873	70,000	47,887	71,831	
4						

Green Earth's Corporate Ov... - Datasheet

4. Edit the information as needed.
5. Press Enter.

Dragging Data Markers in 2D Charts

If your chart is two-dimensional, you can also change the value of a single data series item by dragging the data marker. Data marker dragging, shown in Figure 19.4, gives you a quick and easy way to edit a chart.

A *data series* is the group(s) of related information on your chart. In a bar chart, each bar with the same color is part of the complete series, as in East, West, North, and so forth. A pie chart has only one data series. A *data marker* is a single item in a data series, such as the first quarter information for the East.

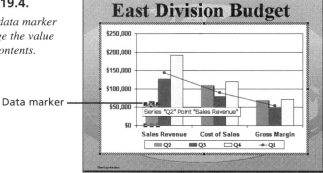

FIGURE 19.4.

Drag a data marker to change the value of cell contents.

Data marker

To Do: Change Data Using the Mouse

To edit the value of a data marker by dragging, follow these steps:

1. Click once on any part of the data series.

2. Click once again on the data marker you want to edit; make sure that only one data point is selected.

3. Place the mouse on the top selection handle (for bar charts) and hold down the mouse button.

4. Drag the marker to the location you want.

5. Release the mouse button.

Some chart types, such as 3D charts, do not permit you to edit the value of a data point in this manner.

Although dragging the data point can be an easy way to edit the value of a data marker, it's difficult to be accurate. If you need to enter accurate information, use the datasheet.

Plotting by Row or Column

Microsoft Graph usually plots the data series based on the information you enter in the datasheet rows. You can easily modify a chart's display by changing the graph's plot axis. The information is exactly the same, but you have a different view. For example, instead of comparing the sales figures of individual territories, you could compare how each product is selling.

To Do: Plot by Rows or Columns

To change how Microsoft Graph plots the data series, do one of the following:

- Choose Data, Series in Rows (to plot by datasheet rows) or Data, Series in Columns (to plot by datasheet columns) from the menu.
- Click the By Row (to plot by datasheet rows) or By Column (to plot by datasheet columns) button on the standard toolbar.

Figure 19.5 shows a chart that's plotted on the datasheet rows, and Figure 19.6 illustrates the same information plotted by using the datasheet columns.

FIGURE 19.5.

Information plotted using the datasheet rows.

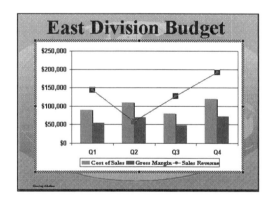

FIGURE 19.6.

The same information shown plotted on the datasheet columns.

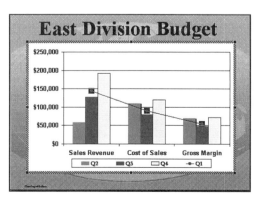

19

Selecting Chart Objects

It's important to understand that when you're editing and customizing a chart, there are many objects that can be customized. A chart consists of not only the data information, but also other items that make the chart readable. A chart may include the following objects:

- Legend
- Chart floor
- Axis (X and Y)
- Description text
- Chart background and walls

How do you know which object you have selected? Look for the small, black, square selection handles on the chart. There should be one handle in each corner of the area you have selected. Also, take a look at the Chart Objects drop-down list on the Standard toolbar. (See Figure 19.7.) The Chart Objects list tells you the name of the object that's currently selected.

FIGURE 19.7.

The Chart Objects list shows you which chart item is currently selected.

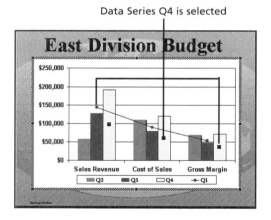

Data Series Q4 is selected

Using the Mouse

You can use the mouse to select any chart object. Simply click the object you want to select. Some objects, such as data series, data labels, and legend items, are grouped together. To select a single item in a group, you need to click once to select the group and then click a second time (do not double-click) to select the individual item. (See Figure 19.8.)

Don't double-click. When you double-click an item, you jump directly into the Format dialog box for the particular item that was double-clicked. For this task, click, pause, and then click again on the item.

FIGURE 19.8.

Click the mouse twice on a grouped chart object to select a single object from the group.

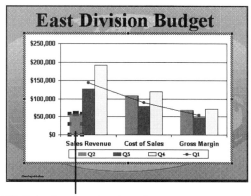

Q2's Sales Revenue is selected

Using the Toolbar

Use the Chart Objects button on the Standard toolbar to quickly select any main chart object, as shown in Figure 19.9.

FIGURE 19.9.

The Chart Objects list on the Standard toolbar allows quick access to selecting chart items.

19

The toolbar doesn't have options for selecting individual items from a data series, data label, or legend. Use the mouse selection method described previously to select these items.

Changing Chart Object Attributes

Every chart object attribute can be changed and customized to match your needs. The following sections cover the most frequently made changes for the axis, legend, and series objects. However, when you have time, experiment with each chart object to find how you can customize its attributes.

To Do: Customize a Chart Object

To customize any chart item, use the following steps:

1. Select the chart item you want to change.

2. Choose Format, Selected [chart item name] from the menu to open the Format dialog box, as shown in Figure 19.10.

   The [chart item name] changes depending on which item you have selected. In Figure 19.10, the chart item selected was Data Series.

Dialog box title bar

FIGURE 19.10.

The Format dialog box title bar displays what chart object is being formatted.

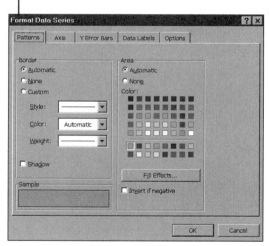

3. Make any changes you want from the Format dialog box.

4. Click the OK button when you're finished.

Axis Labels

The most popular items to change on a chart are the axis labels. Usually, people want to change the font, the font size, or the placement of the labels.

To Do: Format Axis Labels

Use the following instructions to format the axis label with different font attributes:

1. Select the axis you want to change.

2. Choose Format, Selected Axis from the menu to open the Format Axis dialog box.

3. Click the Font tab to change the font settings, as shown in Figure 19.11.

FIGURE 19.11.

Use the Font tab of the Format Axis dialog box to change the font used for the labels.

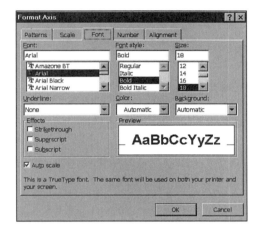

4. Change the font.

▲ 5. Click the OK button.

To Do: Rotate Axis Labels

Rotating the axis labels is just as easy and can help make some labels easier to read. Use the following steps to rotate the axis labels:

1. Select the axis you want to change.

2. Choose Format, Selected Axis from the menu.

3. Click the Alignment tab to change the label alignment options, as shown in Figure 19.12.

19

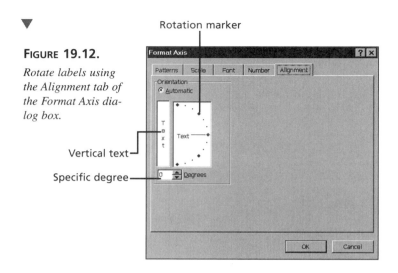

FIGURE 19.12.

Rotate labels using the Alignment tab of the Format Axis dialog box.

4. Under the Orientation section, click or drag the text rotation marker to the angle you want.

> You also can enter a rotation angle, if you like, in the Degrees box. Type a positive number (up to 90) to rotate the text upward; use a negative number (up to –90) to rotate the text downward.

5. Click the OK button.

> Microsoft Graph also enables you to quickly change the text orientation from horizontal to vertical by simply clicking the vertical text option in the Orientation section.
>
> To quickly rotate text to a 45-degree angle, use the Angle Text Downward or Angle Text Upward buttons on the formatting toolbar.

Legends

You can also format the font attributes for legends. Their placement, for example, is frequently changed. The legend is typically displayed on the right of the chart. However, you can place the legend anywhere you want, as shown in Figure 19.13.

FIGURE 19.13.

Placing the legend at the bottom of the chart makes the chart easier to read.

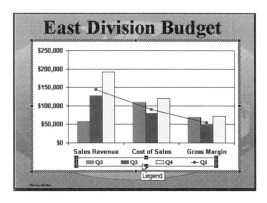

To Do: Change the Placement of the Legend

To format the legend, use the following steps:

1. Select the legend.

2. Choose Format, Selected Legend from the menu. The Format Legend dialog box opens.

3. Click the Placement tab to change the legend location.

4. Select the location you want for the legend.

5. Click the OK button.

 You can also simply drag the legend to the location you want. However, this will not resize the chart.

Data Series Colors and Patterns

The last item up for discussion this hour is the data series—specifically, how to change the color or pattern of the series. Figure 19.14 shows the sample chart that has been formatted to display a pattern for the data series. Using a pattern for the data series is great when you aren't giving a color presentation (as in this book).

19

FIGURE **19.14.**

A chart with each data series represented by a different pattern.

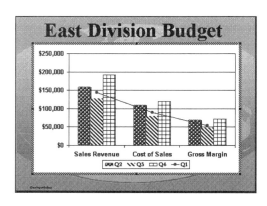

To Do: Format a Data Series

▼ To Do

To change the color or pattern of a data series, follow these steps:

1. Select the data series you want to change.
2. Choose Format, Selected Data Series from the menu to open the Format dialog box.
3. Click the Patterns tab.
4. Select the color you want for the series.
5. For a pattern, click the Fill Effects button to open the Fill Effects dialog box.
6. In the Fill Effects dialog box, click the Pattern tab, as shown in Figure 19.15.

FIGURE **19.15.**

Format the data series with a pattern using the Pattern tab of the Fill Effects dialog box.

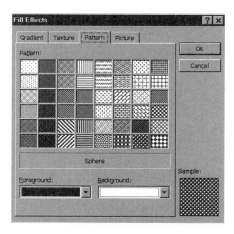

7. Select a pattern.

> There are two things you should be aware of: First, choose a pattern that's
> easy to recognize onscreen, usually the simpler the better; second, make
> sure the background color is white, or the pattern might be hard to see.

8. Click the OK button in the Fill Effects dialog box.

▲ 9. Click the OK button in the Format Data Series dialog box.

Summary

In this hour, you learned how to edit information in the datasheet and explored a few of
the formatting options available when using Microsoft Graph 2000. Although you have
seen only the options specific to the axis, legend, and data series objects, all the attribute
changes mentioned apply to any chart object. There are so many options available when
formatting a chart that the only way to learn every option is to experiment.

Q&A

**Q I want my legend on the bottom of the chart, but in two rows instead of one.
How can I do this?**

A Format the legend so that it's placed on the bottom of the chart. Then resize the
legend so that it's shorter. You will see a ghost outline of the legend when you're
resizing to let you know that the legend is going to be two rows of text.

Q I want to make the legend appear transparent. Can I do that?

A Yes. Simply format the legend by first selecting the legend and choosing Format,
Selected Legend from the menu. Then click the Patterns tab and under Border and
Area, select None. Then click the OK button. This procedure simply turns off the
border line and any fill for the legend. You should now have a transparent legend.

19

Hour 20

Using Microsoft Organization Chart

Most of us work with other people, and a lot of us work for companies that have five or more (many, many more) employees. How do the powers that be (in other words, the Human Resources department) keep track of where everyone belongs as well as the corporate pecking order? How do you know that Charlie is really your supervisor? Enter the Microsoft Organization Chart application.

In this hour, you learn about the following topics:

- What an organizational chart is and why you might need one
- How to enter information into a Microsoft organizational chart
- How to add and delete a position

Organizational charts can be useful in a PowerPoint presentation. PowerPoint integrates closely with the Microsoft Organization Chart software to make creating and embedding organizational charts a simple task.

What Is an Organizational Chart?

An organizational chart is a graphical representation of the personnel structure for a corporation, committee, or any other collaborative team. Organizational charts are useful when you need to visually portray the team members and their respective relationships. Figure 20.1 shows the organizational structure of King Arthur's Court.

FIGURE 20.1.

The organization of Camelot.

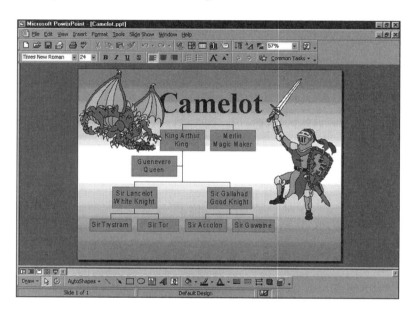

Inserting an Organizational Chart

When you insert an organizational chart into your presentation, you're embedding a chart created with Microsoft Organization Chart 2.0. There are two simple ways to insert an organization chart into your presentation slide. The method you choose is just a matter of personal preference.

To Do: Insert an Organizational Chart in a Slide

To insert an Organizational Chart in a slide, use the following steps:

1. Start a new slide.
2. Select the Organization Chart layout.
3. Double-click the organization chart placeholder.

Another method uses the Insert menu item, as follows:

1. Display the slide where you want to insert an organizational chart.

▲ 2. Choose Insert, Picture, Organization Chart from the menu.

Either method starts the Microsoft Organization Chart program (notice the button on your taskbar) and displays the screen shown in Figure 20.2. If you're not entering information right away, click outside the top box on any white area of the window.

FIGURE 20.2.

A new organizational chart using the Microsoft Organization Chart program.

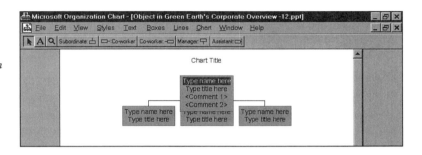

All the embedded objects covered so far have used the PowerPoint window for their operations. The toolbars and menu commands in PowerPoint have changed to reflect that you have been working on an embedded object. Microsoft Organization Chart is a much older program, so it reacts differently. When you embed an organizational chart, you're actually starting the Microsoft Organization Chart program in a separate window. You should notice that there's an additional button on the Windows taskbar to represent Microsoft Organization Chart.

Microsoft has been using the Microsoft Organization Chart 2.0 program since PowerPoint 4.0, and there has been no update to the program. Usually it works just fine, but on occasion the computer has stopped responding while using this feature. Even though you probably save your work all the time, be extra careful to do so while using the Microsoft Organization Chart program.

20

Components of an Organizational Chart

An organizational chart is composed of boxes connected to one another by lines. Each box represents an individual in the organization. The lines that connect a box to other boxes illustrate the relationship of the individuals. There are four types of individual relationships: manager, co-worker, subordinate, and assistant.

In the Camelot example, King Arthur is the uppermost manager with Merlin as a co-worker (or partner) and Guenevere as an Assistant. Sir Lancelot and Sir Gallahad are both subordinates of King Arthur. Sir Lancelot is the manager of both Sir Trystram and Sir Tor, and Sir Gallahad is the manager of Sir Accolon and Sir Gawaine.

Entering Information

When you first insert an organizational chart, you will probably see a sample chart containing four boxes. The top box should be the one that's selected and ready for you to start typing in the information. When a box is selected for editing, you will see four lines available to insert information. Each line is a field that contains information for the name, title, and two comments, as shown in Figure 20.3.

Sometimes you won't see the last two lines in a box unless the box is selected for editing. However, after the box is selected, you can type information in all four lines. If you don't use all the field labels, they won't be displayed in your organizational chart.

These field labels are simply placeholders that show where you can enter information. The labels also indicate the type of information you might want to include.

To Do: Enter Information in a Personnel Box

To enter information in a personnel box, follow these steps:

1. Click once on the box to select it (if it's not already selected).
2. Click a second time on the box (don't double-click; for this task, click, pause, and then click again on the personnel box). The box should expand to display all the fields available for text entry, as shown in Figure 20.4.

FIGURE 20.3.

Each personnel box can contain up to four lines for infor-

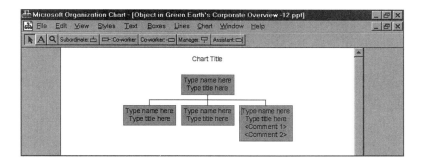

3. Press the Tab key until the field you want to enter information into is selected.

4. Type the information.

5. Press the Tab key to move to the next field.

6. Repeat steps 4 and 5 as necessary.

▲ 7. Click outside the box to deselect it.

If you make a mistake in Microsoft Organization Chart, you can use the Undo command. You have only one chance to undo your mistake, however—much like working in Microsoft Graph. If you make a mistake, undo it right away. To undo a mistake, just choose Edit, Undo from the menu.

Selected personnel box

FIGURE 20.4.

A selected box in Microsoft Organization Chart, expanded and ready for data entry.

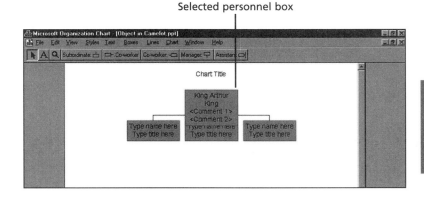

20

Adding, Deleting, and Moving Positions

All organizational charts initially start with four default personnel boxes. Although these initial boxes are a great start, the folks at Microsoft realized that every organization would be different, so they've made it very easy to add, delete, or move boxes as you see fit. The Camelot example required that several boxes be inserted and some needed to be moved around. It was especially necessary when Merlin got promoted to the same level as King Arthur. Actually, no one can supervise Merlin.

Adding Positions

Adding positions is probably the easiest task to master of the three box commands. You just need to decide what type of relationship to add and whom you want to append the new box to. Table 20.1 shows the five types of relationship buttons available in Microsoft Organization Chart, with a corresponding explanation of the relationship.

TABLE 20.1.   ORGANIZATIONAL RELATIONSHIPS.

Button	Relationship Explanation
Subordinate:	The Subordinate button attaches a new position box under another box. Subordinates report to a Manager box.
:Co-worker	The left Co-worker button attaches a new position box to the left of another box. Coworkers all have the same manager, and form a group.
Co-worker:	The right Co-worker button attaches a new position box to the right of another box as a co-worker.
Manager:	The Manager button attaches a new position box above another box. Managers have other Subordinate boxes reporting to them.
Assistant:	The Assistant button attaches a new position box to another box. Assistant boxes can be used to represent a variety of positions, from secretarial to managerial assistance.

To Do: Insert a New Position Box

To insert a new position box into your organizational chart, follow these steps:

1. Click the Position Box button that represents the type of position you want to insert.

2. Click the existing box you want the new box to branch off from as shown in Figure 20.5.

FIGURE 20.5.

Add a new personnel box with a quick click.

Merlin gets to supervise

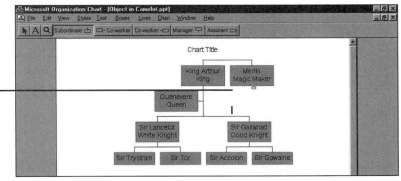

> If you need to add several new position boxes to an existing box, you can click the Position Box button enough times to equal the number of boxes you need to add. For example, to add three subordinates to Merlin, click the Subordinate Position Box button three times and then click the Merlin box.

Using Zoom

After you have added new boxes, you might find it difficult to see the box text or the entire organizational structure. With Microsoft Organization Chart, you have several options available with the zoom feature.

To Do: Use the Zoom Feature

Pick one of the zoom options outlined in Table 20.2 to zoom in to or out of organizational charts.

TABLE 20.2.   ZOOM OPTIONS.

Size	Menu Choice	Keyboard
Fit in window	View, Size to Window	F9
50%	View, 50% of Actual	F10
Actual size	View, Actual Size	F11
200%	View, 200% of Actual	F12

20

You can also use the Zoom tool on the Microsoft Organization Chart toolbar to adjust the screen area. You can quickly magnify the screen area to actual size, or reduce the screen area to the size of the window. The tool changes to reflect which option is currently available: A magnifying glass, Figure 20.6, indicates that you can magnify, and a chart, Figure 20.7, means you can reduce. Simply click the tool and then click your chart.

FIGURE 20.6.   **FIGURE 20.7.**

Zoom tool ready   *Zoom tool ready to*
to magnify.   *reduce to window size.*

To Do: Select Boxes

Before deleting boxes, you must first be able to select the box you want to delete. (Otherwise, how will Microsoft Organization Chart know which boxes you want to delete?) To select a box, click once on it.

Wow, that was easy! A box is selected when it's highlighted in black, but not expanded as when you are editing the information it contains.

You can select or deselect additional boxes by holding down the Shift key as you click each box you want to select.

To Do: Delete Boxes

Deleting positions in Microsoft Organization Chart is easier than it is in real life. Organizational charts don't show emotions or ask for termination pay. To delete a position, use this method:

1. Select the box(es) you want to delete.
2. Press the Delete or Backspace key.

Remember that the Microsoft Organization Chart program permits only one Undo operation. When you delete a position, you delete not only the box, but also the information inside the box. Use caution when you're deleting multiple boxes.

Moving Personnel Around

In the Camelot example, Sir Gawaine and Sir Gallahad have agreed to change places. You could simply delete the existing boxes and insert new ones, but that would take a lot of time and retyping effort. A quicker alternative is to move the boxes around a bit to get the layout you want.

In Figure 20.8, Sir Gawaine was moved up to the new position of co-worker with Sir Gallahad. Next, Sir Gallahad will be moved, and then Sir Accolon, to the subordinate position under Sir Gawaine.

FIGURE 20.8.

Making Sir Gawaine a co-worker of Sir Gallahad is the first step before he becomes a full-fledged manager.

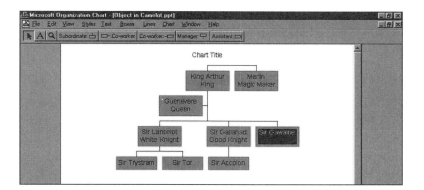

To Do: Move Boxes

Use the following steps to move a box to a new position:

1. Click and hold the mouse button on the box you want to move.
2. Drag the box to the new location.

Before performing these steps, the personnel box you want to move must not be selected. If you accidentally select the box before moving, simply click any other area of the organization chart and then try again.

20

The mouse pointer changes to reflect the type of position you're moving a box to. An arrow represents a co-worker, and a box with a line coming out of it represents a subordinate.

Exiting Microsoft Organization Chart

When you have finished with the organizational chart, you exit Microsoft Organization Chart a little bit differently than you do with other screens containing embedded objects.

 Remember that the Microsoft Organization Chart is a separate program that is actually running in another window separate from the PowerPoint 2000 window.

 ### To Do: Exit Microsoft Organization Chart and Return to PowerPoint

Here's how you exit Microsoft Organization Chart and return to PowerPoint:

1. Choose File, Exit and Return to [PowerPoint filename].

2. Click Yes, in the confirmation window, to update the organization chart in your presentation.

 If you make a really big mess of things and want to start over fresh, just exit without updating.

Summary

In this hour, you learned how to create an organizational chart and embed the information into a PowerPoint presentation. Organizational charts are useful tools for outlining the responsibilities of individuals and defining the chain of command back to the eminent leader. Creating and modifying an organizational chart should be a quick task when you're using the Microsoft Organization Chart application. Go ahead and create some charts of your organization. The next hour teaches you how to customize the organizational chart display to seamlessly integrate the picture with your professional presentation.

Q&A

Q **I want to format all the boxes to look the same. Is there an easy way to select all the boxes?**

A Absolutely. Use the Edit, Select, All menu command or simply press Ctrl+A (my personal favorite). If you use the Edit, Select menu command, you can see several options besides selecting all the boxes. You can just as quickly select all the managers in a chart or all the co-workers.

Q **Is there a way to move an entire group of boxes to a new location?**

A Yes. You must select all the boxes you want to move first by holding the Ctrl key and clicking each box. Then select Edit, Cut from the menu. Click once on the Manager box they should be under and then choose Edit, Paste Boxes from the menu.

20

PART VI

Multimedia, the World Wide Web, and Other Cool Stuff

Hour

HOUR 21

Multimedia

This hour introduces you to the basics of inserting multimedia elements into a PowerPoint 2000 presentation, expanding on what was covered in Hour 6, "Working with Clip Art and Pictures." Hour 6 covered many aspects of working with clip art and pictures. This hour expands on what you learned previously and enhances your PowerPoint 2000 presentations with photos, sound, music, narration, and video.

As you work your way through this hour, you will learn about the following:

- Sound files
- CD music
- Narration
- Adding video
- Finding multimedia files on the Web

What Is Multimedia?

Multimedia is sound, pictures, and video that can be used in a presentation to dazzle and entertain an audience. You use multimedia objects, such as clip art, photos, pictures, sound clips, music files you may have on your computer, music or other CD tracks, custom soundtracks, voice narration, and video—in other words, the things that make people say "ooh" and "aah" as you present your PowerPoint slide show.

Other than a gratifying audience response, why would you want to add these fancy multimedia objects to your PowerPoint 2000 presentation? After all, you might already have some nice clip art built into your slide show. You can add more pizzazz to your presentation by incorporating multimedia files. It's been said that a picture is worth a thousand words, so imagine how much more you can say when you can add a photo, music, or video clip to your presentation!

Inserting Sound Files

With slides of information, clip art, and pictures, PowerPoint presentations are effective by themselves. However they can be even more attention-grabbing with sound effects added to the presentation. These sound effects can come from many sources, including a prerecorded sound file, a music track from a CD, or a custom narration for your presentation. To use sound files effectively, you must have the proper hardware installed on your computer and the computer that will be used to give the presentation: a sound card, speakers, and a microphone to record narration. If you will be playing a music CD, your computer will also need a CD-ROM drive. Most new computers and many laptop computers have everything you need built-in, so they should be able to play sound effects.

 PowerPoint 2000 recognizes different types of sound files. The more popular of these are WAV, which are more like real recordings of actual sounds, and MID, which are MIDI (musical instrument digital interface) music files. Depending on your computer's sound card, these files can sound like either an organ or a full-size orchestra.

Inserting Sound Files from the Clip Gallery

PowerPoint 2000's Clip Gallery might also include a few sound clips that you can include in your presentation. You maneuver through the Clip Gallery the same way you browse for clip art.

> If you find that there are no sound files in the Clip Gallery, never fear—the next few sections cover how to find files on your computer. You can also download some really fantastic sounds from the Web at Microsoft's Clip Gallery Live site. You may need to come back to this section.

To Do: Open the Clip Gallery and Browse the Sound Clips Available

To browse the Clip Gallery, use the following steps:

1. Select Insert, Movies and Sounds, Sound from Gallery from the menu. This opens the Insert Sound dialog box, as shown in Figure 21.1.

FIGURE 21.1.

You can insert sounds by using the Insert Sounds dialog box.

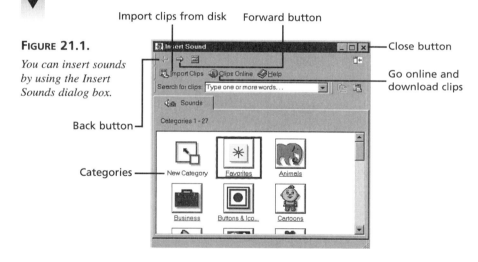

2. Click a Category button (such as Downloaded…) to display a list of the sound clips available for that category.

3. Use the Back and Forward navigation buttons, as shown, to help in the viewing of the gallery categories.

4. When you are done browsing, you can insert a sound clip, import a sound clip into the gallery, go to the Web to download sound clip(s), or close the gallery. These options are discussed in detail in the following sections.

When you find a sound clip that you want to play in your presentation, inserting it into your presentation is as easy as inserting a clip art image.

To Do: Insert a Sound Clip into a PowerPoint 2000 Presentation

To insert a sound clip from the Clip Gallery, use the following steps:

> Skip steps 1–3 if you have already been browsing the Clip Gallery.

1. Select Insert, Movies and Sounds, Sound from Gallery from the menu to open the Insert Sounds dialog box of the Clip Gallery.
2. Click a Category button to display a list of the sound clips available for that category.
3. Use the Back and Forward navigation buttons, as shown, to help in the viewing of the gallery categories.
4. Click the sound clip you want to insert and the Pop-up menu will display.

> Before you insert a sound clip, you may want to listen to it first to see whether it meets your needs. To preview a sound clip, simply click the clip and then click the Play Clip button from the Pop-up menu.

5. Click the Insert Clip button, as shown in Figure 21.2.
6. Close the Insert Sound dialog box by clicking on the Close button in the upper-right corner.
7. PowerPoint will ask whether you want the sound to play automatically in the slide show. This means that when this particular slide displays, the sound will automatically play. If this is what you want, click Yes. Otherwise, the sound will play only if you click the sound icon that is inserted onto your slide.

FIGURE 21.2.

Click the Insert Clip button on the Pop-up menu to insert a sound clip into a slide.

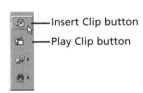

Insert Clip button

Play Clip button

You can change the way the sound clip plays, if you change your mind. To change the autoplay option for a sound clip, use the Custom Animation dialog box as discussed in Hour 10, "Adding Pizzazz to a Slide Show."

After the sound clip has been inserted into a slide, you will see a small speaker icon that represents the sound. You can double-click the icon to play the sound anytime you desire. You can also move or resize the icon just as you would a clip art image, if desired.

The speaker icon is there to remind you that there's a sound associated with the slide.

Inserting Other Sound Files

PowerPoint 2000 also enables you to insert Sound Files that are not in the Clip Gallery, but that you might have on disk or downloaded (see the later section on downloading clips from Microsoft). You probably have many sound files that are available on your computer of which you are unaware. Many of these may have been installed with other software. If you do not know whether you have other sounds, or if you do not know the correct location, PowerPoint 2000 comes to your aid once again.

To Do: Insert a Sound File from Disk

To insert sound files you might have on disk, use the following steps:

1. Select Insert, Movies and Sounds, Sound from File from the menu to open the Insert Sound dialog box.
2. Specify the correct folder location in the Look In box, as shown in Figure 21.3.

Specify the correct folder location in the Look In box

Use Tools to find a sound file (see the next To Do)

FIGURE 21.3.

You can insert any sound file from disk using the Insert Sound dialog box.

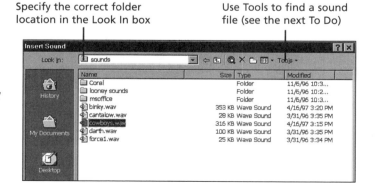

21

▼   3. Click the file you want to insert to select it.

4. Click the OK button to insert the file into your presentation slide.

5. PowerPoint will ask whether you want the sound to play automatically in the slide show. This means that when this particular slide displays, the sound will automatically play. If this is what you want, click Yes. Otherwise, the sound will play only
▲   if you click the sound icon.

Playing a CD Track

You can also play music or other sound track from a CD. This does require that you have a CD-ROM drive and a sound card in your computer. Most computers sold now, including many laptop and notebook computers, have these components built in.

To Do: Insert a CD Audio Track into a Presentation

To insert an audio track (an icon will be inserted that you can click so the track can be played from the CD), use the following steps:

1. Select Insert, Movies and Sounds, Play CD Audio Track from the menu to open the Movie and Sound Options dialog box, as shown in Figure 21.4.

FIGURE 21.4.
Use the Movie and Sound Options dialog box to insert a song from a music CD

2. Enter the track number you want to start with and the start time.

3. Enter the track number you want to end with and the end time, as shown in Figure 21.5. The total playing time will be displayed.

FIGURE 21.5.

Setting a music CD track to play in a PowerPoint 2000 presentation.

Enter starting track and time ⟶

Total CD playing time ⟶

⟶ Enter ending track and time

Movie and Sound Options

Play options
- ☑ Loop until stopped
- ☐ Rewind movie when done playing

Play CD audio track
Start: End:
Track: 2   Track: 2
At: 00:00   At: 04:53

Total playing time: 04:53
File: [CD Audio]

OK   Cancel

4. Click the OK button when finished.

5. PowerPoint will ask whether you want the sound to play automatically in the slide show. This means that when this particular slide displays, the sound will automatically play. If this is what you want, click Yes. Otherwise, the sound will play only if you click the sound icon.

To determine the start and end times of a certain portion of a CD music track, use the Windows CD Player program. Click the Start button and then choose Programs, Accessories, Multimedia, CD Player. The CD Player shows you the running time of a music track. Under the View menu, make sure Track Time Elapsed is checked so you can time the track from beginning to end.

If you're running Office 2000 from the CD-ROM, you can't play a CD music track unless you have two CD-ROM drives (which is not very common). You must also have the correct music CD available for the presentation and in the drive when it's time to give your presentation. You probably would not want to accidentally have Led Zeppelin playing "Stairway to Heaven" in the middle of a presentation to a group of more conservative investors. Always check to make sure the CD in your drive is the right one!

Recording Narration

To record narration for your PowerPoint presentation, you need a sound card with a microphone plugged in. You should also have a script prepared for whatever you want to say.

21

The sound quality of your narration is directly linked to the quality of your microphone and the amount of ambient noise. Ambient noise can be minimized by closing the door or windows to the room you're in, turning off the radio or TV, waiting for that noisy jet airplane to pass overhead, and so forth. An inexpensive microphone will probably do for the occasional narrative. However, you might want to consider purchasing a good-quality microphone if you plan on creating many high-quality, professional presentations. We do not suggest using built-in microphones as the quality can be extremely poor.

To Do: Record Narration for a Single Slide

To record narration for a single slide, use the following steps:

1. Choose Insert, Movies and Sound, Record Sound from the menu to open the Record Sound dialog box. (See Figure 21.6.)

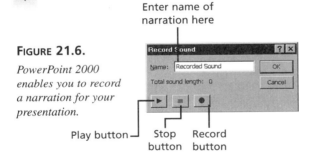

FIGURE 21.6.

PowerPoint 2000 enables you to record a narration for your presentation.

2. Enter the name of your narration in the Name field.

3. To start recording your narration, click the Record button and start talking into the microphone.

4. When you have finished your narration, click the Stop button. To check your recording, you can play it by clicking the Play button.

5. When you're finished recording, click the OK button. As with other sounds, a speaker icon will appear in the middle of your slide. If you want to play the narration, double-click the speaker icon.

Another option available to you is to record your narration while viewing the slides for your presentation.

To Do: Record Narration While Viewing All Your Slides

To record a narration for the entire show, use the following steps:

1. Select Slide Show, Record Narration from the menu to open the Record Narration dialog box shown in Figure 21.7.

FIGURE 21.7.

Record your narration while you view the slides for your presentation.

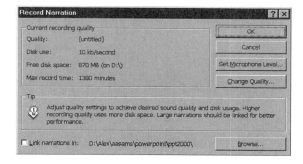

2. Click the Change Quality button to set the recording's sound quality in the Sound Selection dialog box. This enables you to have higher-quality recordings, such as CD quality. After you have set the sound quality, click the OK button.

> The higher the sound quality, the more disk space you use.

3. Click the OK button to start the narration.
4. Click the First Slide button to start the narration at the first slide.
5. Record your narration, clicking the mouse to advance to each new slide.
6. When you are finished, you're asked whether you want the save the new timings (because of your added narration) and review them in Slide Sorter View. Click Yes.

You may want to preview your presentation again to see how the narration sounds and then rerecord if necessary.

Adding Video

Video is perhaps the ultimate multimedia object you can add to your PowerPoint presentation. You have a moving picture, as well as sound in a video clip. A video clip, even a short one, can help you make a point in your presentation. Just as with sound clips and photo files, you can get video clips by using either the PowerPoint Clip Gallery or other video files.

21

Inserting Video Files from the Clip Gallery

As with clip art, pictures, and sound clips, you can also use PowerPoint's built-in Clip Gallery to browse through a selection of video clips.

To Do: Open the Clip Gallery to Browse and Insert a Video Clip

To use PowerPoint's built-in Clip Gallery to browse through a selection of video clips, use the following steps:

1. Choose Insert, Movies and Sounds, Movie from Gallery to open the Videos tab of the familiar Clip Gallery.

2. Click a Category button (such as Downloaded Clips) to display a list of the video clips available for that category.

3. Use the Back and Forward navigation buttons to help in the viewing of the gallery categories.

4. Click the video clip you want to insert.

 Before you insert a video clip, you can preview it, just as with a sound clip. To preview a video clip, simply click the clip and then click the Play Clip button.

5. Click the Insert Clip button.

6. Close the Insert Movie dialog box by clicking on the Close button in the upper-right corner.

Inserting Other Video Files

If you have video clips that didn't come with PowerPoint, you can incorporate them, too, just as you can use picture and sound files from other folders on your hard drive. The most common video file formats that work with PowerPoint are AVI, MPG, FLC, and FLI files. AVI and MPG files produce movie-like and television-like video clips. Just as with sound files, you might not even be aware of video files you already have available. You can also download files from the Web or purchase video files if you desire.

To Do: Insert a Video File from Disk

To add one of these files to your PowerPoint presentation, use the following steps (they are exactly the same as when you inserted a sound file):

1. Choose Insert, Movies and Sounds, Movie from File to open the Insert Movie dialog box.

2. Specify the correct folder location in the Look in box.

3. Click the file you want to insert to select it.

4. Click the OK button to insert the file into your presentation slide.

5. If you want the video to play automatically in the slide show, click Yes; otherwise, click No.

▲

As with pictures and sound clips, you can resize the video clip and move it to anywhere on the slide. To play the video clip, double-click its icon on the slide (in Slide Show view, just single-click).

You can also search for video files, as you have done for sound files. To search for video files, use the same steps you performed for sound files; simply substitute Movies from File in step 1.

Microsoft's Online Clip Gallery

If you like free stuff—and don't we all—those nice folks at Microsoft have much to offer. If you are having a hard time finding just the right sound or video clip for your presentation, check out the Clip Gallery Live site at Microsoft. In order to access this site, you must have an Internet account and be online.

To Do: Download Clips from the Clip Gallery Live

If you are online, you can download clips by using the following steps:

1. Open the Clip Gallery by selecting Insert, Picture, Clip Art to open the Insert ClipArt dialog box.

2. Click the Clips Online button.

3. After you have read the End User Licensee Agreement, click the Accept button to go to the online Clip Gallery, as shown in Figure 21.8.

4. Click the Clip Art, Pictures, Sounds, or Motion tabs to display the type of clip art you can download. Figure 21.9 shows the Sounds tab displayed. There are several ways to find clips relevant to your needs. You can search for clips by entering a keyword and clicking the Go button, selecting a category from the Category drop-down list, or, after you click a clip, you can browse using any of the quick search keywords. Take a few minutes to browse around and see what Microsoft has to offer. If you need help at any time, you can click the Help icon in the upper-right corner.

▼

21

▼

FIGURE 21.8.

The Microsoft Clip Gallery Live Internet site has hundreds of clips for you to select and download for free.

Clip Art tab
Sounds tab
Pictures tab
Motion tab

5. After you have found a clip you want to download, simply click the selection check box to add the clip to your Selection Basket. You can then browse for more clips, selecting any that you want.

6. After you are finished, click the Selection Basket to preview your selections before downloading. When you are done, click Download in the How To area.

7. Read the download instructions and then click Download Now!, as shown in Figure 21.10.

▲

After you have downloaded clips, they will be placed in the Clip Gallery, in the Downloaded category.

Selection   Selection
check box   Basket

FIGURE 21.9.

*Click a selection
check box to add a
clip to the Selection
Basket to download
later, or click the
Download Now
arrow to download
the clip right now.*

Search on a Keyword

Browse by a Category

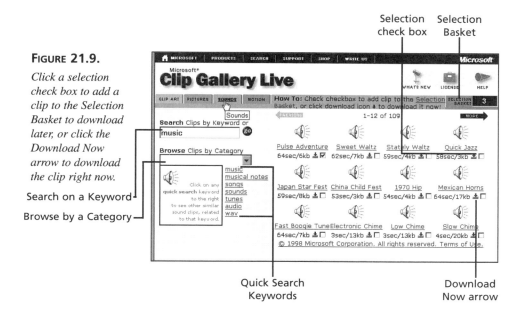

Quick Search
Keywords

Download
Now arrow

FIGURE 21.10.

*Click Download Now!
to start downloading
the clips you have
selected.*

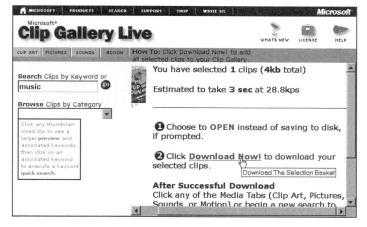

Importing Picture, Sound, and Video Clips into the Clip Gallery

Although you can insert a picture, sound, or video clip into a slide from any location on
your computer, you will probably find that having the clips you use most often in the
Clip Gallery is more convenient. If you have files that you have downloaded from the
Web or that you have found on your computer, you can import them into the Clip Gallery
to make them more accessible.

21

To Do: Import a Clip into the Clip Gallery

To import a picture, sound, or video file into the Clip Gallery, use the following steps:

1. Open the Clip Gallery and select the appropriate tab for the clip you are importing: Pictures, Sounds, or Motion clips.

2. Click a category to store the clip in—for example, Favorites.

3. Click the Import Clips button. The Add Clip to Clip Gallery dialog box will open, as shown in Figure 21.11.

FIGURE 21.11.

You can add clips to the Clip Gallery using the Add Clip to Clip Gallery dialog box.

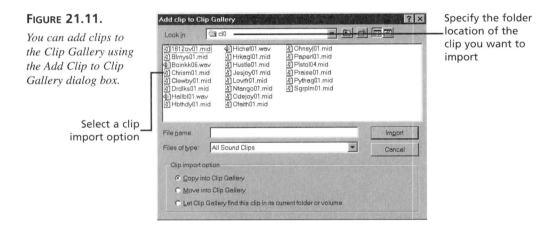

Select a clip import option

Specify the folder location of the clip you want to import

4. Specify the file's folder location in the Look In box.

5. Select the file or files you want to import. You can select multiple files by holding the Ctrl key while you click the filename.

6. Select a clip import option.

7. Click the Import button and the Clip Properties dialog box will open. If you choose Move into Clip Gallery as an Import option, you will be asked to confirm that this is what you want to do.

8. Enter a description of the clip.

9. Click the Categories tab to add the clip to other categories by clicking the appropriate check boxes.

For example, you might want a Christmas sound clip to be available in the Favorites, Miscellaneous, Cartoons, Entertainment, and Seasons categories. You can also create a new category from this location, such as Holidays or Christmas, to store a clip in. This does not create multiple copies of the same sound clip; it simply tags the clip for easy retrieval.

▼ 10. Click the Keywords tab to specify keywords that may be helpful when you want to search for an appropriate sound. Simply click the Keyword button, enter a key-word, such as Christmas, and press enter.

▲ 11. Click the OK button when finished.

Summary

You have just had a solid hour of learning how to add multimedia object files to your PowerPoint 2000 presentation. You now know that in addition to adding clip art to your PowerPoint presentation, you can insert sound and video from the Clip Gallery or from files outside PowerPoint. You also know how to create a narration for your presentation. Finally, you know where to look for new multimedia files if you run out of ones that you want to use.

Q&A

Q I have a graphics program. Can I use the graphics files from that program with PowerPoint?

A Yes, you can.

Q This multimedia stuff is fun. Should I insert multimedia files into each and every PowerPoint presentation I create?

A Although the answer to this question really depends on the presentation topic and the target audience, the answer is no. You probably will not need to insert multime-dia files into every PowerPoint presentation. Remember, less is usually more when creating a presentation.

You should keep the topic and target audience in mind at all times. Use multimedia whenever you think it might be helpful to your presentation. Do you think the pre-sentation topic will be enhanced or overshadowed by the special effects? If so, maybe you should save them for another time. However, if you feel that your audi-ence and the discussion topic would benefit from multimedia, by all means, go for it. Multimedia files are there to enhance your presentation, not detract (or distract) from it.

Q Can I listen to a sound file that I have found from the Insert Sound dialog box *before* I insert it?

A Not from the dialog box. When you insert Sound Files from outside the Clip Gallery, you can't preview them as you can from the Clip Gallery. One option is to use the Windows Media Player program, which is built into Windows. Just click

21

the Start button and choose Programs, Accessories, Multimedia, Media Player. Use Media Player's File, Open command to open a sound file. When you have found it, load it and click the Play button (the button with the triangle pointing to the right) to hear what the file sounds like.

Q I have several different sound clips in my presentation. However, they all have the same little speaker icon. How can I keep track of the different sounds?

A You could insert a text box under each sound icon and enter the name of the sound; or if you have several sounds on one slide, you may want to use the Custom animation dialog box to control the autoplay of each sound.

Q I did not fill in the properties completely when I imported some clips. Can I go back and update the properties.

A Yes. In the Clip Gallery, right-click the clip you want to modify the properties for and select Clip Properties from the shortcut menu. Follow the To Do steps as listed previously this hour.

Q Can I save my narration to use for another time?

A Not in PowerPoint 2000. However, you can use the Windows Sound Recorder program to record a slide narration and then save it as a WAV file. Click the Start button and then choose Programs, Accessories, Multimedia, Sound Recorder.

HOUR 22

Creating Web Pages

PowerPoint 2000 enables you to save presentations in the HTML World Wide Web format so that you can post them on a Web site. This allows people from all over the globe to see your presentation. Although PowerPoint makes converting a presentation into the standard Internet file format very easy, it is not the best tool to use to create an entire Web site. Use PowerPoint 2000's Web publishing option to make your presentation available to others.

In this hour, you learn about the following:

- Considerations when publishing on the Web
- Viewing and saving a presentation in Web format
- Inserting hyperlinks and action buttons

Publishing Considerations

There are many benefits available to you when you publish your presentation online. Your presentation can contain hyperlinks to appropriate Web sites anywhere on the Internet. In addition, your audience is not limited to viewing your presentation in a linear format—from slide one, to slide two, to slide three, and so on. Individuals can quickly jump to only the topics in which they are inter-ested, if you have provided the appropriate links. An added bonus is that your audience can view your presentation at any time, from any location, without your assistance.

> A *hyperlink* is text or some other PowerPoint object that has been format-ted so that the user can click on it and go to the designated destination. For example, you can click on the words corvette fever, in Figure 22.1, and go to the *Corvette Fever* online magazine.

FIGURE 22.1.

Click the words Corvette Fever Magazine *to link to the online magazine* Corvette Fever.

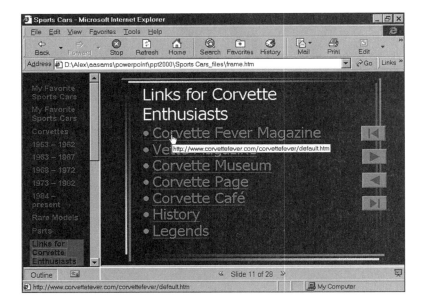

Although you can save any PowerPoint 2000 presentation file as a Web page, taking advantage of already completed work, some of the more advanced PowerPoint features, such as animation and sound, may not perform as desired for all your viewers. You need to carefully consider incorporating these features before adding them to an Internet pre-sentation. You should know your target audience's limitations for viewing special effects, large multimedia clips, and complex graphics. For optimum results on the Web, you should design the presentation specifically for the Internet medium.

Unless everyone in your audience will be using Internet Explorer 5.0 or better, you should keep your presentation simple. PowerPoint 2000 presentations look and behave best using Internet Explorer 5.0; however, all Internet users do not use Internet Explorer 5.0 as their Web browser. If you design your Web pages for the least capable of browsers, everything should look just fine for everyone. It is a very good idea to preview your presentation using every anticipated browser that your audience might be using, to ensure that everyone gets the same picture. It would be very disappointing to have all your hard work go to waste simply because no one could view the presentation.

22

The Internet offers unique benefits and limitations for a presentation. For the best results, you should keep a few guidelines in mind when you're creating a presentation that will be viewed on the Internet. The next two sections outline the limitations and benefits you need to remember.

Internet Limitations

Unlike standard presentations that rely on a projection screen or printout, the Internet doesn't provide a consistent canvas for your presentation. You must pay attention to the typical hardware and connection limitations of your target audience, as well as the software the viewers will be using. Does your average viewer have a 28.8 modem and 16-color screen display or a T1 communication line and a true-color screen display? The impact of your presentation depends on how well you target the capabilities of your viewers' machines.

You should estimate the page download times and what presentation hardware is likely to be needed. In general, the fancier the presentation, the longer it will take to view it. Using animation, for example, means that the people in your audience must install a special PowerPoint viewer to work with their Web browsers. Most of the time, audience participants don't want to go to the trouble. Therefore, for most projects, you should stay away from animation and large multimedia files. The use of sound, another effective presentation component, depends on an active sound card. Sound cards are not always available in the corporate world and are rare in the educational arena (although it does seem that sooner or later everyone will have these capabilities).

Multimedia items make computer files larger, and the more multimedia, the larger the file. The larger the file, the longer the download time. Therefore, when creating Web pages, you should try to have some idea of who your target audience is and how users will be accessing your Web page(s).

Are you targeting the computer-savvy folks who create games or graphics and have the most up-to-date equipment, including a fast modem or Internet connection? If so, go ahead and throw in some really cool multimedia stuff to attract their attention. They probably wouldn't give your page a second look without it.

If, on the other hand, your target audience is Joe and Jane America, who might be connecting with a much slower modem, keep the graphics and other multimedia stuff to a minimum. If the page takes too long to download, Joe and Jane will usually not stick around long enough to see what you've done.

Internet Benefits

The most compelling benefit of the Internet is being able to gather knowledge from resources around the world. You can greatly enhance your presentation by supplying links to other relevant Internet resources. For example, a presentation on Corvettes can have links to major magazines, company fact sheets, and where to find those hard-to-find parts, as shown in Figure 22.2.

FIGURE 22.2.

A presentation designed for the Web about Corvettes has links to other Web sites that may contain useful information.

Navigation buttons

Links to other pages in the presentation

Links to other Internet sites

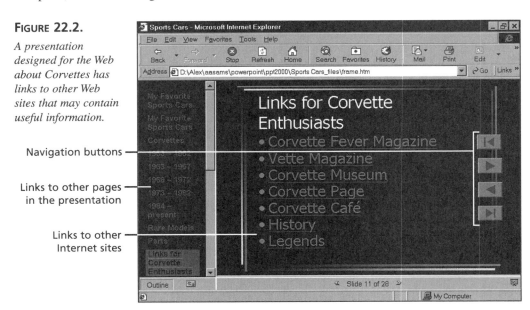

A Web presentation can be more dynamic than an auditorium demonstration because it's not constrained by the one-way dialogue usually associated with standard presentations. On the Internet, the audience is encouraged to interact with the presentation. You can also change the dynamics of the presentation experience; the slide order, for example, could be constructed in a tree hierarchy as opposed to a linear progression.

22

If you are planning on creating a large Web site, you should spend some time doing research on how good sites are constructed. There are some really good books available that teach how to design and create killer Web sites. A personal favorite is Laura Lemay's *Sams Teach Yourself Web Publishing with HTML 3.2 in a Week*. Get it. Read it. Apply it.

Publishing a Presentation As a Web Page

If you have already created your presentation in PowerPoint 2000, you can quickly publish it for the Web. Before posting the presentation on the Internet, you must first convert the PowerPoint presentation file into the appropriate format. An Internet presentation is a set of HTML and graphics files that can be viewed by any graphical Web browser. PowerPoint 2000 has an option that enables you to easily save and transform a standard presentation into the Internet format.

HTML, which stands for Hypertext Markup Language, is the way all documents on the World Wide Web are created. HTML enables every document to be viewed, on the Web, by any type of computer, anywhere in the world. When PowerPoint 2000 creates a Web document it uses the standard .HTM extension. All Web pages use this format.

Previewing the Presentation As a Web Page

Before you publish your presentation as an HTML document, you may want to see how it will appear as a Web page. You might be surprised how some things that look just fine in PowerPoint 2000 will look a little different on the Web.

To Do: Preview an Existing Presentation As a Web Page

To preview your presentation as a Web page (without publishing), use the following steps:

1. If it is not already open, open the presentation by selecting File, Open from the menu. If it is open, save the file by selecting File, Save from the menu.

2. Select File, Web Page Preview from the menu.

PowerPoint 2000 will start the Internet Explorer program and open your presentation file in Internet Explorer, as shown in Figure 22.3. You may want to maximize the Internet Explorer window to better see your presentation.

Back button   Forward button

FIGURE 22.3.

You can preview your presentation before you save it as a Web page.

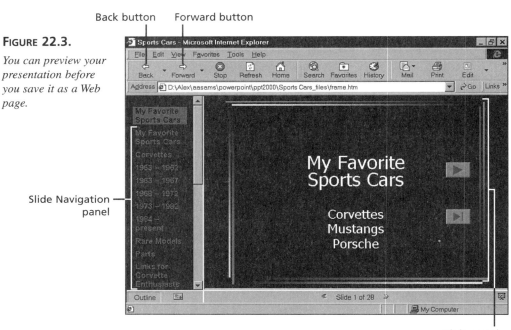

Slide Navigation panel

Slide panel

When you preview or publish your presentation as a Web page, PowerPoint 2000 uses the title of each slide for its Slide Navigation frame, as shown in Figure 22.3.

To view each page in the presentation, click the appropriate title in the Slide Navigation pane. When you are finished, you can exit the Internet Explorer program. If you do not have a Slide Navigation pane in your Web page, this option has not been selected. This option, slide navigation controls, automatically generates the Slide Navigation pane, using the title of each slide as a hyperlink to that slide. This option saves you from hours of work adding links to each slide.

Some older browsers do not support the pane view that the slide navigation controls use. Before you publish your presentation on the Web, you should determine which browser(s) your target audience uses. If you find that they are using older browsers, you will want to add navigation controls, as discussed in the next section, to each slide.

22

To Do: Turn On (or Off) Automatic Slide Navigation

To turn this option on (or off, if you desire), use the following steps:

1. In PowerPoint 2000, select Tools, Options from the menu to open the Options dialog box.
2. Click the General tab in the Options dialog box, as shown in Figure 22.4.

General tab

FIGURE 22.4.

You can change the options of your Web page from the Options dialog box.

Web Options button

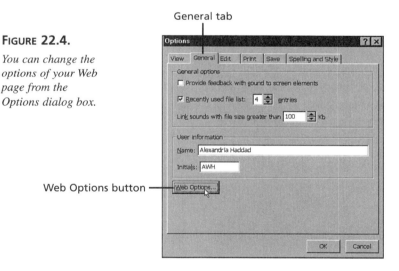

3. Click the Web Options button to open the Web Options dialog box.
4. Click the General tab, if it is not already displayed.
5. Click the Add slide navigation controls check box to turn the feature on, as shown in Figure 22.5. Uncheck this option to turn the feature off.

▼

FIGURE 22.5.

With the Add slide navigation controls check box selected, your presentation will be viewable with a minimum of work.

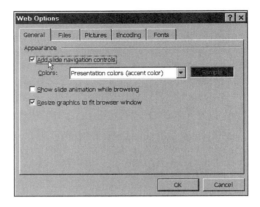

6. Click the OK button in the Web Options dialog box to close it.

7. Click the OK button in the Options dialog box to close it and accept your changes.

You may find that while viewing your presentation, some items do not look the same on a Web page as they did in a regular presentation. If this is the case, you may need to do a bit of editing to make your presentation Internet-ready. Always keep your pages simple. You do not want your message being overwhelmed by the special effects. Also note that many presentation options do not work well or at all in a Web page, including the following:

- There is no Shadow or Embossed font formatting.
- There are no Spiral, Stretch, Swivel, and Zoom paragraph effects.
- Chart special effects do not work.
- Some animation effects do not work.

For a more complete listing, search the Office Assistant or help files for troubleshooting Web page options.

Publishing the Presentation As a Web Page

After you have your presentation formatted so that it previews nicely, and you have created any navigation buttons necessary, you are ready to publish the presentation as a Web page. When you publish a presentation as a Web page, PowerPoint 2000 re-creates the presentation in HTML format. All the graphics that your presentation uses are also saved as separate, supporting files.

Although you can publish a presentation at any time as a Web page on your own computer, it will not be available on the World Wide Web unless you save the file (and all supporting files) to a Web server. Your company may already have access to a Web server; ask your network administrator about the procedures that you need to follow. You can also contact an Internet service provider (ISP) in your area to obtain access to a Web server, to host your Web page, for a small fee. Check with your local library or the Yellow Pages under Internet Services if you do not already have Internet access. There are hundreds of Internet service providers to choose from, so shop around.

When you have access to a Web server, you need to find out where you should save your Web page and supporting files. After you have gotten all this information together, you are ready to go live.

To Do: Publish a Presentation As a Web Page

To publish your presentation as a Web page, use the following steps:

1. Save the presentation as you normally would by selecting File, Save from the menu. This step can be skipped if you want to publish your presentation only on the Web and not use it for any other purpose.

2. Select File, Save As Web Page from the menu to open the Save As dialog box, as shown in Figure 22.6.

Select the folder location here

FIGURE 22.6.

Save a presentation to the World Wide Web using the Save As Web Page command.

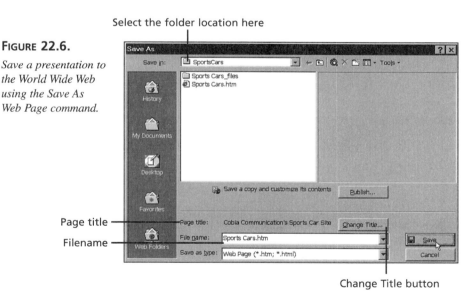

Page title

Filename

Change Title button

3. Select the location where you want to save your Web page and supporting files. You should obtain this information from your network administrator or Internet service provider.

4. Enter the filename for your Web page.

5. To change the title that will be displayed in the title bar for all your Web pages, click the Change Title button, enter a new title, and click OK.

▲ 6. Click the Save button to save and publish your presentation.

You can also click the Publish button to select and customize the way your presentation will be published.

Adding Links in Presentation

With PowerPoint 2000, you can add features quickly to your presentation that are unique to the Internet. Creating a home page, adding hyperlinks to Internet resources, and building action buttons to control the presentation are all tasks you need to learn to build an Internet-ready presentation.

Creating a Home Page

A *home page* is a Web page that acts as an introduction to your presentation. It serves as a type of table of contents for the presentation, providing hyperlinks to the important components. A home page should contain only the main items of interest, so try to keep the home page list of topics as short as possible. Four or five main topic items, at most, are best.

One way to create a home page quickly is to use the summary slide feature of PowerPoint 2000. The summary slide feature enables you to select specific slides, and PowerPoint 2000 will create a new slide using each selected slide title as a bullet item on the new slide. Another term for this feature is agenda slide.

To Do: Use the Summary Slide Feature to Quickly Create a Home Page

To create a summary slide to use for a home page for your Internet presentation, use the following steps:

1. Switch to Slide Sorter view by selecting View, Slide Sorter from the menu or clicking the Slide Sorter button.

2. Select the slides you want to include on the home page (hold down the Ctrl key and click on the slides you're selecting).

3. Click the Summary Slide button on the Slide Sorter toolbar to create the summary slide. (See Figure 22.7.)

Summary Slide button

FIGURE 22.7.

Click the Summary Slide button to create a slide with a bullet item by using the title of each selected slide.

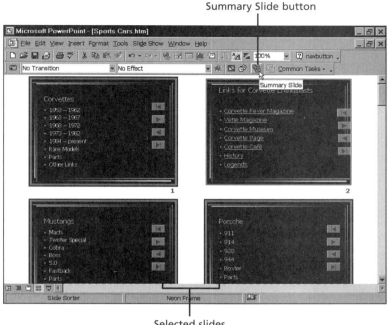

Selected slides

4. After the summary slide has been generated, you may want to move the slide to the beginning of the presentation.

> If you select more than eight slides when creating the home page list, more than one summary slide will be generated. Because Internet browsers enable viewers to scroll the presentation screen, you might want to combine the separate summary screens into one long slide.

After the summary slide has been generated, you should change the generic title "Summary Slide" to something that is more relevant to your presentation's subject. Simply double-click the summary slide in Slide Sorter view to change to Normal view. You can then edit the title as desired. After you have created a home page, you can format each bullet item with a hyperlink action setting to take your viewers to the appropriate slide, as discussed in the next section.

Hyperlinking to Presentation Resources

A hyperlink is a connection between two locations; your presentation viewers can use hyperlinks to guide them to other presentation slides, Internet pages, or even computer files. After you have created the home page for your presentation, you should format each bullet item as a hyperlink to the appropriate page.

To Do: Format a Bullet Item As a Hyperlink

Creating a hyperlink is very simple; just follow these steps:

1. Select a presentation item to associate with the hyperlink, such as the first bullet item on your summary slide/home page.

2. Choose Insert, Hyperlink from the menu or click the Insert Hyperlink button on the standard toolbar to open the Insert Hyperlink dialog box.

3. Click the Place in This Document button, as shown in Figure 22.8.

FIGURE 22.8.

Use the Insert Hyperlink dialog box to format any PowerPoint 2000 object as a hyperlink.

Display text for link

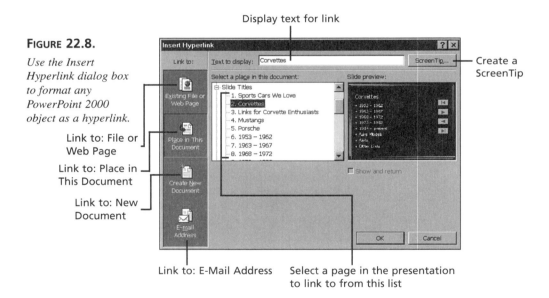

Create a ScreenTip

Link to: File or Web Page

Link to: Place in This Document

Link to: New Document

Link to: E-Mail Address

Select a page in the presentation to link to from this list

4. Select the page you want to link to from the list of slides.

5. Change the display text, if desired.

6. Create a screen tip, if desired, by clicking the ScreenTip button, entering a tip, and then clicking OK.

7. Click the OK button to complete the hyperlink.

PowerPoint 2000 enables you to create hyperlinks that point to many types of resources, including

22

- Presentation slides
- Internet Web pages or resources
- Email addresses

Slides

A hyperlink can point to any existing presentation slide. In the Insert Hyperlink dialog box, you can select the self-explanatory First Slide, Last Slide, Next Slide, or Previous Slide. These options enable you to provide basic navigation for your viewers. Because most home pages are the first page and "table of contents" of a Web site, you might consider putting a link on each slide that will take your viewer back to the First Slide. Each of your slides should also contain a link to another slide, depending on the course you want your viewers to take while viewing your presentation.

Internet Resources

The most common hyperlink destination added to Internet presentations is the URL hyperlink. A *URL* (uniform resource locator) is the unique address for an Internet resource. When possible, type the full path to the resource so that there are no name conflicts if the presentation is moved to another location. For example, `http://www.mcp.com/` is the full path that points to the main index document for the book directory on Macmillan Computer Publishing's server.

To Do: Link to an Internet Site

To add an Internet resource, use the following steps:

1. Select a presentation item to associate with the hyperlink, such as the first bullet item on your summary slide/home page.
2. Choose Insert, Hyperlink from the menu or click the Insert Hyperlink button on the standard toolbar to open the Insert Hyperlink dialog box.
3. Click the Existing File or Web Page button, as shown in Figure 22.9.

▼ To Do

▼

Enter the Web address

FIGURE 22.9.

The Insert Hyperlink dialog box also enables you to insert a link to any Web page available on the Internet.

Click Recent Files to see files you have recently viewed that are located on your computer

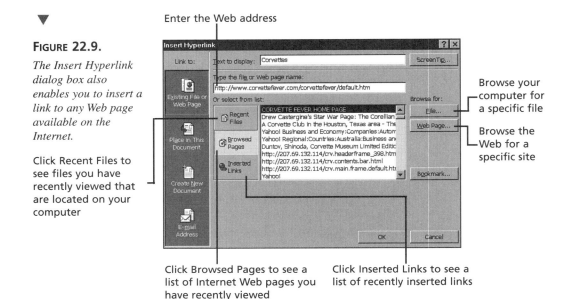

Browse your computer for a specific file

Browse the Web for a specific site

Click Browsed Pages to see a list of Internet Web pages you have recently viewed

Click Inserted Links to see a list of recently inserted links

4. Enter the complete Web address in the filename text box or select a Web address from the list of recent files or browsed Pages.

▲ 5. Click the OK button when finished.

> The URL must be entered as it appears in the address box for the page. URL addresses are also case-sensitive. An easy way to get the address absolutely correct is to copy the address from your Web browser.

Using and Adding Action Buttons or Navigation Controls

You can supply action buttons to help your viewers find useful features. When a user clicks an action button, PowerPoint performs a particular action. There are standard icon images that represent common functions or features, or you can create your own custom button image. Here's a list of some common action buttons, although there are several to choose from:

- Home
- Back or Previous
- Forward or Next
- Beginning
- End

Navigation controls can be added to your slide to enable viewers in your audience to view every slide in your presentation without using the Slide Navigation pane. This is necessary, especially for those viewers who do not have browsers that support frames. If you find that you need to add navigation controls to your presentation, it is an easy and painless task. You simply insert a button on each slide that your audience can click to move on to the next slide. Although you need at least one button to go to the Next slide, you are not limited to the number of buttons you can put on your slides.

You can really jazz up your presentation by adding navigation controls. These controls enable the viewer to go to the next slide as well as another section of the presentation. Later this hour, we discuss adding action settings for any PowerPoint 2000 object.

To Do: Add a Navigation Button to a Slide

Use the following steps to add a navigation button to a slide:

1. Display the slide, in PowerPoint 2000, that requires a navigation button.
2. Select AutoShapes, Action buttons from the Drawing toolbar.
3. Click the appropriate button. Figure 22.10 shows the Next button being chosen.

FIGURE 22.10.

Select the action button that best represents the type of navigation you want the viewer to perform—for example, move to the next slide.

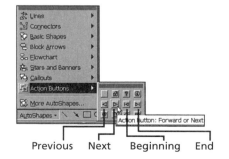

The Action buttons menu is a tear-away menu. If you will be creating many buttons for your presentation, you may want to tear this palette off the menu for easy access. Refer to Hour 2, "Quick Start: Creating Your First Presentation," to refresh yourself about tear-away menus.

4. Drag the mouse on the slide to draw the button, just as if you were drawing any other AutoShape.

5. When you release the mouse button, the Action Settings dialog box will open, as shown in Figure 22.11. If you chose the correct button, you should not need to change any of the settings. Simply click the OK button.

If you want the button to perform in some other way, simply select the options you want from the Action Settings drop-down list and then click the OK button. You can always change the Action Settings at a later time. These buttons can also be formatted just as any other AutoShape.

If you have many slides that need the same navigation buttons, you can create all buttons on the first slide, select them all, and then paste them on each slide. For example, suppose you have 50 slides and want each slide to have a Back, Forward, Beginning, and End button. Instead of creating each button one at a time, create all four buttons on slide one. Then select them all (using the lasso method or Shift+Click) and click the Copy button (or select Edit, Copy from the menu). Go to each slide and click the Paste button (or select Edit, Paste from the menu). You will probably want to delete the Back and Beginning buttons from the first slide and the Forward and End buttons from the last slide.

FIGURE 22.11.

PowerPoint 2000 automatically sets the hyperlink for you when you use the correct action button.

Action setting drop-down list

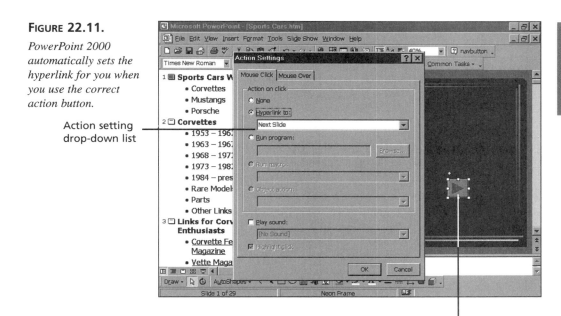

Action button

Summary

With PowerPoint 2000, you can display your presentation on the Internet. The presentation is converted into industry-standard HTML pages and graphics files that can be posted on the World Wide Web. Creating an Internet presentation is useful if the audience can't be present in the conference room or auditorium. After reading the material in this hour, you are now familiar with the steps for creating, saving, and viewing an Internet presentation.

Q&A

Q **How do I post the presentation on my Web site?**

A The process varies based on your particular Web server. You can usually post Web pages through your Internet service provider (ISP). If you're creating a company Web page, ask your Web site administrator for details. Although exact procedures vary among the options, the general procedure is to copy all the files for the site to the Web space. If you're copying to a company server, you need rights to the network directories. Then, just use Windows Explorer to copy the files. You may be able to use the new Web Folders option available. If you're copying to an Internet service provider or some other remote computer, you usually use an FTP client to copy the files. Again, check with your ISP for the specific steps you need to take.

Q **Can I move a PowerPoint Internet presentation after it's been generated?**

A Yes. Just make sure that any external links use the full path to their location.

Q **Can I find out who has viewed my presentation?**

A You can't really see who has viewed your Web page, but you can find out which other computers have visited your site. Ask the Webmaster or Web site administrator to give you a report listing the visitors to the presentation pages. However, the report might supply only IP (Internet provider) addresses or machine names.

Q **Can I post a quiz at the end of my presentation to check whether someone actually understood the material?**

A Not by using just PowerPoint. You'll have to call in the experts to build an online data-entry form.

Q **Can I add other program components to an Internet presentation?**

A No, you can't directly add Java applets, JavaScript, VBScript, or ActiveX controls. You'll have to import the HTML presentation pages into an HTML editor to spruce them up.

Q **I like the contents frame that PowerPoint 2000 creates for me; however, I don't want every slide listed. How can I avoid this?**

A This can be done; however, it requires a bit of planning and work. One option is to create two presentation files, the first file with only the three or four pages that you want listed in the contents frame. The second file would be all the other pages that are in your presentation. You could then publish the first presentation with hyperlinks to the relevant slides in the second presentation. You may want to provide a link back to the first presentation.

HOUR 23

Using and Creating Macros to Automate Tasks

The true power of computers lies in their capability of automating work that would otherwise have to be done by people. Even though PowerPoint 2000 embodies years of user feedback and incorporates many time-saving features, sometimes the developers at Microsoft didn't include a feature or shortcut that you would find useful. What they did include with PowerPoint, however, is a powerful programming language. PowerPoint 2000 contains Visual Basic for Applications (VBA), a subset of the Visual Basic programming language. With VBA, you can create macros that go way beyond mere keystroke recording. In fact, by using the language, macro programmers can now work with many of PowerPoint 2000's internal components.

With VBA, you can "teach" PowerPoint 2000 to automatically perform many routine tasks at the click of a toolbar button. Here are a few common operations that could be automated:

- Adding several new slides to a presentation
- Inserting a title slide and title text
- Turning bullets on and off
- Creating or deleting a custom show
- Manipulating command bars
- Copying slides between presentation
- Printing a presentation
- Naming a slide
- Opening a Web site

This hour covers the features available in the PowerPoint 2000 Macro dialog box and also introduces you to the Visual Basic Editor (VBE). After you have successfully created your first macro scripts, you might want to learn more about the VBA programming capabilities by reading other books devoted solely to that topic.

Creating and Working with Macros

The Macro dialog box is a centralized location for managing your presentation macros. You can view, run, edit, step into, create, or delete macros. To view all the macros in your presentation, open the Macro dialog box by choosing Tools, Macro, Macros from the menu. Or, you can open the Macro dialog box quickly, shown in Figure 23.1, by pressing Alt+F8 while you're in any presentation view (Slide, Outline, Slide Sorter, or Notes Page).

If you have opened a blank presentation without selecting any special templates, the Macro dialog box doesn't list any macros. PowerPoint 2000 has three methods you can use to add macros to a presentation file:

- You can record a macro that contains keystrokes, mouse movements, and menu commands.
- You can open a presentation from a macro template.
- You can directly code or copy VB macro subroutines.

FIGURE 23.1.

The Macro dialog box shows the macros that are available to use in a presentation.

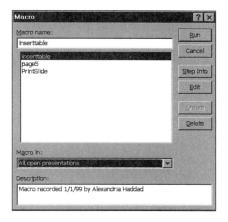

23

Copying existing macros from sample code files is a quick way to become familiar with the power and flexibility of the Visual Basic for Applications language. The section "Finding More Macro Information," later in this chapter, will teach you the steps for finding a wealth of sample code available from the Microsoft Web site.

Creating Macros

The easiest way to create a macro is to record the keystrokes as you replicate the task you want automated.

To Do: Create a Macro

To record a new macro, follow these steps:

1. Choose Tools, Macro, Record New Macro from the menu to open the Record Macro dialog box. (See Figure 23.2.)

2. Enter a name for your macro in the Macro name box. You can also enter a description for the macro in the Description text box to give a short explanation of its purpose.

> Macro names cannot contain spaces. Use the underscore character (_) if you want to add a "space" to the name for readability.

3. The information in the Store macro in field should indicate which presentation file will contain the macro. You can select the current presentation or select All open presentations from the drop-down list to apply the macro to presentations that are currently open.

FIGURE 23.2.

Enter a Name for your macro in the Record Macro dialog box.

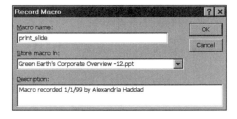

4. Click OK to start recording.

5. Execute the keystrokes or commands.

6. Click the Stop Recording button when you are finished. (See Figure 23.3.)

FIGURE 23.3.

The Macro toolbar is displayed while you record a macro.

Stop button ⌐

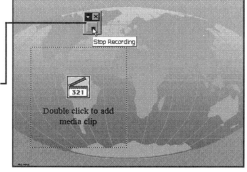

Because PowerPoint doesn't actually record keystrokes in a macro, some actions cannot be used. For example, you can't modify the Tools, Options dialog box using a macro. When you are recording a macro, PowerPoint 2000 analyzes your mouse and keyboard actions and converts them into the appropriate VBA text command. If there is no corresponding VBA command for the operation, the macro will not work as intended.

Running a Macro

After you have created a macro, you can run it at any time. Running a macro means executing the programming commands within the macro. There are two ways to run a macro: You can use the menu, or add a button to a toolbar that represents the macro.

To Do: Run a Macro from the Menu

To run the macro from the menu, use the following steps:

1. Select Tools, Macro, Macros from the menu.
2. Click the macro name you want to run.
3. Click the Run button.

To quickly access and run a PowerPoint macro with a single click, you may want to attach it to a button on either a built-in or custom toolbar. You can then run the macro by clicking the toolbar button.

To Do: Add a Macro Button to a Toolbar

To add a macro button to a toolbar, use the following steps:

1. Select View, Toolbars to display the toolbar you want to add the macro button to, if it is not already displayed.
2. Choose Tools, Customize to open the Customize dialog box.
3. Click the Commands tab and select Macros from the Categories list, as shown in Figure 23.4.

FIGURE 23.4.

Use the Customize dialog box to assign a macro to a toolbar button.

4. Click and drag the macro name onto the appropriate toolbar. A large I-beam will display where the button will appear.
5. Click the Close button.

After you have added a macro button to a toolbar, you may want to customize the button's display attributes so that it is a small icon instead of the macro name.

To Do: Change a Macro Button's Display Attributes to an Icon

To add a macro button to a toolbar, use the following steps:

1. Select Tools, Customize from the menu to open the Customize dialog box, if it is not already open.

2. Click once on the macro button you want to customize to select it.

3. Click the Modify Selection button to open the drop-down list shown in Figure 23.5.

FIGURE 23.5.

The Modify Selection drop-down list offers many choices.

Modify Selection drop-down list

4. Select Default Style from the menu. This will change the button to a blank button.

5. Click the Modify Selection button again, select Change Button Image, and click a button image from the choices available.

6. Click the Close button when finished.

To Do: Remove a Macro Toolbar Button

To remove a macro button from a toolbar (but not delete the macro), use the following steps:

1. Select Tools, Customize from the menu.

2. Drag the button off the toolbar into the presentation window to remove the button from the toolbar.

Deleting Macros

In PowerPoint 2000, you can also remove unused macros. If you frequently use preexisting macro templates, you might want to delete the unused macros to conserve memory resources.

To Do: Delete an Unused Macro

Here's how to delete a macro:

1. Choose Tools, Macro, Macros from the menu.
2. Select the macro you want to delete.
3. Click the Delete button.
4. Click the Yes button to verify that you do want to delete the macro.

The macro is then deleted from the presentation file.

Using Preexisting Template Macros

Macros can be stored in presentation template files and "copied" into your existing presentation. To use template macros in a presentation, you need to create the presentation from the preexisting template.

To Do: Use a Template with Macros

Follow these steps to embed template macros in your presentation:

1. Choose File, New from the menu.
2. Select the template containing the macros you want to use.
3. Click OK.

If you have already built slides that you want to include in the new presentation, add them to the newly created presentation by choosing Insert, Slides from Files from the menu.

> When you apply a template to an existing presentation, the macros in the template are not added to the presentation.

Using the VBA Editor

After recording a macro, PowerPoint tries to reduce the sequence of recorded PowerPoint commands to a series of VBA commands that would have the same effect. If you find that you want to record more powerful macros, you may need to use the VB Editor. The VB Editor is a separate program you can use to customize, create, and debug macros using the VB programming language.

23

Editing a Macro Using the VB Editor

You may find that sometimes a macro is not working the way you had intended. This may be caused by the way your mouse and keystrokes were converted into Visual Basic. For example, if you record a macro and press the Page Down key five times (from slide one), it will be rewritten in Visual Basic as a macro that goes to slide six. To create a macro that would move down five slides, you would have to use the Visual Basic Editor to edit the default macro and make it work the way you intended.

To Do: Use the VB Editor to Edit a Macro

To use the VB Editor and edit a specific macro:

1. Choose Tools, Macro, Macros from the menu.

2. Select the name of the macro to edit.

3. Click Edit. The Visual Basic Editor is then launched, as shown in Figure 2.6, with the edit cursor positioned at the macro you chose. You can now edit the macro commands to modify how it works.

FIGURE 23.6.

The Visual Basic Editor enables you to manually edit a macro.

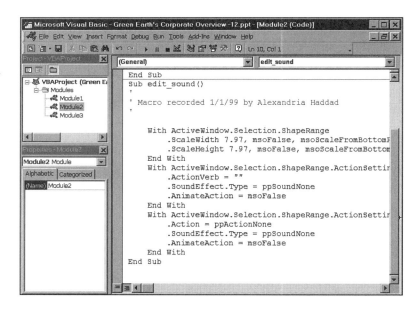

4. Edit the macro as desired.

5. Select File, Close and Return to Microsoft PowerPoint from the menu.

> The Visual Basic Editor has a different Help file than PowerPoint does. To view VBE's Help file, choose Help, Contents and Index from the Visual Basic menu.

Using the VB Editor to Create a Macro

By including the Visual Basic Editor (VBE), PowerPoint 2000 gives you a built-in programming environment with a wealth of features. The editor is a subset of the popular Visual Basic language. Use the editor to edit, write, debug, and manage macro script code. The editor also has many useful windows that help you explore the VBA language.

You can open the editor in one of two ways:

- Choose Tools, Macro, Visual Basic Editor from the main menu.
- Press Alt+F11 while you're in any view.

There are entire books that focus on Visual Basic's impressive capabilities, but in the following sections, I'll try to highlight just the basic features you need to create cool macros.

You can easily cut and paste or drag and drop sample code into a macro module. Open the Visual Basic Editor and choose View, Code from the menu, or press F7 to display the Visual Basic Editor window. After you copy or add VBA code to the window, the macros are automatically displayed and available in PowerPoint's Macro dialog box.

The Visual Basic Help files and Object Browser are useful reference sources; they can give you insight into the objects with which macro subroutines can work.

Finding More Macro Information

To find the latest information about using Visual Basic for Applications with PowerPoint 2000, check out the Microsoft Support Page on the Web. You can find sample code for common automation tasks and useful tips and tricks that can save you time when programming PowerPoint 2000 macros.

To Do: Go to the Microsoft Support Site and Search for PowerPoint Macros

To search for PowerPoint 2000 macro samples and tips using the Microsoft Support Page, use the following steps:

1. Log on to the Internet and point your browser to
   `http://support.microsoft.com/support/default.asp`.
2. Go to the Basic view if you are not already there.

23

▲ To Do

▼   3. Select Visual Basic for Applications in step 1.

        4. For step 2, enter `PowerPoint Macros`, as shown in Figure 23.7.

▲   5. Click find.

FIGURE 23.7.

Use the Microsoft Support Page to search for PowerPoint 2000 sample macros.

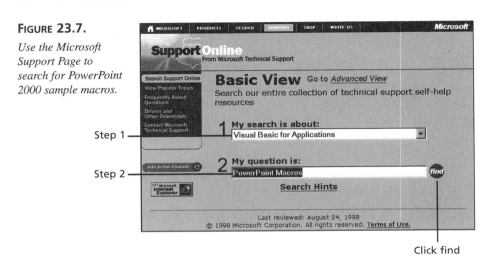

At the time this chapter was written, the search returned 107 matches. Many items pointed to valuable sample code written by Microsoft experts.

Summary

PowerPoint 2000 can be completely customized by adding macros written in the Visual Basic for Application programming language. You can create presentation macros to automate a wide variety of tasks. You might want to invest some time creating macros for tasks you perform often. Macros are also helpful for reducing complex command sequences to a simple button click. Exploring the VBA language and macro capabilities could keep you intellectually challenged for the next 24 hours or more.

Q&A

Q I applied a template to my presentation, but no macros are available. What happened?

A Simple—when you apply a template to an existing presentation, the macros in the template aren't added to the presentation. You should create a new presentation using the template file and then insert the slides into the newly created presentation.

Q While recording a macro, I entered the keystrokes out of order. Is there a way to reverse the key after it's typed?

A You must either delete the macro and then record it again, or try to edit the macro in the Visual Basic Editor after the keystroke recording has stopped.

Q My macro doesn't always run properly. What could be wrong?

A The macro might depend on the particular view or active settings to work correctly. The Visual Basic Help files have pages that explain the error message returned by PowerPoint. To consult them, choose Help, Contents and Index from the Visual Basic menu.

Q Can I stop a macro after it has started running?

A Yes. To stop a macro that's running, press Ctrl+Break on the keyboard. This action interrupts the macro.

23

HOUR 24

PowerPoint Power Hour

Whew! You've made it through 23 hours of PowerPoint. What, you haven't had enough yet? Well, during this last hour, you will touch on a few of PowerPoint's neat features and learn how to really customize PowerPoint to work best for you. This last hour covers the following topics:

- AutoCorrect: what it is and how to make it work for you
- Toolbars: how to create your own special toolbar with only your favorite buttons
- Options: how to get the most from PowerPoint 2000
- Hyperlinks: how you can use them in a slide show
- Presentation designs: some ideas for creating your own custom template

Relax, and go get an espresso (decaf is okay, but just this once). You've come so far—now it's time to put the power into PowerPoint 2000.

AutoCorrect

You might have noticed something strange happening while you have been creating slide presentations during the To Do sections (or maybe not). If you forget to capitalize the first letter of a sentence, it has magically been capitalized for you. If you type adn, it magically changes to and. Try to type (c) or :), and you get © or ☺ instead. Or have you ever accidentally left the Caps Lock key on and had to go back and retype all the text again? Well, there's no need for that now.

PowerPoint automatically corrects all these common mistakes and more with the IntelliSense of AutoCorrect. Want to know more about this fabulous feature, and all that it will do for you?

To Do: Take a Look at the AutoCorrect Features of PowerPoint 2000

Just use the following steps to take a peek at what's going on behind the scenes:

1. Choose Tools, AutoCorrect from the menu to open the AutoCorrect dialog box.

2. Scroll through the Replace Text As You Type list to see everything that can be corrected for you as you type. (See Figure 24.1.)

FIGURE 24.1.

The AutoCorrect dialog box provides many corrections for common typing errors.

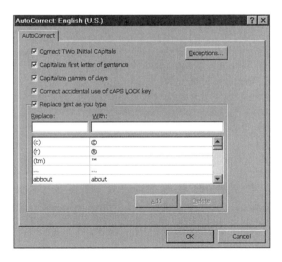

3. Click the OK button when you're finished.

You can add entries to AutoCorrect for those frequent typographical mistakes that only you make. You can also use the AutoCorrect feature as a kind of typing shorthand to help save time. This feature comes in handy, especially when writing these "Sams Teach Yourself Whatever in 24 Hours" books. You can add unique abbreviations for lengthy or odd words that you need to type over and over again. Figure 24.2 shows how to add initials that will be replaced with a name in the AutoCorrect dialog box.

To Do: Add a Personal Entry to the AutoCorrect List

To add your own AutoCorrect items to the AutoCorrect list, use the following steps:

1. Choose Tools, AutoCorrect from the menu.
2. In the Replace box, type the text you want to replace, such as your initials.
3. In the With box, type the correct text.

FIGURE 24.2.

Adding a personal entry to the AutoCorrect list helps speed up your work.

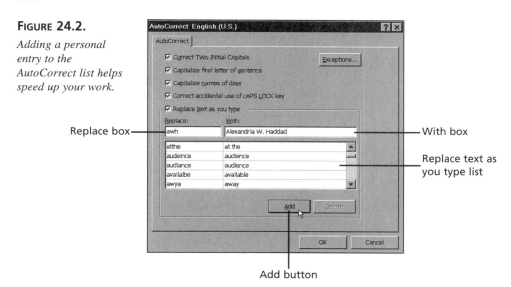

Replace box — Replace box

With box — With box

Replace text as you type list

Add button

4. Click the Add button.
5. Repeat steps 2–4 for each entry you want to add.
6. Click the OK button when you're finished.

24

When using AutoCorrect as a shorthand tool, make sure you think of unique entries for the Replace option. For example, if your company's name is "Anderson's Naughty Desserts," you wouldn't want the AutoCorrect Replace entry to be and because that would be more hindrance than help. A better Replace entry might be /and/ or something else just as unique that you wouldn't otherwise type.

Although AutoCorrect entries are helpful, there might be a few you don't want to have around. Maybe you type (c) on a daily basis and don't want the © symbol to keep popping up.

To Do: Delete an AutoCorrect Entry

To delete an AutoCorrect entry, use the following steps:

1. Choose Tools, AutoCorrect from the menu.
2. Select the entry you want to delete from the Replace Text As You Type list.
3. Click the Delete button.
4. Repeat steps 2 and 3 for each entry you want to delete.
5. Click the OK button when you're done.

You can also turn off any of the other AutoCorrect features, such as the Correct Accidental Use of CAPS LOCK Key option.

To Do: Turn Off or On Automatic Corrections

To turn off any automatic corrections, use the following steps:

1. Choose Tools, AutoCorrect from the menu.
2. Uncheck any check boxes you won't be using.
3. Click the OK button.

There are some exceptions to the Correct TWo INitial CApitals and the Capitalize First Letter of Sentences options. To see a list of these exceptions, click the Exceptions button. In the AutoCorrect Exceptions dialog box, as shown in Figure 24.3, you can even add your own exceptions.

24

FIGURE 24.3.

You can set the exceptions that PowerPoint 2000 uses for AutoCorrect using the AutoCorrect Exceptions dialog box.

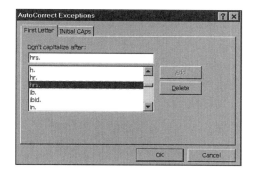

Toolbars

So many toolbars, so little screen space. Although PowerPoint comes with several toolbars to choose from, did you ever wish there was just one toolbar with all your favorite tools on it? Well, welcome to the wonderful world of PowerPoint. You can create your own toolbar with only those items you use most often, and therefore free up some of that valuable screen space. You can add menus to toolbars, too! You can even customize any of the existing toolbars (or even the menu bar), if you desire.

To Do: Create a Custom Toolbar

To create a new custom toolbar, use the following steps:

1. Choose Tools, Customize from the menu to open the Customize dialog box.
2. Click the Toolbars tab.
3. Click the New button.
4. Type a name for the toolbar, such as My Favorite Tools, in the New Toolbar dialog box.
5. Click the OK button in the New Toolbar dialog box. The new toolbar is then displayed as a very small floating toolbar.
6. Double-click the title bar of the new toolbar to dock it on the top of the screen, as shown in Figure 24.4. It will be blank, but you'll fill it up with commands soon enough.

FIGURE 24.4.

Creating a custom toolbar is easy with the Customize dialog box.

New toolbar docked

New toolbar floating

Toolbar names

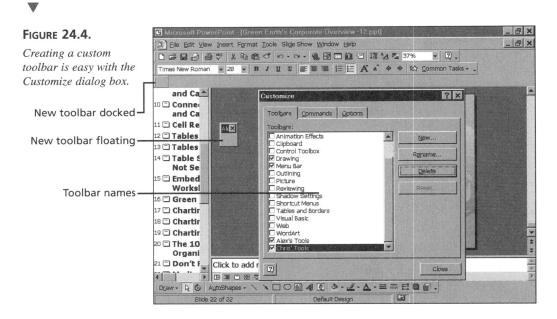

7. Click the Commands tab. (See Figure 24.5.)

FIGURE 24.5.

Use the Commands tab of the Customize dialog box to add buttons to your custom toolbars.

Click the Description button for a description of the selected command

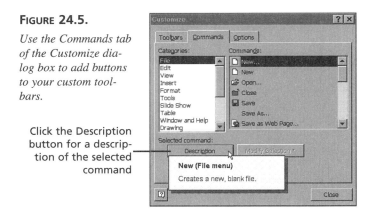

8. Select a category from the Categories list.

9. Select a command from the Commands list. If you're not sure what the command does, click the Description button after selecting the command.

▼   10. Drag the command to your new toolbar. A dark I-beam shows where the button will be placed. Release the mouse button when the I-beam is in the position you want.

11. Repeat steps 8–10 to add any other tools you want to the toolbar.

▲   12. Click the Close button when you're finished.

> You can use any category and add as many command buttons as needed to a toolbar. However, keep in mind that a toolbar is supposed to make tasks easier and quicker to perform. If you're spending a lot of time searching through all the buttons on a toolbar, the toolbar isn't serving its purpose.

24

To Do: Customize an Existing Toolbar

To customize an existing toolbar and add command buttons, use the following steps:

1. Choose View, Toolbars, Customize from the menu to open the Customize dialog box.

2. Click the Toolbars tab.

3. If the toolbar you want to customize isn't currently displayed, click the check box next to the toolbar name to display the appropriate one. A toolbar must be displayed to customize it.

4. Click the Commands tab.

5. Select a category from the Categories list.

6. Select a command from the Commands list.

7. Drag the command to the desired toolbar. A dark I-beam shows where the button will be placed. Release the mouse button when the I-beam is in the position you want.

▲   8. Click the Close button.

To Do: Delete Command Buttons from a Toolbar

To customize an existing toolbar and delete command buttons, use the following steps:

1. Choose View, Toolbars, Customize from the menu.

2. Click the Toolbars tab.

3. If the toolbar you want to customize isn't currently displayed, click the check box next to the toolbar name to display the appropriate one.

▼

▼   4. Drag the command button you want to delete off the toolbar. When the mouse
       pointer has a little x in the lower-right corner, as shown in Figure 24.6, release the
       mouse to delete the command button.

FIGURE 24.6.

*Buttons that you no
longer need can be
easily deleted.*

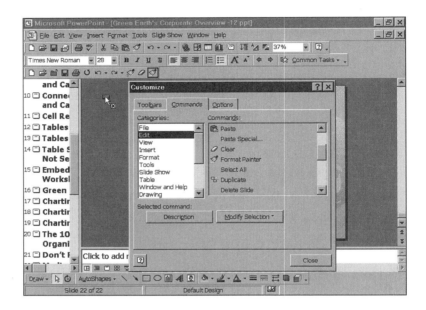

▲   5. Click the Close button.

It is strongly suggested that you create your own toolbar and leave the ones
that came with PowerPoint alone (this especially applies to the menu bar).
You can accidentally delete something that you might need at a later date.
If this happens to you, you can reset the toolbar, but all your changes will be
gone. To reset a toolbar, from the Customize dialog box, select the toolbar
(or menu bar) and click the Reset button. Click Yes to reset the selected bar.
The reset message is a little cryptic, but it does reset the bar to the original
settings.

Customizing PowerPoint 2000

There are many options you can change to customize PowerPoint 2000 to work with you in the best way possible. For example, when you save a file, is there a specific folder you're always switching to? You might want to change the File option in PowerPoint to always point to that folder. Or how often do you want PowerPoint to save your work in case of a power outage? These options and more can all be customized in the Tools, Options dialog box. To help you on your way, Table 24.1 lists all the options available, explains what they do, and offers some suggestions.

A check mark next to an option indicates that the option is active.

Table 24.1 lists the tab of the Options dialog box in boldface type before explaining each of the options you can customize in that tab.

24

TABLE 24.1. OPTIONS AVAILABLE FOR CUSTOMIZATION.

Option	Description
View	
Startup dialog	Shows the PowerPoint dialog box when you first start PowerPoint.
New slide dialog	When you insert a new slide, PowerPoint displays the New Slide dialog box so you can select a layout for the slide. If this option is not checked, you won't automatically see this box.
Status bar	Displays the status bar at the bottom of the screen.
Vertical ruler	Displays a vertical ruler on the left of the screen if you have selected View, Ruler from the menu.
Windows in taskbar	Displays each open presentation as a button on the Windows taskbar.
Pop-up menu on right mouse click	Allows using the right mouse button to quickly perform certain tasks during a slide show.
Show pop-up menu button	During a slide show, displays the very dim menu button (in the lower-left corner of the slide) for selecting slide show commands.
End with black slide	Ends a slide show with a black screen.

continues

TABLE 24.1.   CONTINUED.

Option	Description
General	
Provide feedback with sound to screen elements	Plays a sound when certain actions are performed. Requires sound capabilities with your machine.
Recently used file list: xx entries	Determines whether (and how many) recently used files show up at the bottom of the File menu.
Link sounds with file size greater than xxx Kb	PowerPoint automatically creates a link to sound files bigger than the amount specified.
Name	The name that automatically appears in the properties sheet for the presentation.
Initials	The initials that automatically appear in the properties sheet for the presentation.
Web Options button	Allows the user to set the default options desired for published Web pages.
Edit	
Replace straight quotes with smart quotes	Automatically replaces plain old straight quotes ("") with pretty curly quotes (" ").
When selecting, automatically select entire word	Automatically selects whole words.
Use smart cut and paste	Adds or removes extra spaces or returns when you cut and paste.
Drag-and-drop text editing	Allows using the mouse to cut or copy selected text by dragging.
Auto-fit text to text placeholder	PowerPoint 2000 automatically adjusts text to fit in the current placeholder.
AutoFormat as you type	Automatically formats a presentation with bullets, numbers, borders, and so forth.
New charts take on PowerPoint font	All new charts start with 18-point Arial font.
Maximum number of undos: xx	The number of actions PowerPoint remembers to undo.
Print	
Background printing	Allows printing to be done in the background so you can continue working.
Print TrueType fonts as graphics	Prints Windows TrueType fonts rather than text.
Print inserted objects at printer resolution	Uses the printer's default resolution.

Option	Description
When printing *Presentation NAME* via toolbar button or binder	You have two choices when you click the Print button: 1. Print using the most recent print settings (those you used the last time you chose File, Print from the menu). 2. Print using the default settings.

Save

Allow fast saves	Fast saves speed up saving a file, but increase the file size.
Prompt for file properties	When you save a file, displays the File Properties dialog box.
Save AutoRecover info every xx minutes	How often PowerPoint saves your work in case of a power outage.
Convert charts when saving as a previous version	Automatically converts charts to the correct format.
Save PowerPoint files as:	The default file type.
Default file location:	The folder PowerPoint looks in first when you choose either Save or Open from the menu.

Spelling and Style

Check spelling as you type	Displays red squiggly underlines under misspelled words.
Hide spelling errors in this document	Hides the red squiggly underlines under misspelled words.
Always suggest corrections	Always suggests possible correct spelling during a spellcheck.
Ignore words in UPPERCASE	Ignores uppercase words during a spellcheck.
Ignore words with numbers	Ignores words with numbers during a spellcheck.
Check style	Checks that the style options you set are being applied throughout your presentation.
Style Options button	Enables you to set style options to help keep your presentation style consistent for such items as spelling, capitalization, font size, and so forth.

24

To Do: Change Any PowerPoint 2000 Options

To change any PowerPoint options, use the following steps:

1. Choose Tools, Options from the menu.
2. Change any settings you want.
3. Click the OK button.

Creating a Custom Template

If you have created a custom look for presentations that you would like to use over and over again, you can save your presentation as a presentation design template.

To Do: Save a Presentation As a Template

To do that, follow these steps:

1. Open the presentation on which you want to base the template.

2. Delete all the slides, text, and other objects that you don't want to appear on every new presentation you create when you use this template.

3. Choose File, Save As from the menu.

4. Type a name for the template, such as XYZ Corp.

5. Select Design Template from the Save As Type drop-down list, as shown in Figure 24.7.

FIGURE 24.7.

Save your presenta-tion as a template for future use.

     6. Click the Save button.

Summary

In this final hour of PowerPoint 2000, you learned about some of the features that will really show off what a power user you have become. You can save lots of typing time by using AutoCorrect, and you can now customize or create toolbars. PowerPoint 2000 has many options you can change so that it works better for you. The sections on hyperlinks and presentation designs had several ideas to help you on your way to complete cus-tomization of PowerPoint 2000.

I hope you have as much fun learning about PowerPoint 2000 as I have had writing about it. You've been a great audience.

Q&A

Q Mommy, are you done yet?

A Yes.

PART VII

Appendixes

APPENDIX A

Hotkeys and Menus

The following tables outline most of the shortcut keys available in PowerPoint, but PowerPoint lists many other shortcut keys in the Help Index, too.

Table A.1 lists, in alphabetical order, the shortcut key combinations that use the Ctrl key.

TABLE A.1. SHORTCUTS USING THE CTRL KEY.

Shortcut Key Combination	Action Performed
Ctrl+A	Slide View: Select all objects
	Outline View: Select all text
	Slide Sorter View: Select all slides
Ctrl+B	Bold
Ctrl+C	Copy
Ctrl+D	Duplicates selected object
Ctrl+E	Center align
Ctrl+F	Find
Ctrl+G	Turn guides on or off
Ctrl+H	Replace
Ctrl+I	Italic
Ctrl+J	Justify-align
Ctrl+K	Insert a hyperlink
Ctrl+L	Left-align
Ctrl+M	Insert a new slide
Ctrl+N	Start a new presentation
Ctrl+O	Open a presentation
Ctrl+P	Print a presentation
Ctrl+Q	Exit from PowerPoint
Ctrl+R	Right-align
Ctrl+S	Save a presentation
Ctrl+T	Format the font
Ctrl+U	Underline
Ctrl+V	Paste
Ctrl+W	Close the presentation
Ctrl+X	Cut
Ctrl+Y	Repeat the last action (or command)
Ctrl+Z	Undo last action (or command)

Table A.2 lists some other shortcuts that I've found useful.

TABLE A.2. OTHER SHORTCUTS WITH THE KEYBOARD AND FUNCTION KEYS.

Shortcut Key Combination	Action Performed
Cursor Movement Using the Keyboard	
Ctrl+left arrow	Move one word to the left
Ctrl+right arrow	Move one word to the right
End	Move to the end of the line
Home	Move to the beginning of the line
Ctrl+up arrow	Move up one paragraph
Ctrl+down arrow	Move down one paragraph
Ctrl+Home	Go to the first slide (if no object is selected), or go to the beginning of all text (if object is selected)
Ctrl+End	Go to the last slide (if no object is selected), or go to the end of all text (if object is selected)
Selection Options Using the Keyboard	
Shift+right arrow	Select one character to the right
Shift+left arrow	Select one character to the left
Ctrl+Shift+right arrow	Select to end of a word
Ctrl+Shift+left arrow	Select to beginning of a word
Shift+up arrow	Select one line up
Shift+down arrow	Select one line down
Tab (with nothing selected)	Select an object on a slide
Other Shortcuts and Function Keys	
Ctrl+Backspace	Delete one word to the left (going back) of the cursor
Ctrl+Delete	Delete one word to the right (going forward) of the cursor
Ctrl+F9	Minimize the presentation window
Ctrl+F10	Maximize the presentation window
F1	Help
F2	Toggle between selecting all the text in an object or selecting the object
F5	Run presentation
F7	Spelling

A

Hotkeys for Slide Show

Table A.3 lists hotkeys used during slide shows.

TABLE A.3.   SLIDE SHOW HOTKEYS.

Hotkey	Action Performed
Click, space, N, right arrow, down arrow, enter, page down	Advance to next slide
Backspace, P, left arrow, up arrow, page up	Return to previous slide
Any number followed by Enter	Go to slide
B or . (period)	Black screen on/off
W or , (comma)	White screen on/off
A or = (equal)	Arrow pointer on/off
S or + (plus)	Automatic Show start/stop
Esc, Ctrl+Break, or - (hyphen)	End slide show
E	Erase Drawing on screen
H	Go to hidden slide
T	Rehearse using new times
O	Rehearse using original times
M	Rehearse using mouse click to advance
Ctrl+P	Pointer to pen
Ctrl+A	Pointer to arrow
Ctrl+H	Hide pointer and button (dim in lower-left section of screen)
Ctrl+U	Pointer and button show/hide

Menus

As with any Windows program, you can choose any menu command by using the keyboard. Press the Alt key followed by the underlined letter in the main menu (for example, pressing Alt+F opens the File menu). Pressing any underlined letter in a menu, without using the Alt key, chooses the menu command. For example, to print a presentation, use the following keystrokes:

1. Alt
2. F
3. P

If you like this method of choosing menu commands, you will find that the more you use it, the faster you get.

You can customize any menu by using the following instructions. First, to add a command to a menu, follow these steps:

1. Choose View, Toolbars, Customize from the menu.
2. Click the Toolbars tab.
3. Select Menu Bar from the list of toolbars.
4. Click the Commands tab.
5. Select a category from the Categories list.
6. Click the menu heading you want to edit to open the menu.
7. Drag the command to the menu.
8. Repeat the previous steps, if needed.

Here's how you can delete a command from a menu:

1. Choose View, Toolbars, Customize from the menu.
2. Click the Toolbars tab.
3. Select Menu Bar from the list of toolbars.
4. Click the menu heading you want to edit to open the menu.
5. Drag the command off the menu.
6. Repeat the previous steps, if needed.

A

Don't customize your menu so much that you (or someone else who shares your machine) can't get your work done. If you accidentally get carried away with all this cool customization stuff and you fall off the wall, you can put everything back together (unlike Humpty Dumpty). To reset your menu to the original settings, follow these steps:

1. Choose View, Toolbars, Customize from the menu.

2. Click the Toolbars tab of the Customize dialog box.

3. Select Menu Bar from the list of toolbars.

4. Click the Reset button; the Reset Toolbar dialog box pops up.

5. Click the OK button in the Reset Toolbar dialog box.

6. Click the Close button in the Customize dialog box.

Only ten seconds, and you have put Humpty Dumpty back together again.

APPENDIX B

Common Mouse Pointer Shapes in PowerPoint 2000

Table B.1 illustrates the most common mouse pointer shapes and their meaning.

TABLE B.1.   MOUSE POINTER SHAPES.

Pointer Shape	What It Does
▷	When the mouse pointer appears as a white or black arrow (the most commonly seen pointer), you can select any object by clicking on it.
I	When the mouse pointer appears as an I-beam, you can select text.
↔	When the mouse pointer appears as a double arrow (usually when it's placed on a resize handle), you can resize an object by dragging the handle to a new location.
✛	When the mouse pointer appears as a four-headed arrow, you can move an object by dragging it to a new location.
⌛	When the mouse pointer appears as an hourglass, Windows is asking you to be patient and wait a few seconds. Although sometimes you can perform another task when you see the hourglass, it's usually a good idea to let Windows finish the operation it's working on first.

INDEX

brightness of image
objects, 96
browsers, publishing
presentations online, 297
browsing Clip Gallery,
281, 288
bulleted slides, creating,
56-59
bulleted text
characters or pictures,
changing, 77
entering in Outline pane,
58-59
symbols, changing, 76-77
working with, 75
bullets
font sources for, 127
overview of, 5
Bullets and Numbering
dialog box, 76
buttons, deleting from
toolbars, 331-332

C

callouts, drawing, 179
cancelling presentations, 28
CDs
determining start and end
times of tracks, 285
inserting sound files from,
284-285
cells
description of, 212
selecting, 231
Cells command (Format
menu), Excel, 235
changing
chart type, 246
color of 3D effects for
objects, 204

data series plotting, 255
default chart type, 249
images to watermarks, 97
options, 335
shadow colors for
objects, 202
shape of WordArt
objects, 170
text anchor point, 81-82
text object attributes,
79-81
text orientation, 260
text properties
alignment, 74-75
font size, 78
fonts, 72-74
chart edit mode,
entering information in
datasheets, 241
chart items, selecting, 247
Chart menu commands
(Microsoft Graph), Chart
Type, 246
chart objects
attributes, changing
axis labels, 259-260
data series, 261-262
legends, 260-261
overview of, 258
customizing, 258
selecting
mouse, using, 256-257
toolbar, using, 257
Chart Objects button
(Standard toolbar),
Microsoft Graph, 257
Chart Type dialog box
(Microsoft Graph), 246
charts
changing type of, 246
choosing type of, 245

combining types of,
246-247
components of, 256
creating, 240
custom types, 248-249
datasheets, editing,
252-253
default type,
changing, 249
editing
dragging data markers,
253-254
overview of, 251
selecting cells, 243
selecting
datasheets, 244
inserting, 240-241
organizational
adding positions, 270
components of, 268
deleting boxes, 272
description of, 266
entering text, 268-269
inserting, 266
inserting position
boxes, 270
moving boxes, 273
selecting boxes, 272
choosing
chart type, 245
fonts, 72
clip art
copyright issues, 86
customizing color of, 97
deleting, 88
grouping and ungrouping,
91-93
inserting, 86-88
Web sites, 86
Clip Gallery
browsing, 281
images, adding to, 88-89

Get FREE books and more...when you register this book online for our Personal Bookshelf Program

http://register.samspublishing.com/

SAMS

 Register online and you can sign up for our *FREE Personal Bookshelf Program*—immediate and unlimited access to the electronic version of more than 200 complete computer books! That means you'll have 100,000 pages of valuable information onscreen, at your fingertips!

 Plus, you can access product support, including complimentary downloads, technical support files, book-focused links, companion Web sites, author sites, and more!

 And, don't miss out on the opportunity to sign up for a *FREE subscription to a weekly email newsletter* to help you stay current with news, announcements, sample book chapters, and special events, including sweepstakes, contests, and various product giveaways.

 We value your comments! Best of all, the entire registration process takes only a few minutes to complete, so go online and get the greatest value going—absolutely FREE!

Don't Miss Out On This Great Opportunity!

Sams®is a brand of Macmillan Computer Publishing USA. For more information, visit *www.mcp.com*